A DICTIONARY OF MARKS

A DICTIONARY OF

MARKS

CERAMICS METALWORK FURNITURE

The Identification Handbook for Antique Collectors

Edited by
MARGARET MACDONALD-TAYLOR

With an Introduction by L. G. G. Ramsey
Editor of *The Connoisseur*

HAWTHORN BOOKS
A division of Elsevier-Dutton
NEW YORK

Contents

Introduction

To collectors and to those who live and work among antiques, an unfamiliar mark is an intriguing, provocative challenge. Only admire an old dinner service and more than one guest round the table will be tempted to risk disaster by scanning the underside of his plate. Mention hallmarks and every detective instinct will be aroused. Nevertheless, I never cease to be astonished at the owners of antiques who have never really searched for marks – tiny, inconspicuously placed and often worn almost illegible, that can yet tell the whole fascinating story of date, maker and material and thereby contribute not only interest but value to a piece.

Collectors are aware today that marks on their own can never be regarded as substitutes for real study of the antiques concerned, whether in metal, ceramics or wood. But, more especially among the lesser makers, they are of inestimable value in establishing the detailed history of a craft. That is why, especially, I welcome and commend this volume. Within a single book may be found the essential basis constantly required by collector, dealer, and even the chance inheritor of what may be valuable antiques, whether they are American, English, or Continental. To many this will mean a widening of the field of interest, a welcome realisation of much individual talent, especially among a range of nineteenth-century ceramics, formerly obscured by the few most famous craftsmen in eighteenth-century porcelains.

Among silversmiths Britain is world-renowned for the system of hallmarking that has not changed in principle since the Middle Ages. Even in England one may encounter marks tantalisingly distorted by time and even by deliberate forgery. But the law established by the London goldsmiths more than six hundred years ago, and still strictly enforced, requires every individual piece of silver to pass through an assay office to be tested for its proportion of alloy and either punch-marked or rejected and broken up accordingly. Collectors quickly learn to recognise the marks used by different assay offices and at different periods. There is a peculiar pleasure in identifying the small mark that distinguishes a provincial assay office. This was often adapted from the city's coat of arms; but two of the most familiar, the anchor of Birmingham and the crown of Sheffield, introduced in 1773 through the praiseworthy determination of Matthew Boulton, have a more interesting history. There were the chance results of the toss of a coin when the men responsible completed their negotiations at the Strand's Crown and Anchor Inn.

Careful study of these pages will make the silver collector familiar with the different forms of the London "leopard's head" and lion, the head bereft of its crown from 1821 and the lion facing forward instead of "gardant". The changing shape of the puncheon outlines is also essential knowledge. The "lion's head erased", found with the Britannia figure on silver of a purer standard, is a reminder of another small detail of history associated especially with the flamboyant days of silver shortage and consequent coin clipping at the turn of the seventeenth-eighteenth century but encountered, too, on silver of this "high standard" made more recently. (Occasionally, it may be mentioned here, Britannia herself is confused with Ireland's Hibernia.)

7

Always the collector's hope is for a clear date letter, and here again the puncheon outline is important. General study of form and ornament, a feeling for right design and an acquaintance with customs and the vessels that served them will guide the collector puzzled by the occasional repetition of certain styles of alphabet and punch outline at different periods.

Of particular interest are the touch marks on pewter, Sheffield plate and the later developments such as British plate. Every tyro collector has to learn caution among the pseudo silvermarks so often found on nineteenth-century metal alloys, and to accept defeat when a piece reveals the letters *EPNS* of post-1842 electro plate.

Likewise among ceramics the collector also practises caution. The most familiar English marks, such as Chelsea gold anchors, all too seldom designate true products of the famous potteries. Few makers had the scruples of Thomas Randal who steadfastly refused to give his superb Madeley porcelain the coveted mark of early Sèvres. Incised and impressed marks such as the Chelsea raised anchor are a little more reliable. But the innumerable marks and minute initials of lesser potters are fascinating and endlessly informative. Dates included in ceramics marks usually refer merely to the founding of the potteries concerned.

Dates are more frequent than other marks on English furniture but frequently testify to a Victorian foible. This volume must deal mainly with French pieces. Nevertheless occasional impressed marks are to be found, and even printed labels. This is a quest that is endless. Always, after intensive search, a new acquisition may contribute another tiny fragment to our knowledge of antiques and of the men and women who created them. There, assuredly, where others glanced unseeing, the "bargain" is to be found among antiques today.

L. G. G. RAMSEY

Editor's Preface

The interest in pictures and antiques of all kinds has gathered increasing momentum of recent years, and books and articles of generalised or particular interest continue to delight and inform a wide public. It is not necessary to be rich to indulge one's taste for fine things. Many people today can see objects of the highest quality in the surroundings most fitted to show them to advantage, especially in the many country houses open to visitors. More people than ever before are appreciating the great store of beauty housed in museums and art galleries, and by frequent visits learn to train the eye to see quality and to remember shapes and ornamentation. At previews of auction sales, and in the more intimate atmosphere of antique dealers' shops, even the most diffident enthusiast can find opportunities to go further than simply looking. The experience of actually touching a piece of Chippendale or of holding in the hand some fine piece of porcelain or silver brings closer acquaintance with its character, and stimulates the desire for even more detailed knowledge. For some people this particular interest may be encouraged by having a good eye for fine design and workmanship, and perhaps by being able to acquire a few antiques to add grace to their homes. Others, again, may be happy in the possession of some heirlooms, such as family silver, which has been lovingly cherished from one generation to the next, or old porcelain, carefully preserved. In the case of inherited treasures, some intimate story connected with them will doubtless also be handed down; in very fortunate circumstances there may exist the original bills which record the name of the maker and details of the purchase. Here there is not only valuable documentary proof, so much prized by the art historian and the connoisseur, but, for everyone interested, expert and amateur alike, an additional savour given to appreciation of the pieces concerned.

Where such documentary proof is lacking, knowledge of the provenance, period, and maker's name may be gained by other means, notably by deduction from marks, especially in ceramics and metalwork. To search out these marks and identify them is a detective exercise which brings both pleasure and reward, but the hunt may be rather protracted and full of complications, if reference works are out of print or otherwise inaccessible; and not everyone has time for lengthy research in reference libraries.

Signatures, or other inscriptions, on pictures and prints do not here concern us, but rather the marks of differing kinds and purposes on ceramics, metalwork, furniture and tapestry. These marks are now put into one book, although they are kept in separate sections. Each category receives the particular form of presentation felt to be best suited to it.

Metalwork is a complex subject and has therefore been subdivided, for the convenience of the reader, into several sections. On old English silver, of course, several marks will be found, including the standard mark, town mark, and date mark. These are grouped in historical sequence under the chief towns, and can be checked easily from the object being studied. English silversmiths were further required to identify their wares by using initials. A selective list of such initials (including compound initials indicating more than one person) has been compiled, in alphabetical order, including those silversmiths whose work is most commonly met with. The reader can run his finger down the list, and find the name of the person given alongside, with approximate dates, and brief indication of the shape in which the initials are enclosed. Taking together the initials, the town mark and its date letter, the maker can be traced with reasonable confidence. Where two different makers with the same initials are found, the year mark is a useful counter-check. Changes of initials are recorded separately, even where they refer to the same silversmith. In English pewter, an enormous number of makers' "touches", as they are called, have been officially recorded. Lack of space did not permit of depicting these here by drawings. To aid the enquirer, however, a selective list of English pewterers, arranged alphabetically by surname, has been included, with approximate dates and a brief description of the touch. Reference to the metalwork index for the emblems will lead the reader to the page, but most touches have readily identifiable names still to be seen, where not partially erased by domestic polishing. Entries recorded under Sheffield plate need no comment.

Many people now take a keen interest in American silver; it was not normally required to bear standard or other marks, but the makers' marks often consist of the straightforward use of the name. Numbers of American silversmiths, however, not only had a taste for imitating the shapes of English silver, but, copying from choice a practice that was followed by regulation in England, used initials only, to mark their work. A selective list of such initials given here follows the method of entry used for English silversmiths, and the selective list of American pewter touches is again in line with that used for English pewter.

Marks on furniture and tapestry also have their appeal for the connoisseur, although in regard to furniture the French claim the largest share of attention. Since, by regulation, the various French master craftsmen, cabinet-makers, clockmakers, bronze workers and others (except those holding special royal privilege) were required to "sign" their pieces, this category takes the form of a selective list, arranged in alphabetical order, with a brief note of dates, together with those few emblems which occur. Marks on tapestry, a practice initiated in Brussels and soon imitated elsewhere, sometimes take almost cabalistic forms, which are therefore not susceptible of being put in an index. The chief English and European centres, and some makers, appear, with their marks, in alphabetical order.

On ceramics, i.e. pottery and porcelain, all kinds of marks are found, sometimes in the form of emblems, anchor, crossed swords, and so on; these may be tracked down by using the ceramic index. Except in the case of Oriental marks, the entries are not separated; English and European appear together in alphabetical order, according to the name of the factory, with a separate entry for an artist if conspicuously famous. Each ceramics entry gives a brief note on date, country, type of ware (i.e. maiolica, porcelain, etc.), with, wherever possible, a facsimile representation of known marks, whether name or emblem. In the case of much English nineteenth-century work, however, an entry giving the firm's name in type only has been deemed sufficient. Decorators' marks, where known and identified, and thought useful to record, are normally here included under the factory entry. In using this book, therefore, the reader should first check the factory mark; if an emblem is used, this will be traced by the ceramics index. Once the factory mark has been identified, it is a simple matter to trace under the particular entry any additional mark (e.g. date letter, artist's initials, etc.) which may occur on the piece being examined. As regards Oriental marks, the dynasty marks of China and the year marks of Japan have been illustrated. Although so foreign in appearance to Western eyes, constant study soon makes them familiar, especially since their number is not large. As some European and English factories have used imitation Oriental marks, it is interesting to refer to the genuine, original mark, and to note the differences between the two.

In short the essential marks to be recognised when studying or collecting antiques have been included in this book, and no claim to be all-embracing is made. To extend his knowledge yet further, the reader is referred to those specialised books listed in the bibliography. All such study will contribute greatly to the appreciation of those works of the past which were such a source of pride and pleasure to the original owners, and which continue to delight us today.

M. M. T.

Acknowledgment

The editor would like to record sincere appreciation of the work done by Mrs Mary Platford who drew, with great care and precision, the metalwork marks and those relating to Oriental pottery and porcelain, and who brought unfailing patience to the lengthy task of deciphering the editor's notes, sketches, and directions. Her invaluable help is hereby gratefully acknowledged.

Metalwork

British Silver

Four marks are usually found stamped on silver, namely: the hall, or town, mark, indicating the assay office; the maker's mark; the annual mark or date letter, indicating the year of assay; the standard mark, indicating sterling quality. Other marks are: the Britannia mark, used 1697 to 1719, to indicate the higher standard of silver required during that period; the Sovereign's head or duty mark, used 1784 to 1890, to indicate duty had been paid on the piece so stamped; the Jubilee mark, used in addition to other marks, on pieces with date letters from 1933/4 to 1935/6, celebrating the silver jubilee of King George V. and Queen Mary; the Coronation mark of 1953 (the head of Queen Elizabeth II) to mark her accession.

The following is a guide to the letters at the head of each table: **LH** Leopard's head; **DL** Date letter; **LP** Lion passant; **LHC** Leopard's head crowned; **B** Britannia; **LHE** Lion's head erased; **TM** Town mark; **RC** Rose crowned; **DM** Deacon's mark; **AM** Assay mark; **T** Thistle; **LR** Lion rampant; **H** Hibernia; **SH** Sovereign's head.

London

Goldsmiths' Company empowered to assay and stamp gold or silver articles in 1327. Marks: the **leopard's head** (i.e. a lion's face) at first uncrowned; crowned 1478–1697; not used during "Britannia" period (1697–1719); crowned 1720–1823, thereafter uncrowned; the **lion passant**, indicating sterling standard, at first "guardant", and crowned until 1550; disused during "Britannia" period (1697–1719); the **Britannia figure**, and the **lion's head erased** (profile head, cut off at neck), both used during Britannia period (1697–1719); **Sovereign's head**, as duty mark, 1784–1890; **date letter**, changed annually in May; **maker's mark.**

| | | 1558–1578 | | | | | |
LHC	LP	DL		LHC	LP	DL	
👑	🦁	𝖆	1558/59	👑	🦁	𝖍	1565/66
		𝖇	1559/60			𝖎	1566/67
		𝖈𝖈	1560/61			𝖐𝖐	1567/68
		𝖉	1561/62			𝖑	1568/69
		𝖊	1562/63			𝖒 𝖒	1569/70
		𝖋𝖋	1563/64			𝖓	1570/71
		𝖌	1564/65			𝖔	1571/72

15

LHC	LP	DL		LHC	LP	DL	
		p	1572/73			P	1592/93
		q	1573/74			Q	1593/94
		r	1574/75			R	1594/95
		s	1575/76			S	1595/96
		t	1576/77			T	1596/97
		u	1577/78			V	1597/98

1598–1618

LHC	LP	DL	
		T	1598/99
		B	1599/1600
		C	1600/1
		D	1601/2
		E	1602/3
		F	1603/4
		G	1604/5
		h	1605/6
		I	1606/7
		K	1607/8
		L	1608/9
		M	1609/10
		N	1610/11
		O	1611/12
		P	1612/13

1578–1598

LHC	LP	DL	
		A	1578/79
		B	1579/80
		C	1580/81
		D	1581/82
		E	1582/83
		F	1583/84
		G	1584/85
		H	1585/86
		I	1586/87
		K	1587/88
		L	1588/89
		M	1589/90
		N	1590/91
		O	1591/92

LHC	LP	DL	
		Q	1613/14
		R	1614/15
		S	1615/16
		T	1616/17
		V	1617/18

1618–1638

LHC	LP	DL	
		a	1618/19
		b b	1619/20
		c	1620/21
		d	1621/22
		e	1622/23
		f	1623/24
		g	1624/25
		h	1625/26
		i	1626/27
		k k	1627/28
		l	1628/29
		m	1629/30
		n	1630/31
		o	1631/32
		p	1632/33
		q	1633/34

LHC	LP	DL	
		r	1634/35
		s	1635/36
		t	1636/37
		v	1637/38

1638–1658

LHC	LP	DL	
		a b	1638/39
		b	1639/40
		c	1640/41
		d	1641/42
		e	1642/43
		ff	1643/44
		g	1644/45
		h	1645/46
		i	1646/47
		k	1647/48
		l	1648/49
		m	1649/50
		n	1650/51
		o	1651/52
		p	1652/53
		q	1653/54
		r	1654/55

17

LHC	LP	DL		LHC	LP	DL	
🛡	🦁	O	1655/56	🛡	🦁	T	1676/77
		P	1656/57			U	1677/78
		Q	1657/58				

1658–1678

LHC	LP	DL	
🛡	🦁	A	1658/59
		B	1659/60
		C	1660/61
		D	1661/62
		E	1662/63
		F	1663/64
		G	1664/65
		H	1665/66
		I	1666/67
		K	1667/68
		L	1668/69
		M	1669/70
		N	1670/71
		O	1671/72
		P	1672/73
		Q	1673/74
		R	1674/75
		S	1675/76

1678–1697

LHC	LP	DL	
🛡	🦁	a	1678/79
		b	1679/80
		c	1680/81
		d	1681/82
		e	1682/83
		f	1683/84
		g	1684/85
		h	1685/86
		i	1686/87
		k	1687/88
		l	1688/89
		m	1689/90
		n	1690/91
		o	1691/92
		p	1692/93
		q	1693/94
		r	1694/95
		s	1695/96
		t	1696/97

		1697–1716					1716–1736	
LHC	LP	DL		B	LHE	DL		
🦁	🦁	—	1697	🏛	🦁	A	1716/17	
		—	1697/98			B	1717/18	
		—	1698/99	LHC	LP	C	1718/19	
		—	1699/1700	🦁	🦁	D	1719/20	
		—	1700/1			E	1720/21	
		—	1701/2			F	1721/22	
		—	1702/3			G	1722/23	
		—	1703/4			H	1723/24	
		—	1704/5			I	1724/25	
		—	1705/6			K	1725/26	
		—	1706/7			L	1726/27	
		—	1707/8			M	1727/28	
		—	1708/9			N	1728/29	
		—	1709/10			O	1729/30	
		—	1710/11			P	1730/31	
		—	1711/12			Q	1731/32	
		—	1712/13			R	1732/33	
		—	1713/14			S	1733/34	
		—	1714/15			T	1734/35	
		—	1715/16			V	1735/36	

		1736–1756	
LHC	LP	DL	
🛡	🦁	a	1736/37
		b	1737/38
		c	1738/39
		d	1739/40
		d	1739/40
		e	1740/41
		f	1741/42
		g	1742/43
		h	1743/44
		i	1744/45
		k	1745/46
		l	1746/47
		m	1747/48
		n	1748/49
		o	1749/50
		p	1750/51
		q	1751/52
		r	1752/53
		r	1753/54
		t	1754/55
		u	1755/56

		1756–1776	
LHC	LP	DL	
🛡	🦁	A	1756/57
		B	1757/58
		C	1758/59
		D	1759/60
		E	1760/61
		F	1761/62
		G	1762/63
		H	1763/64
		J	1764/65
		K	1765/66
		L	1766/67
		M	1767/68
		N	1768/69
		O	1769/70
		P	1770/71
		Q	1771/72
		R	1772/73
		S	1773/74
		T	1774/75
		U	1775/76

		1776–1796	
LHC	LP	DL	
🛡	🦁	a	1776/77

LHC	LP	DL	SH	
👑	🦁	b		1777/78
		c		1778/79
		d		1779/80
		e		1780/81
		f		1781/82
		g		1782/83
		h		1783/84
		i	head	1784/85
		k		1785/86
		l	head	1786/87
		m		1787/88
		n		1788/89
		o		1789/90
		p		1790/91
		q		1791/92
		r		1792/93
		s		1793/94
		t		1794/95
		u		1795/96

1796–1816

LHC	LP	DL	SH	
👑	🦁	A	head	1796/97
		B		1797/98
		C		1798/99

LHC	LP	DL	SH	
👑	🦁	D	head	1799/1800
		E		1800/1
		F		1801/2
		G		1802/3
		H		1803/4
		I		1804/5
		K		1805/6
		L		1806/7
		M		1807/8
		N		1808/9
		O		1809/10
		P		1810/11
		Q		1811/12
		R		1812/13
		S		1813/14
		T		1814/15
		U		1815/16

1816–1836

LHC	LP	DL	SH	
👑	🦁	a	head	1816/17
		b		1817/18
		c		1818/19
		d		1819/20
		e	head	1820/21

LH	LP	DL	SH		LH	LP	DL	SH	
🦁	🦁	**f**	👤	1821/22	🦁	🦁	**G**	👤	1842/43
		g		1822/23			**H**		1843/44
		h		1823/24			**I**		1844/45
		i		1824/25			**K**		1845/46
		k		1825/26			**L**		1846/47
		l		1826/27			**M**		1847/48
		m		1827/28			**N**		1848/49
		n		1828/29			**O**		1849/50
		o		1829/30			**P**		1850/51
		p		1830/31			**Q**		1851/52
		q	👤	1831/32			**R**		1852/53
		r		1832/33			**S**		1853/54
		s		1833/34			**T**		1854/55
		t		1834/35			**U**		1855/56
		u		1835/36					

1836–1856

LH	LP	DL	SH	
🦁	🦁	**A**	👤	1836/37
		B	👤	1837/38
		C		1838/39
		D		1839/40
		E		1840/41
		F		1841/42

1856–1876

LH	LP	DL	SH	
🦁	🦁	**a**	👤	1856/57
		b		1857/58
		c		1858/59
		d		1859/60
		e		1860/61
		f		1861/62
		g		1862/63

LH	LP	DL	SH	
🦁	🦁	𝖍	👤	1863/64
🦁	🦁	𝖎		1864/65
		𝖐		1865/66
		𝖑		1866/67
		𝖒		1867/68
		𝖓		1868/69
		𝖔		1869/70
		𝖕		1870/71
		𝖖		1871/72
		𝖗		1872/73
		𝖘		1873/74
		𝖙		1874/75
		𝖚		1875/76

1876–1896

LH	LP	DL	SH	
🦁	🦁	A	👤	1876/77
		B		1877/78
		C		1878/79
		D		1879/80
		E		1880/81
		F		1881/82
		G		1882/83
		H		1883/84

LH	LP	DL	SH	
🦁	🦁	I	👤	1884/85
		K		1885/86
		L		1886/87
		M		1887/88
		N		1888/89
		O		1889/90
		P		1890/91
		Q		1891/92
		R		1892/93
		S		1893/94
		T		1894/95
		U		1895/96

1896–1916

LH	LP	DL	
🦁	🦁	a	1896/97
		b	1897/98
		c	1898/99
		d	1899/1900
		e	1900/1
		f	1901/2
		g	1902/3
		h	1903/4
		i	1904/5

LH	LP	DL		Year
🛡	🛡	k		¹905/6
		l		1906/7
		m		1907/8
		n		1908/9
		o		1909/10
		p		1910/11
		q		1911/12
		r		1912/13
		s		1913/14
		t		1914/15
		u		1915/16

1916–1936

LH	LP	DL	Year
🛡	🛡	a	1916/17
		b	1917/18
		c	1918/19
		d	1919/20
		e	1920/21
		f	1921/22
		g	1922/23
		h	1923/24
		i	1924/25
		k	1925/26
		l	1926/27
		m	1927/28
		n	1928/29

LH	LP	DL	SH	Year
🛡	🛡	o		1929/30
		p		1930/31
		q		1931/32
		r		1932/33
🛡	🛡	s	👑	1933/34
		t		1934/35
		u		1935/36

1936–1956

LH	LP	DL	Year
🛡	🛡	A	1936/37
		B	1937/38
		C	1938/39
		D	1939/40
		E	1940/41
		F	1941/42
		G	1942/43
		H	1943/44
		I	1944/45
		K	1945/46
		L	1946/47
		M	1947/48
		N	1948/49
		O	1949/50
		P	1950/51
		Q	1951/52

LH	LP	DL	SH	
🦁	🦁	R	👤	1952/53
		S		1953/54
		T		1954/55
		U		1955/56

1956-

LH	LP	DL	
🦁	🦁	a	1956/57
		b	1957/58
		c	1958/59

LH	LP	DL	
🦁	🦁	d	1959/60
		e	1960/61
		f	1961/62
		g	1962/63
		h	1963/64
		i	1964/65
		k	1965/66
		l	1966/67

Birmingham

Assay marking begun here 1773, and continues. Marks: an **anchor**, for "town" mark; **lion passant**, as standard mark; **Britannia figure**, for silver of 11 oz. 10 dwts; **date letter**, changed annually in July; **Sovereign's head**, as duty mark (1784–1890); **maker's mark.**

TM	LP	DL	SH		TM	LP	DL	SH	
		1773–1798								
⚓	🦁	A		1773/74	⚓	🦁	U	🛡	1792/93
		B		1774/75			V		1793/94
		C		1775/76			W		1794/95
		D		1776/77			X		1795/96
		E		1777/78			Y		1796/97
		F		1778/79			Z		1797/98
		G		1779/80					
		H		1780/81			**1798–1824**		
		I		1781/82	⚓	🦁	a	🛡	1798/99
		K		1782/83			b		1799/1800
		L		1783/84			c		1800/1
		M	🛡	1784/85			d		1801/2
		N		1785/86			e		1802/3
		O		1786/87			f		1803/4
		P		1787/88			g		1804/5
		Q		1788/89			h		1805/6
		R		1789/90			i		1806/7
		S		1790/91			j		1807/8
		T		1791/92			k		1808/9

TM	LP	DL	SH	
⚓	🦁	l	🦁	1809/10
		m		1810/11
		n		1811/12
		o		1812/13
		p		1813/14
		q		1814/15
		r		1815/16
		s		1816/17
		t		1817/18
		u		1818/19
		v		1819/20
		w		1820/21
		x		1821/22
		y		1822/23
		z		1823/24

TM	LP	DL	SH	
⚓	🦁	K	👑	1833/34
		L		1834/35
		M		1835/36
		A		1836/37
		D		1837/38
		P	👤	1838/39
		O		1839/40
		R		1840/41
		S		1841/42
		T		1842/43
		U		1843/44
		U		1844/45
		W		1845/46
		X		1846/47
		Y		1847/48
		Z		1848/49

1824–1849

TM	LP	DL	SH	
⚓	🦁	A	👤	1824/25
		B		1825/26
		C		1826/27
		D		1827/28
		E		1828/29
		F		1829/30
		G		1830/31
		H		1831/32
		J		1832/33

1849–1875

TM	LP	DL	SH	
⚓	🦁	A	👤	1849/50
		B		1850/51
		C		1851/52
		D		1852/53
		E		1853/54
		F		1854/55
		G		1855/56
		H		1856/57

TM	LP	DL	SH	
⚓	🦁	I	◐	1857/58
		J		1858/59
		K		1859/60
		L		1860/61
		M		1861/62
		N		1862/63
		O		1863/64
		P		1864/65
		Q		1865/66
		R		1866/67
		S		1867/68
		T		1868/69
		U		1869/70
		V		1870/71
		W		1871/72
		X		1872/73
		Y		1873/74
		Z		1874/75

TM	LP	DL	SH	
⚓	🦁	h	◐	1882/83
		i		1883/84
		k		1884/85
		l		1885/86
		m		1886/87
		n		1887/88
		o		1888/89
		p		1889/90
		q		1890/91
		r		1891/92
		s		1892/93
		t		1893/94
		u		1894/95
		v		1895/96
		w		1896/97
		x		1897/98
		y		1898/99
		z		1899/1900

1875–1900

TM	LP	DL	SH	
⚓	🦁	a	◐	1875/76
		b		1876/77
		c		1877/78
		d		1878/79
		e		1879/80
		f		1880/81
		g		1881/82

1900–1925

TM	LP	DL	
⚓	🦁	a	1900/1
		b	1901/2
		c	1902/3
		d	1903/4
		e	1904/5
		f	1905/6
		g	1906/7

TM	LP	DL		TM	LP	DL	SH	
⚓	🦁	h	1907/8	⚓	🦁	H		1932/33
		i	1908/9			J	😊	1933/34
		k	1909/10			K		1934/35
		l	1910/11			L		1935/36
		m	1911/12			M		1936/37
		n	1912/13			N		1937/38
		o	1913/14			O		1938/39
		p	1914/15			P		1939/40
		q	1915/16			Q		1940/41
		r	1916/17			R		1941/42
		s	1917/18			S		1942/43
		t	1918/19			T		1943/44
		u	1919/20			U		1944/45
		v	1920/21			V		1945/46
		w	1921/22			W		1946/47
		x	1922/23			X		1947/48
		y	1923/24			Y		1948/49
		z	1924/25			Z		1949/50

1925–1950

TM	LP	DL	
⚓	🦁	A	1925/26
		B	1926/27
		C	1927/28
		D	1928/29
		E	1929/30
		F	1930/31
		G	1931/32

1950–

TM	LP	DL	SH	
⚓	🦁	A		1950/51
		B		1951/52
		C	😊	1952/53
		D		1953/54

TM	LP	DL		TM	LP	DL	
⚓	🦁	*E*	1954/55	⚓	🦁	*M*	1961/62
		F	1955/56			*N*	1962/63
		G	1956/57			*O*	1963/64
		H	1957/58			*P*	1964/65
		J	1958/59			*Q*	1965/66
		K	1959/60			*R*	1966/67
		L	1960/61				

Chester

Plate assayed here from early 15th century; marks regulated about end 17th century; the Chester assay office re-established 1701; closed end 1961. Marks: **three wheat-sheaves** with **sword**, as "town" mark (1686–1701, and 1779 onward); LING recorded between 1683 and 1700; **three wheatsheaves/three lions halved,** from 1701 to 1779; **leopard's head,** crowned 1719–1823, uncrowned 1823–39, then disused; **lion's head erased** and **Britannia,** 1701–19; **Sovereign's head,** as duty mark, 1784–1890; **date letter,** changed annually in July; **lion passant,** after 1719; **maker's mark.**

 1686/90

1701–1726					TM	LP	LHC	DL	
TM	B	LHE	DL						
🛡	🗡	🦅	**A**	1701/2	🛡	🦁	🐆	**T**	1719/20
			B	1702/3				**U**	1720/21
			C	1703/4				**V**	1721/22
			D	1704/5				**W**	1722/23
			E	1705/6				**X**	1723/24
			F	1706/7				**Y**	1724/25
			G	1707/8				**Z**	1725/26
			H	1708/9					
			I	1709/10	1726–1751				
			K	1710/11	TM	LP	LHC	DL	
			L	1711/12	🛡	🦁	🐆	**A**	1726/27
			M	1712/13				**B**	1727/28
			N	1713/14				**C**	1728/29
			O	1714/15				**D**	1729/30
			P	1715/16				**E**	1730/31
			Q	1716/17				**F**	1731/32
			R	1717/18				**G**	1732/33
			S	1718/19				**H**	1733/34
								I	1734/35

TM	LP	LHC	DL		TM	LP	LHC	DL	
🛡	🦁	👑	K	1735/36	🛡	🦁	👑	K	1760/61
			L	1736/37				L	1761/62
			M	1737/38				m	1762/63
			N	1738/39				n	1763/64
			O	1739/40				O	1764/65
			P	1740/41				P	1765/66
			Q	1741/42				Q	1766/67
			R	1742/43				R	1767/68
			S	1743/44				S	1768/69
			T	1744/45				T	1769/70
			U	1745/46				U	1771/72
			V	1746/47				V	1773
			W	1747/48				W	1774
			X	1748/49				X	1775
			Y	1749/50				Y	1775/76
			Z	1750/51					

1751–1776

TM	LP	LHC	DL	
🛡	🦁	👑	a	1751/52
			b	1752/53
			c	1753/54
			d	1754/55
			e	1755/56
			f	1756/57
			G	1757/58
			h	1758/59
			I	1759/60

1776–1797

TM	LP	LHC	DL	SH	
🛡	🦁	👑	a		1776/77
			b		1777/78
			c		1778/79
👤			d		1779/80
			e		1780/81
			f		1781/82
			g		1782/83
			h		1783/84
			i		1784/85
			i	🦁	1784/85

TM	LP	LHC	DL	SH	
😐	🦁	🐆	K	🛡	1785/86
			l	🛡	1786/87
			m		1787/88
			n		1788/89
			o		1789/90
			p		1790/91
			q		1791/92
			r		1792/93
			s		1793/94
			t		1794/95
			u		1795/96
			v		1796/97

1797–1818

TM	LP	LHC	DL	SH	
😐	🦁	🐆	A	🛡	1797/98
			B		1798/99
			C		1799/1800
			D		1800/1
			E		1801/2
			F		1802/3
			G		1803/4
			H		1804/5
			I		1805/6
			K		1806/7
			L		1807/8
			M		1808/9
			N		1809/10

TM	LP	LHC	DL	SH	
😐	🦁	🐆	O	🛡	1810/11
			P		1811/12
			Q		1812/13
			R		1813/14
			S		1814/15
			T		1815/16
			U		1816/17
			V		1817/18

1818–1839

TM	LP	LHC	DL	SH	
😐	🦁	🐆	A	🛡	1818/19
			B		1819/20
			C		1820/21
		LH	D		1821/22/23
		🐆	E	🛡	1823/24
			F		1824/25
			G		1825/26
			H		1826/27
			I		1827/28
			K		1828/29
			L		1829/30
			M		1830/31
			N		1831/32
			O		1832/33
			P		1833/34
			Q		1834/35
			R	🛡	1835/36

TM	LP	LH	DL	SH		TM	LP	DL	SH	
🛡	🦁	🏵	S	◊	1836/37	🛡	🦁	W	✊	1860/61
			T		1837/38			X		1861/62
			U		1838/39			Y		1862/63
								Z		1863/64

1839–1864

TM	LP	DL	SH	
🛡	🦁	A	☺	1839/40
		B		1840/41
		C		1841/42
		D		1842/43
		E		1843/44
		F		1844/45
		G		1845/46
		H		1846/47
		J		1847/48
		K		1848/49
		L		1849/50
		M		1850/51
		A		1851/52
		O		1852/53
		P		1853/54
		Q		1854/55
		R		1855/56
		S		1856/57
		T		1857/58
		U		1858/59
		V		1859/60

1864–1884

TM	LP	DL	SH	
🛡	🦁	a	✊	1864/65
		b		1865/66
		c		1866/67
		d		1867/68
		e		1868/69
		f		1869/70
		g		1870/71
		h		1871/72
		i		1872/73
		k		1873/74
		l		1874/75
		m		1875/76
		n		1876/77
		o		1877/78
		p		1878/79
		q		1879/80
		r		1880/81
		s		1881/82
		t		1882/83
		u		1883/84

34

1884–1903

TM	LP	DL	SH	
🛡	🦁	A	☺	1884/85
		B		1885/86
		C		1886/87
		D		1887/88
		E		1888/89
		F		1889/90
		G		1890/91
		H		1891/92
		I		1892/93
		K		1893/94
		L		1894/95
		M		1895/96
		N		1896/97
		O		1897/98
		P		1898/99
		Q		1899/1900
		R		1900/1
		A		1901/2
		B		1902/3

1903–1926

TM	LP	DL	
🛡	🦁	C	1903/4
		D	1904/5
		E	1905/6
		F	1906/7

TM	LP	DL	
🛡	🦁	G	1907/8
		H	1908/9
		I	1909/10
		K	1910/11
		L	1911/12
		M	1912/13
		N	1913/14
		O	1914/15
		P	1915/16
		Q	1916/17
		R	1917/18
		S	1918/19
		T	1919/20
		U	1920/21
		V	1921/22
		W	1922/23
		X	1923/24
		Y	1924/25
		Z	1925/26

1926–1951

TM	LP	DL	
🛡	🦁	a	1926/27
		b	1927/28
		c	1928/29
		d	1929/30
		e	1930/31

TM	LP	DL	SH		TM	LP	DL	
🛡	🦁	ff		1931/32	🛡	🦁	W	1947/48
		G		1932/33			X	1948/49
		H	🔘	1933/34			Y	1949/50
		J		1934/35			Z	1950/51
		K		1935/36				

1951–1961

TM	LP	DL	SH	
		L		1936/37
		M		1937/38
		N		1938/39
		O		1939/40
		P		1940/41
		Q		1941/42
		R		1942/43
		S		1943/44
		T		1944/45
		U		1945/46
		V		1946/47

TM	LP	DL	SH	
🛡	🦁	A		1951/52
		B	👤	1952/53
		C		1953/54
		D		1954/55
		E		1955/56
		F		1956/57
		G		1957/58
		H		1958/59
		J		1959/60
		K		1960/61

Dublin

Earliest assay recorded 1638; continues. Marks: **harp crowned,** as "town" mark; **"Hibernia" figure** adopted 1730/1, at first used as duty mark; **Sovereign's head,** as duty mark (1807-90); **date letter,** changed annually in January; **maker's mark.**

	1638–1658				1638-1658 cont	
TM	**DL**			**TM**	**DL**	
	A	1638/39			S	1655/56
	B	1639/40			T	1656/57
	C	1640/41			U	1657/58
	D	1641/42				
	E	1642/43			**1658–1678**	
	F	1643/44		**TM**	**DL**	
	G	1644/45			a	1658/59
	H	1645/46			b	1659/60
	I	1646/47			c	1660/61
	K	1647/48			d	1661/62
	L	1648/49			e	1662/63
	M	1649/50			f	1663/64
	N	.650/51			g	1664/65
	O	1651/52			h	1665/66
	P	1o.2/53			j	1666/67
	Q	1o53/54			k	1667/68
	R	654/55			l	1668/69
					m	1669/70

TM	DL			TM	DL	
	n	1670/71			P	1702/3
	o	1671/72			Q	1703/4
	p	1672/73			R	1704/5/6
	q	1673/74			S	1706/7/8
	r	1674/75			T	1708/9/10
	s	1675/76			U	1710/11/12
	t	1676/77			W	1712/13/14
	u	1677/78			X	1714/15
					Y	1715/16
					Z	1716/17

1678–1717

TM	DL	
	A	1678/79
	B	1679/80
	C	1680/81
	D	1681/82
	E	1682/83
	F	1683/84
	G	1685/86/87
	H	1688/92
	J	1688/92
	K	1693/94/95
	L	1696/99
	M	1699/1700
	N	1700/1
	O	1701/2

1717–1731

TM	DL	
	A	1717/18
	B	1718/19
	C	1719/20
	C	1719/20
	A	1720/21
	B	1721/22
	C	1722/23
	D	1723/24
	E	1724/25
	F	1725/26
	G	1726/27

38

TM	DL		
🛡	H		1727/28
	J		1728/29
	K		1729/30
	L		1730/31

1731–1746

TM	H	DL	
🛡	🛡	L	1731/32
		M	1732/33
		N	1733/34
		O	1734/35
		P	1735/36
		Q	1736/37
		R	1737/38
		S	1738/39
		T	1739/40
		U	1740/41
		W	1741/42/43
		W	
		X	1743/44
		Y	1745
		Z	1746

1747–1772

TM	H	DL	
🛡	🛡	A	1747

TM	H	DL	
🛡	🛡	B	1748
		C	1749
		D	1750
		E E	1751/52
		F	1752/53
		G	1753/54
		H	1754/55
		I	1757
		K	1758
		L	1759
		M	1760
		N	1761
		O	1762
		P	1763
		Q	1764
		R	1765
		S	1766
		T	1767
		U	1768
		W	1769
		X	1770
		Y	1771
		Z	1772

1773–1796 | 1797–1820

TM	H	DL			TM	H	DL	SH
🐚	🦁	A	1773	1797	🐚	🦁	A	
		B	1774	1798			B	
		C	1775	1799			C	
		D	1776	1800			D	
		E	1777	1801			E	
		F	1778	1802			F	
		G	1779	1803			G	
		H	1780	1804			H	
		I	1781	1805			I	
		K	1782	1806			K	
		L	1783	1807			L	👤
		M	1784	1808			M	
		N	1785	1809			N	👤
		O	1786	1810			O	
		P	1787	1811			P	
		Q	1788	1812			Q	
		R	1789	1813			R	
		S	1790	1814			S	
		T	1791	1815			T	
		U	1792	1816			U	
		W	1793	1817			W	
		X	1794	1818			X	
		Y	1795	1819			Y	
		Z	1796	1820			Z	

	1821–1846					1846–1871		
TM	H	DL	SH		TM	H	DL	SH

TM	H	DL	SH	Year	TM	H	DL	SH	Year
☑	☑	A	☺	1821	☑	☑	a	☺	1846/47
		B	☺	1822			b		1847/48
		C		1823			c		1848/49
		D		1824			d		1849/50
		E e	☺	1825/26			e		1850/51
		F	☺	1826/27			f f		1851/52
☑	☑	G	☺	1827/28			g g		1852/53
		H	☺	1828/29			h h		1853/54
☑	☑ I	I	☺	1829/30			j		1854/55
☑		K	☺	1830/31			k		1855/56
	☑	L	☺	1831/32			l		1856/57
		M		1832/33			m		1857/58
		N N		1833/34			n		1858/59
		O O	☺	1834/35			o		1859/60
		P P		1835/36			p		1860/61
		Q Q		1836/37			q		1861/62
		R R		1837/38			r		1862/63
		S	☺	1838/39			s		1863/64
		T		1839/40			t		1864/65
		U U		1840/41			u		1865/66
		V		1841/42			v		1866/67
		W		1842/43			w		1867/68
		X		1843/44			x		1868/69
		Y Y		1844/45			y		1869/70
		Z		1845/46			z		1870/71

1871–1896

TM	H	DL	SH	
		A		1871/72
		B		1872/73
		C		1873/74
		D		1874/75
		E		1875/76
		F		1876/77
		G		1877/78
		H		1878/79
		I		1879/80
		K		1880/81
		L		1881/82
		M		1882/83
		N		1883/84
		O		1884/85
		P		1885/86
		Q		1886/87
		R		1887/88
		S		1888/89
		T		1889/90
		U		1890/91
		V		1891/92
		W		1892/93
		X		1893/94
		Y		1894/95
		Z		1895/96

1896–1916

TM	H	DL	
		A	1896/97
		B	1897/98
		C	1898/99
		D	1899/1900
		E	1900/1
		F	1901/2
		G	1902/3
		H	1903/4
		I	1904/5
		K	1905/6
		L	1906/7
		M	1907/8
		N	1908/9
		O	1909/10
		P	1910/11
		Q	1911/12
		R	1912/13
		S	1913/14
		T	1914/15
		U	1915/16

1916–1941

TM	H	DL	
		A	1916/17
		B	1917/18
		C	1918/19
		D	1919/20

TM	H	DL		TM	H	DL	JM	
🛡	🛡	𝖊 1920/21		🛡	🛡	B		1943
		𝖋 1921/22				C		1944
		𝖌 1922/23				D		1945
		𝖍 1923/24				E		1946
		𝖎 1924/25				F		1947
		𝖐 1925/26				G		1948
		𝖑 1926/27				H		1949
		𝖒 1927/28				I		1950
		𝖓 1928/29				J		1951
		𝖔 1929/30				K		1952
		𝖕 1930/31				L		1953
		𝖖 1932				M		1954
		𝖗 1933				N		1955
		𝖘 1934				O		1956
		𝖙 1935				P		1957
		𝖚 1936				Q		1958
		𝖛 1937				R		1959
		𝖜 1938				S		1960
		𝖝 1939				T		1961
		𝖞 1940				U		1962
		𝖟 1941				V		1963
						W		1964
		1942–				X		1965
TM	H	DL				Y	🍃	1966
🛡	🛡	A 1942						

Jubilee Mark for 1966, used on Irish gold and silver, on all items except jewellery and watch cases, in addition to the normal hallmark during the year 1966

Edinburgh

Plate marked here from 1457 onward. Marks: **three-towered castle**, as "town" mark (from 1485); **deacon's mark** (1457–1681); **Assay Master's mark** (1681–1759); **date letters** (1681 onward) changed annually in October; **thistle mark** (1759 onward); Sovereign's **head**, as duty mark (1784–1890); **maker's mark**.

TM	DM			TM	DM	
🏰		1552/62		🏰		1642
		1563/64				
	IC	1570				1644/46
		1576			GC	1649
		1585/86				'651/59
	M	1590/91				1660
		1591/92			IS	1665/67
		1591/94			Is	1665
	W	1596/1600				1669/75
		1609/10			E	1663/81
🏰		1611/13			W	1675/77
		1617/19				
	G	1617				

1681–1705

TM		1613/21		TM	AM	DL	
		1616/35		🏰	B		1681/82
	R	1633			B		1682/83
						C	1683/84
						D	1684/85
						E	1685/86

1637–1677

TM	DM	
🏰		1637/39
		1640/42

		1686/87
		1687/88

TM	AM	DL		TM	AM	DL	
🏰	ℬ	h	1688/89	🏰	EP	K	1714/15
		i	1689/90			L	1715/16
		k	1690/91			M M	1716/17
		l	1691/92			N N	1717/18
		m	1692/93		EP	N	1717/18
		n	1693/94			O	1718/19
		o	1694/95			P P	1719/20
		p	1695/96		EP	P	1719/20
	𝒫	q	1696/97			q	1720/21
		r	1697/98			R	1721/22
		s	1698/99			S	1722/23
		t	1699/1700			T	1723/24
		u	1700/1			U	1724/25
		v	1701/2			V	1725/26
		w	1702/3			W	1726/27
		x	1703/4			X	1727/28
		y	1704/5			Y	1728/29
						Z	1729/30
					AU	Z	1729/30

		1705–1730	
TM	AM	DL	
🏰	𝒫	A	1705/6
		B	1706/7
	EP	C	1707/8
		D	1708/9
		E	1709/10
		F	1710/11
		G	1711/12
		H	1712/13
		I	1713/14

		1730–1755	
TM	AM	DL	
🏰	AU	A	1730/31
		B	1731/32
		C	1732/33
		D	1733/34
		E	1734/35
		F	1735/36
		G	1736/37

TM	AM	DL	
🏰	AU	H	1737/38
		J	1738/39
		K	1739/40
	GED	L	1740/41
		M	1741/42
	EL	N	1742/43
		O	1743/44
	HG	P	1744/45
		Q	1745/46
		R	1746/47
		S	1747/48
		T	1748/49
		U	1749/50
		V	1750/51
		W	1751/52
		X	1752/53
		Y	1753/54
		Z	1754/55

1755–1780

TM	AM	DL	
HFR	HG	A	1755/56
		B	1756/57
		C	1757/58
	T	D	1758/59
		E	1759/60
		F	1760/61
		G	1761/62
		H	1762/63

TM	T	DL	
🏰		I	1763/64
		K	1764/65
		L	1765/66
		M	1766/67
		N	1767/68
		O	1768/69
		P	1769/70
		Q	1770/71
		R	1771/72
		S	1772/73
		T	1773/74
		U	1774/75
		V	1775/76
		X	1776/77
		Y	1777/78
		Z	1778/79
		U	1779/80

1780–1806

TM	T	DL	SH	
🏰		A		1780/81
		B		1781/82
		C		1782/83
		D		1783/84
		E		1784/85
		F		1785/86
		G		1786/87/88
		H		1788/89
		IJ		1789/90

TM	T	DL	SH		TM	T	DL	SH	
🔲	🛡	K	🔵	1790/91	🔲	🛡	J	🔵	1815/16
		L		1791/92			k		1816/17
		M		1792/93			l		1817/18
		N		1793/94			m		1818/19
		O		1794/95			n		1819/20
		P		1795/96			o		1820/21
		Q		1796/97			p		1821/22
		R	🔵	1797/98			q		1822/23
		S		1798/99			r	🔵	1823/24
		T		1799/1800			s		1824/25
		U		1800/1			t		1825/26
		V		1801/2			u		1826/27
		W		1802/3			v		1827/28
		X		1803/4			w		1828/29
		Y		1804/5			x		1829/30
		Z		1805/6			y		1830/31
							z		1831/32

TM	T	1806–1832 DL	SH		TM	T	1832–1857 DL	SH	
🔲	🛡	a	🔵	1806/7	🔲	🛡	A	🔵	1832/33
		b		1807/8			B		1833/34
		c		1808/9			C		1834/35
		d		1809/10			D		1835/36
		e		1810/11			E		1836/37
		f		1811/12			F		1837/38
		g		1812/13			G		1838/39
		h		1813/14			H		1839/40
		i		1814/15					

47

TM	T	DL	SH		TM	T	DL	SH	
		J		1840/41			I		1865/66
		K		1841/42			K		1866/67
		L		1842/43			L		1867/68
		M		1843/44			M		1868/69
		N		1844/45			N		1869/70
		O		1845/46			O		1870/71
		P		1846/47			P		1871/72
		Q		1847/48			Q		1872/73
		R		1848/49			R		1873/74
		S		1849/50			S		1874/75
		T		1850/51			T		1875/76
		U		1851/52			U		1876/77
		V		1852/53			V		1877/78
		W		1853/54			W		1878/79
		X		1854/55			X		1879/80
		Y		1855/56			Y		1880/81
		Z		1856/57			Z		1881/82

		1857–1882					1882–1906		
TM	T	DL	SH		TM	T	DL	SH	
		A		1857/58			a		1882/83
		B		1858/59			b		1883/84
		C		1859/60			c		1884/85
		D		1860/61			d		1885/86
		E		1861/62			e		1886/87
		F		1862/63			f		1887/88
		G		1863/64			g		1888/89
		H		1864/65			h		1889/90

TM	T	DL	SH	
🛡	🌹	î	🦁	1890/91
		k		1891/92
		l		1892/93
		m		1893/94
		n		1894/95
		o		1895/96
		p		1896/97
		q		1897/98
		r		1898/99
		s		1899/1900
		t		1900/1
		u		1901/2
		w		1902/3
		x		1903/4
		y		1904/5
		z		1905/6

TM	T	DL	
🛡	🌹	I	1914/15
		K	1915/16
		L	1916/17
		M	1917/18
		N	1918/19
		O	1919/20
		P	1920/21
		Q	1921/22
		R	1922/23
		S	1923/24
		T	1924/25
		U	1925/26
		V	1926/27
		W	1927/28
		X	1928/29
		Y	1929/30
		Z	1930/31

1906–1931

TM	T	DL	
🛡	🌹	A	1906/7
		B	1907/8
		C	1908/9
		D	1909/10
		E	1910/11
		F	1911/12
		G	1912/13
		H	1913/14

1931–1956

TM	T	DL	SH	
🛡	🌹	A		1931/32
		B		1932/33
		C	🦁	1933/34
		D		1934/35
		E		1935/36
		F		1936/37
		G		1937/38
		H		1938/39

TM	T	DL	SH		TM	T	DL	
		J		1939/40			*Y*	1954/55
		K		1940/41			*Z*	1955/56
		L		1941/42				
		M		1942/43				
		N		1943/44			**1956–**	
					TM	T	DL	
		O		1944/45			**A**	1956/57
		P		1945/46			**B**	1957/58
		Q		1946/47			**C**	1958/59
		R		1947/48			**D**	1959/60
		S		1948/49			**E**	1960/61
		T		1949/50			**F**	1961/62
		U		1950/51			**G**	1962/63
		V		1951/52			**H**	1963/64
		W	●	1952/53			**I**	1964/65
		X		1953/54			**K**	1965/66

50

Exeter

Assay office apparently not legally existing here before 1701, though making of wrought silver recorded in middle ages; office closed 1883. Marks: **Roman capital letter "X"** as "town" mark, 16th and 17th centuries; sometimes found crowned; **three-towered turreted castle,** as "town" mark, from 1700/1; **leopard's head,** up to 1776; **Britannia, and lion's head erased,** to 1719; **Sovereign's head,** as duty mark, 1784–1890; **date letter,** begun November, 1701, then changed annually in August from 1702; **maker's mark.**

1570	1590	1635	1640/50	1646/98	1680

TM	B	LHE	DL		TM	B	LHE	DL	
			A	1701/2				S	1718/19
			B	1702/3				T	1719/20
			C	1703/4		LHC	LP	V	1720/21
			D	1704/5				W	1721/22
			E	1705/6				X	1722/23
			F	1706/7				Y	1723/24
			G	1707/8				Z	1724/25
			H	1708/9					
			I	1709/10					
			K	1710/11			1725–1749		
			L	1711/12	TM	LHC	LP	DL	
			M	1712/13				a	1725/26
			N	1713/14				b	1726/27
			O	1714/15				c	1727/28
			P	1715/16				d	1728/29
			Q	1716/17				e	1729/30
			R	1717/18				f	1730/31
								g	1731/32

TM	LHC	LP	DL	Year
⬟	⬟	⬟	h	1732/33
			i	1733/34
			k	1734/35
			l	1735/36
			m	1736/37
			n	1737/38
			o	1738/39
			p	1739/40
			q	1740/41
			r	1741/42
			s	1742/43
			t	1743/44
			u	1744/45
			w	1745/46
			x	1746/47
			y	1747/48
			z	1748/49

TM	LHC	LP	DL	Year
⬟	⬟	⬟	H	1756/57
			I	1757/58
			K	1758/59
			L	1759/60
			M	1760/61
			N	1761/62
			O	1762/63
			P	1763/64
			Q	1764/65
			R	1765/66
			S	1766/67
			T	1767/68
			U	1768/69
			W	1769/70
			X	1770/71
			Y	1771/72
			Z	1772/73

1749–1773

TM	LHC	LP	DL	Year
⬟	⬟	⬟	A	1749/50
			B	1750/51
			C	1751/52
			D	1752/53
			E	1753/54
			F	1754/55
			G	1755/56

1773–1797

TM	LHC	LP	DL	Year
⬟	⬟	⬟	A	1773/74
			B	1774/75
			C	1775/76
			D	1776/77
			E	1777/78
			F	1778/79
			G	1779/80

TM	LP	DL	LHC	
🛡	🦁	**H**	👑	1780/81
		I		1781/82/83
		K	SH	1783/84
		L	👤	1784/85
		M		1785/86
		N	👤	1786/87
		O		1787/88
		P		1788/89
		q		1789/90
		r		1790/91
		f		1791/92
		t		1792/93
		u		1793/94
		w		1794/95
		x		1795/96
		y		1796/97

1797–1817

TM	LP	DL	SH	
🛡	🦁	**A**	👤	1797/98
		B		1798/99
		C		1799/1800
		D		1800/1
		E		1801/2
		F		1802/3
		G		1803/4
		H		1804/5

TM	LP	DL	
🛡	🦁	**I**	1805/6
		K	1806/7
		L	1807/8
		M	1808/9
		N	1809/10
		O	1810/11
		P	1811/12
		Q	1812/13
		R	1813/14
		S	1814/15
		T	1815/16
		U	1816/17

1817–1837

TM	LP	DL	SH	
🛡	🦁	**a**	👤	1817/18
		b		1818/19
		c		1819/20
		d		1820/21
		e		1821/22
		f	👤	1822/23
		g		1823/24
		h		1824/25
		i		1825/26
		k		1826/27
		l		1827/28
		m		1828/29

TM	LP	DL	SH	
𝔐	🦁	n		1829/30
		o		1830/31
		p	○	1831/32
		q		1832/33
		q		1833/34
		r	○	1834/35
		s		1835/36
		t		
		u		1836/37

1837–1857

TM	LP	DL	SH	
𝔐	🦁	A	○	1837/38
		B	○	1838/39
		C		1839/40
		D		1840/41
		E		1841/42
		F		1842/43
		G		1843/44
		H		1844/45
		J		1845/46
		K		1846/47
		L		1847/48
		M		1848/49
		N		1849/50
		O		1850/51
		P		1851/52
		Q		1852/53
		R		1853/54

TM	LP	DL	
𝔐	🦁	S	1854/55
		T	1855/56
		U	1856/57

1857–1877

TM	LP	DL	SH	
𝔐	🦁	A	○	1857/58
		B		1858/59
		C		1859/60
		D		1860/61
		E		1861/62
		F		1862/63
		G		1863/64
		H		1864/65
		I		1865/66
		K		1866/67
		L		1867/68
		M		1868/69
		N		1869/70
		O		1870/71
		P		1871/72
		Q		1872/73
		R		1873/74
		S		1874/75
		T		1875/76
		U		1876/77

1877–1883

TM	LP	DL	SH		TM	I.P	DL	
🔲	🦁	**A**	⭕	1877/78	🔲	🦁	**D**	1880/81
		B		1878/79			**E**	1881/82
		C		1879/80			**F**	1882/83

Glasgow

Assay office established here in 1819. Marks: **lion rampant**, as "standard" mark; **Tree, fish,** and **bell** (city arms), as "town" mark; **Sovereign's head,** as duty mark, until 1890; **thistle mark,** added 1914; **date letter,** changed annually in July; **maker's mark.** N.B. A date letter was used on Glasgow wrought silver, 1681–1710; discontinued until 1819. Finally closed March 1964

TM	DL		TM	DL	
⊙	a	1681/82	⊙	t	1699/1700
	b	1682/83		u	1700/1
	c	1683/84		v	1701/2
	d	1684/85		w	1702/3
	e	1685/86		x	1703/4
	f	1686/87		y	1704/5
	g	1687/88		z	1705/6
	h	1688/89			

1706–1765

TM	DL	
⊙	A	1706/7
	B	1707/8
	D	1709/10
	S	1728/31
	S	1725/35
	S	1743/52
	S	1747/60
	S	1756/76

i	1689/90
K	1690/91
l	1691/92
m	1692/93
n	1693/94
o	1694/95
p	1695/96
q	1696/97
r	1697/98
s	1698/99

TM	DL		
🔲			1756/76
🔲			1757/80
🔲			1757/80
🔲			1757/80
	S		1758/65

1763–1800

TM			
🔲	E		1763/70
	F		1763/70
	S		1773/80
	O		1776/80
	O		1785/95
	S		1785/95
🔲	S		1781/1800

1819–1845

TM	LR	DL	SH	
🔲	🦁	A	👤	1819/20
🔲		B		1820/21
		C		1821/22
		D		1822/23
		E		1823/24
		F		1824/25
		G		1825/26
		H		1826/27
		I		1827/28
		J		1828/29

TM	LR	DL	SH	
🔲	🦁	K	👤	1829/30
		L		1830/31
		M		1831/32
		N	👤	1832/33
		O		1833/34
		P		1834/35
		Q		1835/36
		R		1836/37
		S		1837/38
		T		1838/39
		U		1839/40
		V		1840/41
		W		1841/42
		X		1842/43
		Y		1843/44
		Z		1844/45

1845–1871

TM	LR	DL	SH	
🔲	🦁	A	👤	1845/46
		B		1846/47
		C		1847/48
		D		1848/49
		E		1849/50
		F		1850/51
		G		1851/52
		H		1852/53
		I		1853/54

TM	LR	DL	SH	Date
(mark)	(mark)	I	(mark)	1854/55
		K		1855/56
		L		1856/57
		M		1857/58
		N		1858/59
		O		1859/60
		P		1860/61
		Q		1861/62
		R		1862/63
		S		1863/64
		T		1864/65
		U		1865/66
		V		1866/67
		W		1867/68
		X		1868/69
		Y		1869/70
		Z		1870/71

TM	LR	DL	SH	Date
(mark)	(mark)	I	(mark)	1879/80
		J		1880/81
		K		1881/82
		L		1882/83
		M		1883/84
		N		1884/85
		O		1885/86
		P		1886/87
		Q		1387/88
		R		1888/89
		S		1889/90
		T		1890/91
		U		1891/92
		V		1892/93
		W		1893/94
		X		1894/95
		Y		1895/96
		Z		1896/97

1871–1897

TM	LR	DL	SH	Date
(mark)	(mark)	A	(mark)	1871/72
		B		1872/73
		C		1873/74
		D		1874/75
		E		1875/76
		F		1876/77
		G		1877/78
		H		1878/79

1897–1923

TM	LR	DL	Date
(mark)	(mark)	A	1897/98
		B	1898/99
		C	1899/1900
		D	1900/1
		E	1901/2
		F	1902/3
		G	1903/4

TM	LR	DI	T	Year
🦁	🦁	H		1904/5
		I		1905/6
		J		1906/7
		K		1907/8
		L		1908/9
		M		1909/10
		N		1910/11
		O		1911/12
		P		1912/13
		Q		1913/14
		R	🌹	1914/15
		S		1915/16
		T		1916/17
		U		1917/18
		V		1918/19
		W		1919/20
		X		1920/21
		Y		1921/22
		Z		1922/23

TM	LR	T	DL	SH	Year
🦁	🦁	👑	f		1928/29
			g		1929/30
			h		1930/31
			i		1931/32
			j		1932/33
			k	●	1933/34
			l		1934/35
			m		1935/36
			n		1936/37
			o		1937/38
			p		1938/39
			q		1939/40
			r		1940/41
			s		1941/42
			t		1942/43
			u		1943/44
			v		1944/45
			w		1945/46
			x		1946/47
			y		1947/48
			z		1948/49

1923–1949

TM	LR	T	DL	Year
🦁	🦁	👑	a	1923/24
			b	1924/25
			c	1925/26
			d	1926/27
			e	1927/28

1949– 1964

TM	LR	T	DL	Year
🦁	🦁	👑	A	1949/50
			B	1950/51
			C	1951/52

TM	LR	T	DL	SH		TM	LR	T	DL	
⬛	⬛	⬛	D	⬛	1952/53	⬛	⬛	⬛	L	1958/59
			E		1953/54				M	1959/60
			F		1954/55				N	1960/61
			Z		1955/56				O	1961/62
			H		1956/57				P	1962/63
			J		1957/58				R	1963/64

Newcastle

Goldsmiths recorded working here from mid 13th century; some examples (later 17th century) have marks including a single castle ("town" mark), and a lion passant. Assay office re-established 1702, closed down 1884. Marks: **three** distinct **castles,** as "town" mark (from city arms), from *c.* 1670; **lion's head erased** and **Britannia,** 1702–19; **lion passant,** recorded 1721–28, facing right; **Sovereign's head,** as duty mark, 1784 to closure; **date letter,** changed annually with some regularity at first, later not consistently carried on; **maker's mark.**

TM	B	LHE	DL	
🏰	🛡	🦁	𝕬	1702/3
			𝕭	1703/4
			𝕮	1704/5
			𝕯	1705/6
			𝕰	1706/7
			𝕱	1707/8
			𝕲	1708/9
				1709/10
				1710/11
				1711/12
			𝕳	1712/13
				1713/14
			𝕷	1714/15
				1715/16
				1716/17
			𝕻	1717/18

1702–1721

TM	B	LHE	DL	
🏰	🛡	🦁	𝕼	1718/19
			𝕽	1719/20
			𝕱	1720/21

1721–1740

LP	LHC	DL	
🦁	🦁	𝖆	1721/22
🦁	🦁	𝖇	1722/23
	🦁	𝖈	1723/24
		𝖉	1724/25
🦁	🦁	𝖊	1725/26
		𝖋	1726/27
		𝖌	1727/28
	🦁	𝖍	1728/29
		𝖎	1729/30
		𝖐	1730/31

TM	LP	LHC	DL	
🛡	🦁	👑	𝕷	1731/32
			𝕸	1732/33
			𝕹	1733/34
			𝕺	1734/35
			𝕻	1735/36
			𝕼	1736/37
			𝕽	1737/38
			𝕾	1738/39
			𝕿	1739/40

1740–1759

TM	LP	LHC	DL	
🛡	🦁	👑	A	1740/41
			B	1741/42
			C	1742/43
			D	1743/44
			E	1744/45
			F	1745/46
			G	1746/47
			H	1747/48
			I	1748/49
			K	1749/50
			L	1750/51
			M	1751/52
			N	1752/53
			O	1753/54

TM	LP	LHC	DL	
🛡	🦁	👑	P	1754/55
			Q	1755/56
			R	1756/57
			S	1757/58
			T	1758/59

1759–1791

TM	LP	LHC	DL		
🛡	🦁	👑	𝓐		1759/60
			𝓑		1760/68
			𝓒		1769/70
			𝓓		1770/71
			𝓔		1771/72
			𝓕		1772/73
			G		1773/74
			H		1774/75
			I		1775/76
			K		1776/77
			L		1777/78
			M		1778/79
			N		1779/80
			O		1780/81
			P		1781/82
			Q		1782/83
			R	SH	1783/84
			S	🔲	1784/85

TM	LP	LHC	DL	SH	
🛡	🦁	👑	T	👤	1785/86
			U	👤	1786/87
			W		1787/88
			X		1788/89
			Y		1789/90
			Z		1790/91

TM	LP	LHC	DL	SH	
🛡	🦁	👑	U	👤	1810/11
			W		1811/12
			X		1812/13
			Y		1813/14
			Z		1814/15

1791–1815

TM	LP	LHC	DL	SH	
🛡	🦁	👑	A	👤	1791/92
			B		1792/93
			C		1793/94
			D		1794/95
			E		1795/96
			F		1796/97
			G	👤	1797/98
			H		1798/99
			I		1799/1800
			K	👤	1800/1
			L		1801/2
			M		1802/3
			N	👤	1803/4
			O		1804/5
			P		1805/6
			Q		1806/7
			R		1807/8
			S		1808/9
			T	👤	1809/10

1815–1839

TM	LP	LHC	DL	SH	
🛡	🦁	👑	A	👤	1815/16
			B		1816/17
			C		1817/18
			D		1818/19
			E		1819/20
			F		1820/21
			G	👤	1821/22
			H		1822/23
			I		1823/24
			K		1824/25
			L		1825/26
			M		1826/27
			N		1827/28
			O		1828/29
			P		1829/30
			Q		1830/31
			R		1831/32
			S	◯	1832/33
			T		1833/34
			U		1834/35

TM	LP	LHC	DL	SH	
🛡	🛡	🛡	**W**	◖	1835/36
			X		1836/37
			Y		1837/38
			Z		1838/39

TM	LP	LH	DL	SH	
🛡	🛡	🛡	**W**	◖	1860/61
			X		1861/62
			Y		1862/63
			Z		1863/64

1839–1864

TM	LP	LHC	DL	SH	
🛡	🛡	🛡	**A**	◖	1839/40
			B		1840/41
			C	◖	1841/42
			D		1842/43
			E		1843/44
			F		1844/45
		LH	**G**		1845/46
		🛡	**H**		1846/47
			I		1847/48
			J		1848/49
			K		1849/50
			L		1850/51
			M		1851/52
			N		1852/53
			O		1853/54
			P		1854/55
			Q		1855/56
			R		1856/57
			S		1857/58
			T		1858/59
			U		1859/60

1864–1884

TM	LP	LH	DL	SH	
🛡	🛡	🛡	**a**	◖	1864/65
			b		1865/66
			c		1866/67
			d		1867/68
			e		1868/69
			f		1869/70
			g		1870/71
			h		1871/72
			i		1872/73
			k		1873/74
			l		1874/75
			m		1875/76
			n		1876/77
			o		1877/78
			p		1878/79
			q		1879/80
			r		1880/81
			s		1881/82
			t		1882/83
			u		1883/84

Norwich

Assay marks recorded here from mid 16th century until end 17th century. Marks: **castle** over a **lion passant; date letter,** changed annually in September, 1565–85, and from 1624–43, again 1688; **crowned rose,** recorded 1610/11, perhaps used as a standard mark; **crown** as separate mark, 1642–88; **rose sprig,** 1643–88; **maker's mark.**

1565–1585					
TM	DL				
	A	1565/66	S	1582/83	
	B	1566/67	T	1583/84	
	C	1567/68	V	1584/85	
	D	1568/69			
	E	1569/70	1600–1610		
	F	1570/71		1600/10	
	G	1571/72			
	H	1572/73	1624–1644		
	I	1573/74	TM RC DL		
	K	1574/75	A	1624/25	
	L	1575/76	B	1625/26	
	M	1576/77	C	1626/27	
	N	1577/78	D	1627/28	
	O	1578/79	E	1628/29	
	P	1579/80	F	1629/30	
RC	Q	1580/81	G	1630/31	
	R	1581/82	H	1631/32	

TM	RC	DL	
		I	1632/33
		K	1633/34
		L	1634/35
		M	1635/36
		N	1636/37
		O	1637/38
		P	1638/39
		Q	1639/40
		R	1640/41
		S	1641/42
		T	1642/43
		V	1643/44

1688–1702

TM	RC	DL	
		a	1688
		b	1689
		C	1690
		D	1691
		E	1692
		F	1693
		G	1694
		H	1695
		I	1696
		K	1697

			1660
			1670
			1675
			1680

TM	LHE	B	DL	
			A	1701/2

Sheffield

Assay office for silver (not "Sheffield plate") established here 1773; continues. Marks: **crown**, as "hall" mark of company; N.B. stamped upside down 1815 to 1819; **lion passant** (11 oz. 2 dwts) and **Britannia** (11 oz. 10 dwts) as standard marks; **Sovereign's head**, as duty mark, 1784–1890; **date letter**, changed annually in July; **maker's mark.**

1773–1799

TM	LP	DL	SH	
⊕	🦁	𝕰		1773/74
		𝕱		1774/75
		𝕹		1775/76
		𝕽		1776/77
		𝕳		1777/78
		𝕾		1778/79
		𝕬		1779/80
		🜨		1780/81
		𝕯		1781/82
		𝕲		1782/83
		𝕭		1783/84
		𝕴	▣	1784/85
		🜨		1785/86
		𝕶	⊘	1786/87
		𝕿		1787/88
		𝖂		1788/89
		𝕸		1789/90
		𝕷		1790/91
		🜨		1791/92

TM	LP	DL	SH	
⊕	🦁	U	⊘	1792/93
		O		1793/94
		m		1794/95
		q		1795/96
		Z		1796/97
		⊗X		1797/98
		V		1798/99

1799–1824

TM	LP	DL	SH	
♔	🦁	E	⊘	1799/1800
		N		1800/1
		H		1801/2
		M		1802/3
		F		1803/4
		G		1804/5
		B		1805/6
		A		1806/7
		S		1807/8
		P		1808/9

TM	LP	DL	SH	
👑	🦁	K	ᘓ	1809/10
		L		1810/11
		C		1811/12
		D		1812/13
		R		1813/14
		W		1814/15
		O		1815/16
		T		1816/17
		X		1817/18
		I		1818/19
		V		1819/20
		v		1819/20
		Q		1820/21
		Y		1821/22
		Z		1822/23
		U		1823/24

1824–1844

TM	LP	DL	SH	
👑	🦁	a	ᘓ	1824/25
		b		1825/26
		c		1826/27
		d		1827/28
		e		1828/29
		f		1829/30
		g		1830/31
		h	ᘓ	1831/32

TM	LP	DL	SH	
👑	🦁	k	⬤	1832/33
		l		1833/34
		m		1834/35
		p		1835/36
		q		1836/37
		r		1837/38
		s		1838/39
		t		1839/40
		u	⬤	1840/41
		v		1841/42
		x		1842/43
		Z		1843/44

1844–1868

TM	LP	DL	SH	
👑	🦁	A	⬤	1844/45
		B		1845/46
		C		1846/47
		D		1847/48
		E		1848/49
		F		1849/50
		G		1850/51
		H		1851/52
		I		1852/53
		K		1853/54
		L		1854/55
		M		1855/56

TM	LP	DL	SH	
🛡	🦁	N	☺	1856/57
		O		1857/58
		P		1858/59
		R		1859/60
		S		1860/61
		T		1861/62
		U		1862/63
		V		1863/64
		W		1864/65
		X		1865/66
		Y		1866/67
		Z		1867/68

TM	LP	DL	SH	
🛡	🦁	O	✊	1881/82
		P		1882/83
		Q		1883/84
		R		1884/85
		S		1885/86
		T		1886/87
		U		1887/88
		V		1888/89
		W		1889/90
		X		1890/91
		Y		1891/92
		Z		1892/93

1868–1893

TM	LP	DL	SH	
🛡	🦁	A	✊	1868/69
		B		1869/70
		C		1870/71
		D		1871/72
		E		1872/73
		F		1873/74
		G		1874/75
		H		1875/76
		J		1876/77
		K		1877/78
		L		1878/79
		M		1879/80
		N		1880/81

1893–1918

TM	LP	DL	
🛡	🦁	a	1893/94
		b	1894/95
		c	1895/96
		d	1896/97
		e	1897/98
		f	1898/99
		g	1899/1900
		h	1900/1
		i	1901/2
		k	1902/3
		l	1903/4
		m	1904/5
		n	1905/6

69

TM	LP	DL		
👑	🦁	o		1906/7
		p		1907/8
		q		1908/9
		r		1909/10
		s		1910/11
		t		1911/12
		u		1912/13
		v		1913/14
		w		1914/15
		x		1915/16
		y		1916/17
		z		1917/18

TM	LP	DL	SH	
👑	🦁	O		1931/32
		P		1932/33
		Q	●	1933/34
		R		1934/35
		S		1935/36
		T		1936/37
		U		1937/38
		V		1938/39
		W		1939/40
		X		1940/41
		Y		1941/42
		Z		1942/43

1918–1943

TM	LP	DL	
👑	🦁	a	1918/19
		b	1919/20
		c	1920/21
		d	1921/22
		e	1922/23
		f	1923/24
		g	1924/25
		h	1925/26
		i	1926/27
		k	1927/28
		l	1928/29
		m	1929/30
		n	1930/31

1943–

TM	LP	DL	SH	
👑	🦁	A		1943/44
		B		1944/45
		C		1945/46
		D		1946/47
		E		1947/48
		F		1948/49
		G		1949/50
		H		1950/51
		I		1951/52
		K	●	1952/53
		L		1953/54
		M		1954/55
		N		1955/56

TM	LP	DL		TM	LP	DL	
👑	🦁	O	1956/57	👑	🦁	T	1961/62
		P	1957/58			U	1962/63
		Q	1958/59			V	1963/64
		R	1959/60			W	1964/65
		S	1960/61			X	1965/66
						Y	1966/67

York

Assay mark used here from mid 16th century; office closed 1717, re-opened *c.* 1774/5, closed finally 1856. Marks: **half leopard's head/half fleur-de-lis,** as "town" mark (1562–1631); **half rose crowned/half fleur-de-lis,** as "town" mark (1632–98); **cross with five lions passant** on it, as "town" mark (from 1700); **Sovereign's head,** as duty mark (1784–1856); **date letter; maker's mark.** N.B. Very few pieces assayed and marked during period *c.* 1716 to 1776.

	1559–1583			TM	DL	
TM	DL				V	1578/79
	A	1559/60			W	1579/80
	B	1560/61			X	1580/81
	C	1561/62			Y	1581/82
	D	1562/63			Z	1582/83
	E	1563/64				
	F	1564/65			1583–1607	
	G	1565/66		TM	DL	
	H	1566/67			a	1583/84
	I	1567/68			b	1584/85
	K	1568/69			c	1585/86
	L	1569/70			d	1586/87
	M	1570/71			e	1587/88
	N	1571/72			f	1588/89
	O	1572/73			g	1589/90
	P	1573/74			h	1590/91
	Q	1574/75			i	1591/92
	R	1575/76			k	1592/93
	S	1576/77				
	T	1577/78				

TM	DL		TM	DL	
🟐	𝕷	1593/94	🟐	𝕴	1615/16
	𝖒	1594/95		𝕶	1616/17
	𝖓	1595/96		𝕷	1617/18
	𝖔	1596/97		𝕸	1618/19
	𝖕	1597/98		𝕹	1619/20
	𝖖	1598/99		𝕺	1620/21
	𝖗	1599/1600		𝕻	1621/22
	𝖘	1600/1		𝕼	1622/23
	𝖙	1601/2		𝕽	1623/24
	𝖚	1602/3		𝕾	1624/25
	𝖜	1603/4		𝕿	1625/26
	𝖝	1604/5		𝖀	1626/27
	𝖞	1605/6		𝖂	1627/28
	𝖟	1606/7		𝖃	1628/29
				𝖄	1629/30
				𝖅	1630/31

1607–1631

TM	DL	
🟐	𝕬	1607/8
	𝕭	1608/9
	𝕮	1609/10
	𝕯	1610/11
	𝕰	1611/12
	𝕱	1612/13
	𝕲	1613/14
	𝕳	1614/15

1631–1657

TM	DL	
🟐	𝖆	1631/32
	𝖇	1632/33
	𝖈	1633/34
	𝖉	1634/35
	𝖊	1635/36
	𝖋	1636/37

TM	DL		TM	DL	
🌀	*g*	1637/38	🌀	*C*	1659/60
	h	1638/39		*D*	1660/61
	i	1639/40		*E*	1661/62
	j	1640/41		*F*	1662/63
	k	1641/42		*G*	1663/64
	l	1642/43		*H*	1664/65
	m	1643/44		*I*	1665/66
	n	1644/45		*K*	1666/67
	o	1645/46		*L*	1667/68
	p	1646/47		*M*	1668/69
	q	1647/48		*N*	1669/70
	r	1648/49		*Ø*	1670/71
	s	1649/50		*P*	1671/72
	t	1650/51		*Q*	1672/73
	u	1651/52		*R*	1673/74
	v	1652/53		*S*	1674/75
	w	1653/54		*T*	1675/76
	x	1654/55		*U*	1676/77
	y	1655/56		*V*	1677/78
	z	1656/57		*W*	1678/79
				X	1679/80
				Y	1680/81
				Z	1681/82

1657–1682

TM	DL	
🌀	*A*	1657/58
	B	1658/59

74

1682–1700

TM	DL	
🦁	A	1682/83
	B	1683/84
	C	1684/85
	D	1685/86
	E	1686/87
	F	1687/88
	G	1688/89
	H	1689/90
	I	1690/91
	K	1691/92
	L	1692/93
	M	1693/94
	N	1694/95
	O	1695/96
	P	1696/97
	Q	1697/98
	R	1698/99
	S	1699/1700

1700–1717

TM	B	LHE	DL	
✠	🦁	👑	A	1700/1
			B	1701/2
			C	1702/3
			D	1703/4
				1704/5

TM	B	LHE	DL	
✠	🦁	👑	F	1705/6
			G	1706/7
				1707/8
			I	1708/9
				1709/10
				1710/11
			m	1711/12
				1712/13
			O	1713/14

1776–1787

TM	LHC	LP	DL	SH	
	👑	🦁	A		1776/77
			B		1777/78
			C		1778/79
			D		1779/80
			E		1780/81
			F		1781/82
			G		1782/83
			H		1783/84
			J	👤	1784/85

1787–1812

TM	LHC	LP	DL	SH	
	👑	🦁	A	👤	1787/88
			b		1788/89
			c		1789/90
			d		1790/91

TM	LHC	LP	DL	SH	
⬤	⬤	⬤	e	⬤	1791/92
			f		1792/93
			g		1793/94
			h		1794/95
			i		1795/96
			k		1796/97
			l		1797/98
			m		1798/99
			n		1799/1800
			o		1800/1
			p		1801/2
			q		1802/3
			r		1803/4
			s		1804/5
			t		1805/6
			u		1806/7
			v		1807/8
			w		1808/9
			x		1809/10
			y		1810/11
			z		1811/12

TM	LHC	LP	DL	SH	
⬤	⬤	⬤	f	⬤	1817/18
			g		1818/19
			h		1819/20
			i		1820/21
			k		1821/22
			l		1822/23
			m		1823/24
			n		1824/25
			o		1825/26
			p		1826/27
			q		1827/28
			r		1828/29
			s		1829/30
			t	⬤	1830/31
			u		1831/32
			v		1832/33
			w		1833/34
			x		1834/35
			y		1835/36
			z		1836/37

1812–1837

TM	LHC	LP	DL	SH	
⬤	⬤	⬤	a	⬤	1812/13
			b		1813/14
			c		1814/15
			d		1815/16
			e		1816/17

1837–1857

TM	LHC	LP	DL	SH	
⬤	⬤	⬤	A	⬤	1837/38
			B		1838/39
			C		1839/40
			D		1840/41
			E		1841/42
			F		1842/43

BRITISH SILVER

TM	LHC	LP	DL	SH		TM	LHC	LP	DL	SH	
⊕	👑	🦁	**G**	👤	1843/44	⊕	👑	🦁	**O**	👤	1850/51
			H		1844/45				**P**		1851/52
			I		1845/46				**Q**		1852/53
			K		1846/47				**R**		1853/54
			L		1847/48				**S**		1854/55
			M		1848/49				**T**		1855/56
			N		1849/50				**V**		1856/57

English Silversmiths' Marks

Four marks are usually found stamped on silver, namely: the hall, or town, mark, indicating the assay office; the maker's mark; the annual mark or date letter, indicating the year of assay; the standard mark, indicating sterling quality. Other marks are: the Britannia mark, used 1697 to 1719, to indicate the higher standard of silver required during that period; the Sovereign's head or duty mark, used 1784 to 1890, to indicate duty had been paid on the piece so stamped; the Jubilee mark, used in addition to other marks, on pieces with date letters from 1933/4 to 1935/6, celebrating the silver jubilee of King George V. and Queen Mary; the Coronation mark of 1953 (the head of Queen Elizabeth II) to mark her accession.

Ab   Abercromby, Robert: London
(in flattened oval punch, recorded 1739)

AC   Augustine Courtauld: London
(Gothic caps in shaped punch, recorded 1708; initials AC with fleur-de-lis over, in plain punch with rounded top, entered 1729; initials AC in italics over fleur-de-lis, in trefoil-shaped punch, recorded 1739)

**AC
EF**   Alex Coates and Edward French: London
(in quatrefoil-shaped punch, recorded 1734)

**AF
SG**   Andrew Fogelberg and Stephen Gilbert: London
(in shaped punch, recorded 1780)

AF   Andrew Fogelberg: London
(in rectangular punch, recorded 1776)

AL   Aug. Le Sage: London
(plain, crowned, in oval, or plain with pellet between in rectangle, or initials in quatrefoil, all recorded 1767)

AN   Anthony Nelme: London
(AN italic caps in monogram in cartouche, 1722)

ANe   Anthony Nelme: London
(AN in monogram with "e", in shield-shaped punch, 1697)

AR   Archambo, Peter: London
(between crown and fleur-de-lis, in shaped punch, recorded 1720)

**AS
JS
AS**   Adey, Joseph, and Albert Savory: London
(in upright rectangular punch, 1833)

AT   Ann Tanqueray: London
(with escallop (?) above and below, in lozenge-shaped punch, 1720)

AV   Aymé Videau: London
(italic caps with star over and pellet below, in near-quatrefoil punch, 1739)

Ba Bamford, Thomas: London
(Gothic letters in small oval punch, recorded 1719)

Ba Barnard, John: London
(Gothic letters over fleur-de-lis (?) in heart-shaped punch, recorded
1702; also "Ba" over pellet, in heart-shaped punch, recorded 1720)

Ba Barnard, John: London
(in heart-shaped punch, recorded 1702)

BA Barnet, Edward: London
(in shaped punch; also BA over pellet in heart-shaped punch,
each recorded 1715)

BA Barrett, Edward: London
(in rough quatrefoil-shaped punch, recorded 1715)

BI Bignell, John: London
(in shield-shaped punch, recorded 1718)

BN Bowles Nash: London
(over fleur-de-lis in heart-shaped punch, 1721)

BS Benjamin Smith: London
(in rectangular punch, found in early 19th century)

BS Benjamin Smith and James Smith: London
IS (in plain rectangle, found in 1810s)

Bu Burridge, Thomas: London
(with rosette and two pellets over and one pellet below, in cartouche,
recorded 1706)

BU Burridge, Thomas: London
(with star over, in trefoil-shaped punch, recorded 1717)

CA Aldridge, Charles: London
(in plain rectangular punch, recorded 1786)

CB Charles Bellassyse: London
(with mitre over, in cinquefoil-shaped punch, recorded 1740)

CF Charles Fox: London
(in plain oval punch, 1822)

CH Charles Hatfield: London
(with rosette above and two pellets below, in rectangular punch with
semicircular top and bottom, 1727; also C·H in quasi-italic caps in
shaped oval, 1739)

CH Chartier, John: London
(initials surmounted by fleur-de-lis, with or without crown, in shaped
punch, recorded 1698)

CK Charles Kandler: London
(in plain rectangular punch, 1778)

Co Cole, John: London
(over star in heart-shaped punch, recorded 1697)

Co   Coles, Lawrence: London
(in shaped punch, recorded 1697)

Co   Collins, Henry: London
(crowned C enclosing "o" in narrow rectangular shield-shaped punch,
recorded 1698)

Co   Cooke, John: London
(crowned letters in shaped punch, recorded 1699)

CO   Cornock, Edward: London
(in bordered oval punch, recorded 1707)

CO   Courtauld, Augustine: London
(fleur-de-lis over initials CO in trefoil-shaped punch, recorded 1708)

CR   Crespin, Paul: London
(italic caps in shaped oblong punch, recorded 1740)

C
T W   Thomas Whipham and Charles Wright: London
(in square punch, 1758)

C
T·W   Thomas Whipman and Charles Wright: London
W   (in upright oval punch, 1757; in circular punch, 1758)

CW   Charles Woodward: London
(in rectangular punch; found in 1760s)

DH   David Hennell: London
(with or without pellet between, in plain rectangle, recorded 1736;
with pellet between and fleur-de-lis over in shaped punch, recorded
1739)

Do   Downes, John: London
(Gothic letters in hexagonal-shaped punch, 1697; also Roman letters
"Do" with fleur-de-lis above and below, in upright oval punch, 1697)

DS
BS   Digby Scott with Benjamin and James Smith: London
IS   (in upright rectangular punch, found in 1810s)

DT   David Tanqueray: London
(with sunburst over and pellet below, in quatrefoil-shaped
punch, 1700)

D.W   David Willaume: London
(with two stars over and trefoil (?) below, shaped shield, 1720; DW
in plain rectangle, 1728)

DW   David Williams: London
(italic caps with a six-point star above and below, in quatrefoil-shaped
punch, 1739)

DY   Dymond, Edward: London
(with star above and below, in diamond-shaped punch, 1722)

EA   Edward Aldridge: London
(Gothic caps in shield-shaped punch; pellet between italic caps, in
oblong punch with rounded ends, recorded 1739; star between
initials E A in plain rectangle, recorded 1739)

EC   **Eckfourd, John:** London
(in nipped oval punch, 1698; also EC with star above and two pellets below, in rounded punch, 1725)

EC   **Edward Cornock:** London
(in bordered oval punch, recorded 1707)

ED   **Edward Dymond:** London
(with pellet above and below, in diamond-shaped punch, 1722)

E E   **Edward Barnard** with **Edward jr, John & William:** London
B   (in quatrefoil-shaped punch, 1829)
J W

E   **Edward Aldridge & Co:** London
E A   (in rectangular cross-shaped punch, found during 1760s)
A

EF   **Edith Fletcher:** London
(with pellet above and below, in lozenge (i.e. diamond) shaped punch, 1729)

EF   **Edward Feline:** London
(with bird over and star under, in shaped punch, recorded 1720; italic caps with pellet over, in cinquefoil punch, recorded 1739; the same in almost shield-shape punch, recorded 1739)

E I   **Elizabeth Tuite:** London
(with ewer emblem between initials, in square punch, 1741)

E·I   **Edward Jennings:** London
(crowned initials in rounded punch, 1720)

E J   **E. J. Barnard,** and **W. Barnard:** London
B   (in quatrefoil-shaped punch, 1846)
& W

EL   **Edward Lambe:** London
(italic caps over a ring, in rounded punch, 1740)

EV   **Edward Vincent:** London
(with crescent above and ring below, 1720; initials EV with crescent above, 1723; each mark in a circular punch; initials E·V in italic caps in an oval punch, 1739)

EW   **Edward Wakelin:** London
(Gothic caps under three feathers (?) in shaped punch, 1747)

EW   **Edward Wood:** London
(with pellet above and below, in oval punch, 1722; with star above and pellet (?) under, in oval punch, 1722; crowned EW in Gothic caps, in oval punch, 1740)

F   **Fawdery, Hester:** London
(in lozenge-shaped punch, recorded 1727)

FA   **Farren, Thomas:** London
(with fleur-de-lis over and star below, in rectangle with semicircular top and bottom, 1707)

FA   **Fawdery, John:** London
(in rectangular punch with canted corners, 1697)

FA   **Fawdery, William:** London
(between six pellets, in oval punch, recorded 1698; also crowned WF
in trefoil, recorded 1720; plain initials FA in oval, ascribed to him)

Fa   **Fawler, Thomas:** London
(in shield-shaped punch, 1707)

Fe   **Feline, Edward:** London
(with trefoil over, in trefoil-shaped punch, recorded 1720; over
six-point star in quatrefoil, recorded 1720)

F   **Francis Crump and Gabriel Sleath:** London
G·S   (in upright rectangle with canted corners, 1753)
C

FG   **Francis Garthorne:** London
(over star in shield-shaped punch, 1721)

FK   **Frederick Kandler:** London
(with crown over and mullet below, in shaped rectangular punch,
recorded 1735; italic caps under fleur-de-lis in shaped punch,
recorded 1735; italic caps with fleur-de-lis over, in rectangular punch
with shaped top, recorded 1739)

FL   **Fleming, William:** London
(crowned, in simple shaped punch, 1697; also FL· crowned with
pellet below, in shaped punch of cartouche form, 1703)

FN   **Francis Nelme:** London
(italic caps in monogram, in shaped shield, 1722; initials FN plain
in cartouche, 1735)

GA   **Garthorne, George:** London
(initials over star, in shield-shaped punch; initials with coronet over,
in different shield-shaped punch; both recorded 1697)

G   **Garthorne, Francis:** London
enclosing A   (in shaped punch, 1697)

Ga   **Garthorne, Francis:** London
(in rounded punch; mark ascribed, dated *c.* 1696)

GA   **George W. Adams:** London
(in shaped punch, 1840)

GH   **George Heming and William Chawner:** London
WC   (in rectangle, recorded 1781)

G·I   **George Jones:** London
(under crowned rose, in shaped punch, 1724; the initials GI in italic
caps in shield-shaped punch, 1739)

G   **George Hindmarsh and Robert Abercromby:** London
R·A   (rectangular punch with canted corners, recorded 1731)
H

GR   **Green, Samuel:** London
(with animal above and pellet below, in shaped quatrefoil-type punch, 1721)

GR   **Greene, Henry:** London
(with two pellets above and a ring below, in shaped rectangular punch, 1700; also GR with animal above and ring below in flattened quatrefoil-shaped punch, 1700)

Gr   **Green, David:** London
(Gothic caps with crown over, in shaped punch, 1701)

Gr   **Greene, Richard:** London
(crowned letters in shaped punch, 1703)

Gr   **Greene, Nathaniel:** London
(Gothic letters over fleur-de-lis in rectangular punch shaped at bottom to include the fleur-de-lis, 1698)

G
enclosing **R**   **Green, Richard:** London
(the G large, enclosing the R small, in shield-shaped punch, 1703)

GS   **Gabriel Sleath:** London
(in shield, 1720; initials GS in italic caps in oval punch, 1735)

GS   **George Smith:** London
(in plain rectangle, 1732; G·S in italic caps in rectangular punch, 1739)

GS
TH   **George Smith** and **Thomas Hayter:** London
(in square punch, or in curved punch with straight sides, 1792)

GU   **Gulliver, Nathaniel:** London
(in diamond-shaped punch, 1722)

GW   **George Wickes:** London
(Gothic caps with fleur-de-lis over, in near-trefoil-shaped punch, 1739)

G
enclosing **W**   **George Wickes:** London
(large G enclosing small W in circular punch, 1721)

HA   **Hanet, Paul:** London
(in plain rectangular punch, 1717)

HA   **Harache, Pierre:** London
(initials under crown and crescent, in shaped punch, recorded 1697)

HA   **Hatfield, Charles:** London
(with pellet above and rose or mullet (?) below, in rectangular punch with semicircular top and bottom, 1727)

HB   **Hester Bateman:** London
(italic initials in plain or shaped rectangular punch, recorded 1774)

HC   **Henry Cowper:** London
(in small rectangular punch, 1782)

HC
IE   **Henry Chawner** and **John Emes:** London
(in oval or plain rectangle, recorded 1796)

HG   **Henry Greene:** London
(with pellet above and below, in quatrefoil-type punch, 1720)

HG   **Henry Greenway:** London
(in plain rectangular punch, 1775)

HH   **Henry Haynes:** London
(initials conjoined, in nearly square punch, 1749)

H·H   **Henry Herbert:** London
(in plain rectangle, 1733; also H·H with three crowns over, in shaped
punch, 1734; crowned HH in shaped rectangle, 1739; HH in italic
caps in plain rectangular punch, 1747)

HN   **Henry Nutting:** London
(in oblong punch, 1809)

HN
RH   **Henry Nutting** and **Robert Hennell:** London
(1808)

H
S·H   **S. Herbert & Co:** London
B   (in shaped quatrefoil, recorded 1750)

I·A   **John Allen:** London
(with fleur-de-lis over, in shaped rectangular punch, recorded 1761)

I·A   **John Arnell:** London
(in plain rectangular punch, recorded before 1773)

IB   **John Bignell:** London
(between two stars or mullets, and pellet between the initials, in
shaped punch, recorded 1718; without the pellet, between two stars,
in oval quatrefoil, recorded 1720)

I·B   **John Bridge:** London
(in plain rectangular punch; or crowned in shaped rectangular punch;
both 1823)

IC   **John Chartier:** London
(with trefoil or fleur-de-lis over, in shaped punch, recorded 1723)

I·C   **John Crouch:** London
(in rectangular punch, 1808)

IC
TH   **John Cotton** and **Thomas Head:** London
(in plain upright rectangular punch, 1809)

IC
TH   **John Crouch** and **Thomas Hannan:** London
(in shaped rectangle, 1773; also I·C over T·H in similarly shaped
punch)

IC
WR   **Joseph Craddock** and **William Reid:** London
(in quatrefoil-shaped punch, 1812)

IE   **Eckford, John:** London
(in small rectangular punch, 1720)

IE   **John Eckfourd, Jr.:** London
(under five-point star, in shaped punch, recorded 1725)

I
EA John Stampen and Edward Aldridge: London
S (in either cartouche-shaped punch, or quatrefoil-shaped punch, recorded 1753)

I·F John Fawdery: London
(in rectangular punch, either with curved ends, or with incurved corners, recorded 1728)

IG James Gould: London
(crowned in shaped rectangular punch, 1741; also initials IG in Gothic caps in quatrefoil-shaped punch, 1743)

IG James Gould: London
(caps in monogram, in heart-shaped shield, recorded 1722)

IG John Gould: London
(Gothic caps with star over, in trefoil-shaped punch, 1739)

I·I James Jenkins: London
(crowned in shaped rectangular punch, 1738)

I·I John Jacob: London
(crowned initials over star (?) or rosette, 1734)

I·I John Jones: London
(crowned initials in tall shaped rectangular punch, 1729)

IL Jane Lambe: London
(with paschal lamb over and pellet below, in lozenge-shaped punch, 1729)

IL
HL John, Henry, and Charles Lias: London
CL (in upright rectangular punch, 1823)

I·L
H·L John and Henry Lias: London
(in square punch, 1819)

I·M Jacob Marsh: London
(in rectangular punch of slightly wavy outline, 1744)

IO Jones, John: London
(under fleur-de-lis in shaped rectangle, 1799)

IO Jones, Lawrence: London
(with crowned star over, in shaped punch; mark ascribed to him, as possibly being 1697)

Io Jones, Edward: London
(in heart-shaped punch, 1697)

IP John Priest: London
(in cartouche, 1748)

IP Joseph Preedy: London
(in rectangular punch, 1777)

I·P
E·W John Parker and Edward Wakelin: London
(with large fleur-de-lis over, in cartouche, found late 1760s)

IS   James Smith: London
(italic caps in plain rectangular punch, 1744)

IS   James Smith: London
(under a star, in shaped rectangular punch, 1720)

IS   John Le Sage: London
(crowned in shaped punch, recorded 1718; also crowned winecup
over IS in shaped punch, recorded 1722)

I·S   Joseph Smith: London
(in dotted oval punch, 1728)

ISH   John S. Hunt: London
(with crown over, in trefoil-shaped punch, 1844)

I T   John Tuite: London,
(with ewer emblem between, in shaped punch, 1739)

IW   J. Wisdom: London
(with half-rosette (?) over, in shaped rectangular punch, 1720; mark
ascribed to him)

IW   John White: London
(italic caps under a pellet, in near-sex-foil shape punch, 1739)

I·W   J. Wakelin and Robert Garrard: London
R·G   (in rectangular punch, 1792)

I·W   John Wakelin and William Taylor: London
W·T   (with fleur-de-lis over, in shaped punch, 1776)

IWS   J. W. Story and W. Elliott: London
WE   (in rectangular punch, 1809)

JA   John Angell: London
(mark ascribed to him; 1823)

JA   Jonathan Alleine: London
(italic caps in plain rectangular punch, recorded 1771; plain caps in
plain rectangle, 1777)

J·A   John and Joseph Angel: London
J·A   (with star between the two sets of initials, in quatrefoil-shaped
punch; found 1840s)

J·A *or* **J·A**   Joseph and John Angel: London
I·A   **&**   (with star between, in quatrefoil, recorded 1843; in quatrefoil,
       J·A   recorded 1844)

JB   James Beebe: London
(in rectangular punch with slightly canted corners, 1811)

JC   John Crouch: London
(in small rectangular punch with canted corners, 1808)

J.C.E   J. Charles Edington: London
(in plain rectangular punch, 1828)

JE John Eckfourd: London
(italic caps in rough quatrefoil-shaped punch, 1739; also JE in italic caps with three pellets between, in shaped rectangle, recorded 1739)

JE John Emes: London
(italics caps in nipped oval punch, found 1790s; also J·E in italic caps, in quatrefoil-shaped punch, found early 19th century)

JJ James Jenkins: London
(sloping italic caps under fleur-de-lis in sloped rectangular punch, 1731)

JJ James Jones: London
(italic caps in sloping indented rectangle, 1755)

JJ John Jacobs: London
(italic caps over fleur-de-lis in shield-shaped punch, 1739; crowned JJ italic caps over fleur-de-lis in upright oval punch, 1739; crowned JJ in italic caps over a pellet, in shaped punch, 1739)

JJ John Jones: London
(italics in small plain rectangular punch, 1733)

Jo Jones, Lawrence: London
(with coronet over and star under, in shaped punch, 1697)

J.W John Wirgman: London
(italic caps in plain oblong punch, 1745)

KA Kandler, Charles: London
(with mitre over, in shield with curved top, recorded 1727)

KA Kandler, Frederick: London
(in shaped shield, recorded 1735)

KA
MU Kandler, Charles, and Murray, James: London
(in shield-shaped punch, recorded 1727)

LA Lambe, George: London
(with animal (? lamb) over and pellet or ring under, in shaped rectangular punch, 1713)

LA Lambe, George, widow of: London
(initials under a sheep, in lozenge-shaped punch, 1713)

LA Lamerie, Paul: London
(initials crowned between mullet and trefoil, in shaped punch; under crowned star, in shaped punch; both recorded in 1712)

LC Lawrence Coles: London
(crowned initials over a pellet, in shield-shaped punch, 1669; also initials L·C crowned, over a crescent and two pellets, noted 1680)

LC Louisa Courtauld: London
(initials in lozenge-shaped punch, 1766)

LC
GC Louisa Courtauld and George Cowles: London
(in rectangle; mark ascribed, 1769)

LC — **Louisa** and **Samuel Courtauld**: London
SC — (in plain rectangle, recorded 1777)

LE — **Ley, Petley**: London
(crowned, with rosette under, in shaped punch, 1715; initials LE under an emblem with a flower under, in cross-shaped rectangular punch, 1715)

L·E — **Ley, Timothy**: London
(surrounded by a ring of six pellets and two stars, in a circular punch, 1697)

LL — **Louis Laroche**: London
(cursive caps with coronet (?) over and two pellets below, in rectangle with rounded corners, 1739)

LP — **Lewis Pantin**: London
(in near-square rectangular punch, 1733; also LP in italic caps with pellet over, in shaped rectangular punch, 1739)

L
S*I — **Samuel Laundry** and **Jeffery Griffith**: London
G — (star between the SI, in oval, entered 1731)

Lu — **Lukin, William**: London
(over a pellet, in shield-shaped punch, 1699)

MA — **Margas, Jacob**: London
(plain in a shaped punch; with coronet over and star (?) under, in shaped punch, both 1706; crowned MA over a fleur-de-lis in shaped punch, 1720)

MA — **Margas, Samuel**: London
(crowned initials over fleur-de-lis (?) in near-cinquefoil-shaped punch)

MC — **Mark Cripps**: London
(in small rectangular punch, 1767)

MC — **Mary Chawner**: London
(in plain rectangle; mark ascribed to her, found 1830s)

MC
GA — **Mary Chawner** and **George W. Adams**: London
(in quatrefoil-shaped punch, 1840)

MF — **Magdalen Feline**: London
(italic caps conjoined with pellet over, in lozenge-shaped punch, recorded 1753)

MI — **Middleton, William**: London
(with two pellets over and one under, in shield-shaped punch, 1697)

MP — **Mary Pantin**: London
(initials with peacock over, in lozenge with semicircular head, 1733)

MS
ES — **Mary** and **Elizabeth Sumner**: London
(in broad oval punch, 1809)

NG — **Nathaniel Gulliver**: London
(in diamond-shaped punch, 1723)

NS   **Nicholas Sprimont:** London
(italic caps with star over, in curved punch, 1742)

P   **Pyne, Benjamin:** London
(crowned in a cartouche-shaped punch, used before 1697; found in 1720s)

PA   **Pantin, Simon:** London
(surmounted by peacock, in shaped punch, 1701)

PA   **Peter Archambo:** London
(in heart-shaped punch, recorded 1739; initials crowned in shaped punch, recorded 1722; italic caps in shaped punch, recorded 1739)

PB   **Peter and Ann Bateman:** London
AB   (in rectangular punch, recorded 1791)

PB   **Peter and Jonathan Bateman:** London
IB   (in rectangular punch, recorded 1790)

PB   **P. and W. Bateman:** London
WB   (in plain rectangular punch, recorded 1805)

PC   **Paul Crespin:** London
(initials between escallop and star, in shaped punch, recorded 1720; with two mullets over and fleur-de-lis below, in seven-lobed punch, recorded 1739; italic initials in quatrefoil recorded 1739)

PE   **Penstone, Henry:** London
(over pellet, in shield-shaped punch, 1697)

PE   **Penstone, William:** London
(with star above and below, in quasi-quatrefoil type of punch, 1712; PE with pellet above and below, in shaped rectangle, 1717)

PE   **Petley, William:** London
(with crown over and bird (?) under, upright rectangle with semicircular top and bottom, 1717)

PG   **Peter Gillois:** London
(recorded 1782)

P·G   **Pierre Gillois:** London
(with crown over in shaped punch, recorded 1754)

PH   **Paul Hanet:** London
(with two pellets (?) over, in shaped punch, 1721)

PI   **Pilleau, Père:** London
(with fleur-de-lis over in shaped punch, 1720)

PL   **Paul Lamerie:** London
(with crowned star over and fleur-de-lis below, incised, 1732; initials crowned, over fleur-de-lis, in shaped punch, recorded 1724; italic caps between crown and pellet, in shaped punch, recorded 1739)

PL   **Platel, Pierre:** London
(with crown and mullet over, and fleur-de-lis under, 1699)

P·P   Père Pilleau: London
(under trefoil (?) in shaped rectangular punch, 1720; PP in italic caps under a star, in rounded punch, 1739)

P·P   Philip Platel: London
(in decorative oval, 1737)

PR or **P.R**   Philip Rundell: London
(in plain rectangle, 1819)

PS or **P·S**   Paul Storr: London
(in shaped punch, 1793)

PY   Pyne, Benjamin: London
(under crowned rose, in shaped punch, 1697; letters "Py" in plain oval, 1697)

RA   Robert Andrews: London
(in shaped oval punch, recorded 1745)

R·A   Robert Abercromby: London
(under a coronet, in plain shaped punch, recorded 1731; in shaped oval punch, with one, or two, pellets between, recorded 1739)

R·B   Richard Beale: London
(in plain rectangular punch, recorded 1731; also RB with two pellets over and one below, in shield-shaped punch, recorded 1731)

RB&R   Rundell, Bridge & Rundell: London
(with crown centrally over, in rectangle with semicircular top arranged to include the crown, found early 19th century)

R
D·H   D. & R. Hennel: London
H   (in cross-shaped rectangle, recorded 1768)

RE
EB   Rebecca Emes and Edward Barnard: London
(in quatrefoil-shaped punch, 1808)

RG   Richard Green: London
(over star in heart-shaped punch, 1726)

RG   Robert Garrard: London
(in rectangular punch with canted corners, 1801; in plain rectangle, recorded 1801; cursive caps with crown over, in shaped rectangular punch, 1821)

RG   Garrard: London
(with crown over in shaped rectangular punch, 1801)

RH
DH   Robert and David Hennell: London
(in rectangular punch, recorded 1795)

RH   Robert Hennell: London
(in oval punch, recorded 1773; also R·H in rectangle)

RM   Richard Mills: London
(in plain rectangular punch, 1755)

RR Robert Rogers: London
(in small rectangular punch, 1773)

RR Robert Ross: London
(italic caps in plain rectangular punch, 1774)

R·R Richard Rugg: London
(in oblong punch, 1754; initials RR in shaped oval punch, 1775)

R·R Robert Rew: London
(in plain rectangle, 1754)

RS Richard Sibley: London
(italic caps in rectangular punch; marks ascribed, and found in 1830s)

R·S Richard Sibley: London
(in curvilinear punch, 1837)

RW Robert Williams: London
(with mitre over, in shaped rectangular punch, 1726)

SA Le Sage, John: London
(crowned, with star, in quatrefoil or shaped punch, recorded 1718)

S·C Samuel Courtauld: London
(in trefoil, or rectangular punch, recorded 1746)

S
G·S G. and S. Smith: London
S (in cross-shaped rectangle, 1751)

SH Samuel Hennell: London
(in plain oval punch, 1811; in oblong punch with rounded ends, 1811)

SL Samuel Lee: London
(crowned initials in shaped shield, 1720)

SL Sleath, Daniel: London
(with escallop (?) over, in shaped punch, 1704)

SL Sleath, Gabriel: London
(with bust (?) or escallop (?) over, in shaped punch; over pellet in cartouche; 1706)

S.L Samuel Laundry: London
(in oval, or crowned in shaped rectangle, recorded 1727; crowned rose over S·L might be his)

S·L Simon Le Sage: London
(italic caps with a goblet over and a star below, in shaped cartouche punch, 1754; initials S·L in italic caps, in nearly square punch, 1754)

SM Samuel Margas: London
(crowned over trefoil (?) in rectangle with shaped top and bottom, 1720)

SM Smith, James: London
(in rectangular punch; also S·M in oval punch; both 1718)

SM   **Smith, Samuel**: London
(with fleur-de-lis over and pellet below, in rectangle with
semicircular top and bottom, 1719)

SP *or* S·P   **Simon Pantin**: London
(with peacock over, in rectangle with semi-circular head, 1717; a
variant has the peacock predominantly larger, over SP in small
space, 1717)

SQ   **Squire, George**: London
(in flattened oval punch, 1720)

S·S   **Samuel Smith**: London
(in quatrefoil-shaped punch, 1754)

S·W   **Samuel Wood**: London
(in flattened oval punch, 1733; initials SW in shaped oblong punch,
1737; S·W in oval punch, 1739; initials S·W in italic caps in rough
quatrefoil-shaped punch, 1746)

TA   **Tanqueray, Ann**: London
(with mullet above and below, in lozenge-shaped punch, 1720)

TA   **Tanqueray, David**: London
(with star above and below, in rectangle with semicircular top and
bottom, 1713)

TB   **Thomas Bamford**: London
(in small oval punch, recorded 1720; also TB in italic caps in
rectangular punch, recorded 1739)

TC   **Thomas Chawner**: London
(with or without pellet between, in rectangular punch, probably
before 1773)

T·C·S   **T. Cox Savory**: London
(in plain rectangular punch, 1827)

T·C
W·C   **T. & W. Chawner**: London
(in a square punch, 1765; mark ascribed)

TE   **Tearle, Thomas**: London
(with crown over and fleur-de-lis under, in lozenge-shaped punch;
TE over a star in a lozenge-shaped punch; both 1719)

T·H   **Thomas Heming**: London
(italic caps with crown over, in shaped rectangular punch, recorded
1744; italic caps with pellet between, in plain or shaped oval,
recorded 1745)

TH
GH   **Thomas and George Hayter**: London
(in quatrefoil-shaped punch, 1816)

TH
IC   **Thomas Hannan and John Crouch**: London
(in quatrefoil-shaped punch, 1799)

T·H
I·C   **Thomas Hannan and John Crouch**: London
(in rectangular punch, found in 1760s)

TL   **Timothy Ley:** London
(in ring of two stars and six pellets in a circular punch, used before 1697, and found again in the 1720s)

TP   **T. Phipps** and **E. Robinson:** London
ER   (in quatrefoil-shaped punch; mark ascribed, occuring *c.* 1810)

T   **Thomas Cook** and **Richard Gurney:** London
R·G   (in rectangular punch as cross, 1734)
C

T
R·G   **Richard Gurney and Co:** London
Co   (in quatrefoil-shaped punch, 1750)

TT   **Thomas Tearle:** London
(crowned in shaped punch, 1720; T T. in italic caps crowned, in curved shaped punch, 1739)

TW   **Thomas Whipham:** London
(italic caps in rectangle of shaped outline, 1737; initials TW under fleur-de-lis in shaped rectangular punch, 1737)

T   **T. and W. Chawner:** London
W·C (in shaped rectangle resembling Maltese cross; ascribed to
C   T. & W. Chawner, *fl.* 1760s)

TW   **Thomas Wallis** and **Jonathan Hayne:** London
JH   (in square punch, 1810)

Wa   **Ward, Jos.:** London
(in plain rectangular punch, 1717)

WB   **William Bateman:** London
(cursive caps conjoined, in plain rectangular punch, 1815)

WB   **William Bellassyse:** London
(with mitre over, in rectangle with semicircular top, recorded 1723)

W·B   **William Bateman:** London
(in curved punch, 1815)

W·B   **Walter Brind:** London
(in plain rectangular punch, recorded 1749; also W·B in shaped punch, recorded 1757)

WB   **William Bateman** and **Daniel Ball:** London
DB   (in quatrefoil-shaped punch, 1839)

W·B   **William Burwash** and **Robert Sibley:** London
R·S   (in plain rectangle, recorded 1805)

WC   **William Cafe:** London
(Gothic caps with rosette over, in trefoil-shaped punch, 1758)

WC.   **William Chawner:** London
(with pellet over, in rectangle with shaped top; without pellet, in plain rectangle; both recorded 1815)

WC   **William Cripps:** London
(in small rectangular punch, 1743)

W·E   **William Elliott:** London
(in plain rectangular punch, 1810)

WF   **William Frisbee:** London
(in rectangular punch, recorded 1792)

WF
PS   **William Frisbee** and **Paul Storr:** London
(in rectangular punch, recorded 1792)

W
G·H   **George Heming** and **William Chawner:** London
C   (in oval, or shaped punch, recorded 1774)

Wh   **White, John:** London
(letters "Wh" conjoined, with pellet above and six-point star below, in cartouche, 1724)

WI   **Wickes, George:** London
(with fleur-de-lis over, in shaped rectangular punch, 1721)

WI   **Willaume, David:** London
(with two stars above, and fleur-de-lis (?) under, in shield-shaped punch, 1697; in plain rectangle, 1728)

WI   **Wisdom, J:** London
(over fleur-de-lis, in cartouche, 1704)

WI   **Williams, Robert:** London
(with mitre over, in shaped rectangle, 1726)

WL   **William Lukin:** London
(over a pellet, in shield-type punch, 1725)

WO   **Wood, Edward:** London
(with pellet above and below, in oval punch, 1718)

WP   **William Penstone:** London
(in rectangular punch, the right end curved, found in 1770s)

WP   **William Petley:** London
(between two pellets, with crown over, in near heart-shaped punch, 1720)

WP
JP   **W.** and **J. Priest:** London
(in square punch with canted corners, found in 1760s, and thus ascribed)

WP
JP   **William Pitts** and **Joseph Preedy:** London
(in circle, 1791; also with a pellet between each set of initials, in a circular punch)

WT   **William Trayes:** London
(in plain rectangular punch, 1822)

WT   **William Tuite:** London
(in flattened shield-shaped punch, 1756; W·T in oblong punch ascribed to him, found 1760s)

WT   William Theobalds and Robert Atkinson: London
RA   (in plain square punch, 1838)

W   Thomas Whipham and William Williams: London
T·W   (in cross-shaped rectangle, 1740)
W

WW   William Woodward: London
        (with fleur-de-lis (?) above and below, in circular punch, 1731;
        initials W.W in italic caps in oblong punch; 1743)

W   William Shaw and William Priest: London
W·S   (in punch resembling Maltese cross, 1749)
P

Marks on Gold Plate

Up to the year 1798, the marks on gold were identical with those put on silver. In that year the new standard (18-carat) for gold came into use, the mark for this being used in addition to the usual town mark, date letter, and maker's mark. Separate marks were used for the different standards in use at different times. The date letter continued to be the same as that found on silver. Foreign gold and silver wares imported into England received (from 1876 to 1904) the mark of the Assay Office concerned and an "F" in an oval, or in a rectangle. From 1904 onwards, individual Assay Offices received distinctive marks to use.

Higher Standard Marks		Lower Standard Marks	
	19·20 carat (1300–1476)		15 carat (1854–1932)
18	carat (1477–1544)		12 carat (1854–1932)
18	carat (1544–1574)		9 carat (from 1854)
22	carat (1575–1797)		14 carat (from 1933)
18	carat (1798–1843)		9 carat („)
22	carat (1844–1853)		
22	carat (1932 onwards)		
18	carat („)		

Assay Office Marks on Imported Gold Plate

	Birmingham (1904–)		Glasgow	(1904–1906)
	Chester (1904–1961)			(1906–1964)
	Dublin (1904–1906)		London	(1904–1906)
	(1906–)			(1906–)
	Edinburgh (1904–)		Sheffield	(1904–1906)
				(1906–)

Marks on Sheffield Plate

No date letters are to be found, since none were in use. Makers of Sheffield plate mark their wares (*c.* 1750–*c.* 1785) with their initials, following the practice of the London goldsmiths and silversmiths. From 1784 makers of Sheffield plate were permitted by law to use an emblem or device with their names. By the early 19th century, the emblem may be found alone, a practice fairly general during that period. Makers often used in addition the mark of a crown to indicate quality, but in 1896 this practice was forbidden.

ALL GOOD	Allgood, John	(*c.* 1812)	Birmingham
ASHFORTH & CO	Ashforth & Co	(*c.* 1784)	Sheffield
ASH LEY	Ashley	(*c.* 1816)	Birmingham
BANI STER	Banister, William	(*c.* 1808)	Birmingham
BARNET	Barnet		
BEL DON	Beldon, George	(*c.* 1809)	Sheffield
BELDON HOYLAND & CO	Beldon, Hoyland & Co	(*c.* 1785)	Sheffield
BEST	Best, Henry	(*c.* 1814)	Birmingham

BEST	Best & Wastidge	(*c.* 1816)	Sheffield
W.BINGLEY	Bingley, William	(*c.* 1787)	Birmingham
BOULTON	Boulton	(*c.* 1784)	Birmingham
BRAD SHAW	Bradshaw, Joseph	(*c.* 1822)	Birmingham
BRITTAIN.WILKINSON & BROWNILL	Brittain, Wilkinson & Brownill	(*c.* 1785)	Sheffield
BUTTS	Butts, T.	(*c.* 1807)	Birmingham
CAUSER	Causer, John Fletcher	(*c.* 1824)	Birmingham
Ches-ton	Cheston, Thomas	(*c.* 1809)	Birmingham
CHILD	Child, Thomas	(*c.* 1821)	Birmingham
W.COLDWELL	Coldwell, William	(*c.* 1806)	Sheffield
COPE	Cope, Charles Gretter	(*c.* 1817)	Birmingham
CORN & Cº	Corn, James, & Sheppard, John	(*c.* 1819)	Birmingham

CRACK NALL	Cracknall, John	(c. 1814)	Birmingham
CRESWICKS	Creswick, Thomas, & James	(c. 1811)	Sheffield

DAVIS	Davis, John	(c. 1816)	Birmingham
DEAKIN SMITH&Co	Deakin, Smith & Co	(c. 1785)	Sheffield
J DIXON	Dixon, James, & Son	(c. 1835)	Sheffield
DIXON&Cº	Dixon & Co	(c. 1784)	Birmingham
I·DRABBLE &Cº	Drabble, James, & Co	(c. 1805)	Sheffield
DUNN	Dunn, George Bott	(c. 1810)	Birmingham
S·EVANS	Evans, Samuel	(c. 1816)	Birmingham

FOX·PROCTOR PASMORE·&Cº	Fox, Proctor Pasmore & Co	(c. 1784)	Sheffield
FREETH	Froeth, Henry	(c. 1816)	Birmingham
FROGGATT COLDWELL&LEAN	Froggatt, Coldwell & Co	(c. 1797)	Sheffield

GAINSFORD	Gainsford, Robert	(c. 1808)	Sheffield

	Garnett, William	(c. 1803)	Sheffield
	Gibbs, Joseph	(c. 1808)	Birmingham
	Gilbert, John	(c. 1812)	Birmingham
	Goodman, Alexander & Co	(c. 1800)	Sheffield
	Goodwin, Edward	(c. 1794)	Sheffield
	Green, John, & Co	(c. 1799)	Sheffield
	Green, Joseph	(c. 1807)	Birmingham
	Green, W. & Co	(c. 1784)	Sheffield
	Hall, William	(c. 1820)	Birmingham
	Hanson, Matthias	(c. 1810)	Birmingham
	Harrison, Joseph	(c. 1809)	Birmingham
	Hatfield, Aaron	(c. 1808)	Sheffield

Hatfield, Aaron	(c. 1810)	Sheffield
Hill, Daniel & Co	(c. 1806)	Birmingham
Hinks, Joseph	(c. 1812)	Birmingham
Hipkiss, J.	(c. 1808)	Birmingham
Hipwood, William	(c. 1809)	Birmingham
Holland & Co	(c. 1784)	Birmingham
Holy, Daniel, Parker & Co	(c. 1804)	Sheffield
Holy, Daniel, Wilkinson & Co	(c. 1784)	Sheffield
Horton, David	(c. 1808)	Birmingham
Horton, John	(c. 1809)	Birmingham
Howard, Stanley & Thomas	(c. 1809)	London
Hutton, William	(c. 1807)	Birmingham
Jervis, William	(c. 1789)	Sheffield
Johnson, James	(c. 1812)	Birmingham

Jones	Jones	(c. 1824)	Birmingham
Jordan, Thomas	Jordan, Thomas	(c. 1814)	Birmingham
Kirkby, Samuel	Kirkby, Samuel	(c. 1812)	Sheffield
Law, John, & Son	Law, John, & Son	(c. 1807)	Sheffield
Law, John	Law, John	(c. 1810)	Sheffield
Law, Richard	Law, Richard	(c. 1807)	Birmingham
Law, Thomas, & Co	Law, Thomas, & Co	(c. 1784)	Sheffield
Lea, Abner Cowel	Lea, Abner Cowel	(c. 1808)	Birmingham
Lees, George	Lees, George	(c. 1811)	Birmingham
Lees	"		"
Linwood, John	Linwood, John	(c. 1807)	Birmingham
J. Linwood	"	"	"
Linwood, William	Linwood, William	"	"

Linwood, Matthew, & Son	(c. 1808)	Birmingham
Love, John & Co	(c. 1785)	Sheffield
Love, Silverside, Darby & Co	(c. 1785)	Sheffield
Lylly, John	(c. 1815)	Birmingham
Lylly, Joseph	(c. 1816)	Birmingham
Madin, P., & Co	(c. 1788)	Sheffield
Markland, William	(c. 1818)	Birmingham
Meredith, Henry	(c. 1807)	Birmingham
Moore, Frederick	(c. 1820)	Birmingham
Moore, J.	(c. 1784)	Birmingham
Morton, Richard, & Co	(c. 1785)	Sheffield

Newbould, William, & Sons   (c. 1804)   Sheffield

J·NICHOLDS	Nicholds, James	(c. 1808)	Birmingham

IOHN·PARSONS&Cº	Parsons, John, & Co	(c. 1784)	Sheffield
PEAKE*C	Peake	(c. 1807)	Birmingham
PEAR SON	Pearson, Richard	(c. 1811)	Birmingham
PEAR SON	Pearson, Richard	(c. 1813)	Birmingham
PEMBERTON	Pemberton & Mitchell	(c. 1817)	Birmingham
Pimley	Pimley, Samuel	(c. 1810)	. Birmingham

ROBERTS &CADMAN	Roberts & Cadman	(c. 1785)	Sheffield
I&S. ROBERTS.	Roberts, Samuel, & Co	(c. 1786)	Sheffield
ROGERS	Rogers, John	(c. 1819)	Birmingham
ROD GERS	Rodgers, Joseph, & Sons	(c. 1822)	Sheffield
RYLAND	Ryland, William, & Sons	(c. 1807)	Birmingham
RYLAND	"	"	"

Sansom, Thomas, & Sons	(c. 1821)	Sheffield
Scott, William	(c. 1807)	Birmingham
Shephard, Joseph	(c. 1817)	Birmingham
Silk, Robert	(c. 1809)	Birmingham
Silkirk, William	(c. 1807)	Birmingham
Small, Thomas	(c. 1812)	Birmingham
Smith & Co	(c. 1784)	Birmingham
Smith, Isaac	(c. 1821)	Birmingham
Smith, N. & Co	(c. 1784)	Sheffield
Smith, Nicholson, Tate and Hoult	(c. 1810)	Sheffield
Smith, William	(c. 1812)	Birmingham
Staniforth, Parkin & Co	(c. 1784)	Sheffield

Stot, Benjamin	(c. 1811)	Sheffield
Sutcliff, Robert, & Co	(c. 1786)	Sheffield
..s & Co	(c. 1784)	Sheffield

Thomas, Stephen	(c. 1813)	Birmingham
Thomasons, Edward, & Dowler	(c. 1807)	Birmingham
"	"	"
Tonks, S.	(c. 1807)	Birmingham
Tonks	(c. 1824)	Birmingham
Tudor & Co	(c. 1784)	Sheffield
"	"	"
Turley, Samuel	(c. 1816)	Birmingham
Turton, John	(c. 1820)	Birmingham

Tyndall, Joseph	(*c.* 1813)	Birmingham

Waterhouse & Co	(*c.* 1807)	Birmingham
Waterhouse, J. & Co	(*c.* 1833)	Sheffield
Waterhouse, John, Hatfield, Edward, & Co	(*c.* 1836)	Sheffield
Watson, Fenton & Bradbury	(*c.* 1795)	Sheffield
Watson, Pass & Co	(*c.* 1811)	Sheffield
White, John	(*c.* 1811)	Birmingham
Wilkinson, Henry, & Co	(*c.* 1836)	Sheffield
Willmore, Joseph	(*c.* 1807)	Birmingham
Woodward, William	(*c.* 1814)	Birmingham
Worton, Samuel	(*c.* 1821)	Birmingham
Wright, John, & Fairbairn, George	(*c.* 1809)	Sheffield

 Younge, S. & C., & Co   (*c.* 1813)   Sheffield

British Pewterers' Marks, or "Touches"

It was laid down by law *c*. 1503 that each pewterer should have his own individual mark, which was to be officially recorded on "touch plates". Marks recorded up to the year of the Great Fire of London were unfortunately destroyed in the conflagration. After the rebuilding of the Pewterers' Hall, recording of touches was resumed, and a vast quantity (at least 1,000) accumulated over the years. Individual touches were at first small, but from the early 18th century were more elaborate. The mark of the crowned rose, which previously was supposed to be reserved for use by members of the company only, was from *c*. 1671 intended for use on exported pewter exclusively. By the end of the 17th century it was considerably used as an extra touch by the majority of the London pewterers, and the custom copied by a number of provincial makers also. A series of small marks in shield outlines were also frequently used. Labels with such words as "superfine metal" etc., with or without the maker's name, formed additional touches.

A Selective List

Adams, Henry: (*fl*. 1692–1724) London
Mark used: representation of The Fall, with HEN:ADAMS in curve above, and PICKADILL^v below, in shaped outline.

Adkinson, William: (recorded 1671) London
Mark used: Cupid with bow, between palm leaves, with W. ADKINSON over, curved.

Alder, William: (*fl*. early 18th century) Sunderland, Co. Durham
Mark used: sailing ship between two columns, with WILLIAM curved over, and ALDER below, supported on SUNDERLAND in semicircle, all in shaped outline

Alderson, George *fl*. first half 18th century) London
Marks used: griffin over a coronet, with GEORGE over and ALDERSON below, in cartouche outline; similar cartouche with CARNABY/STREET/LONDON within, in three lines.

Alderson, Sir George: (*fl*. 1817–1826) London
Marks included: lion (?) arising from a coronet, with GEORGE above and ALDERSON below, in cartouche; also ALDERSON forming circle, in circular outline.

Alderson, John: (*fl*. 1764–1792) London
Marks used: lion arising from a coronet with JOHN and ALDERSON under, in rounded outline; crowned rose with LONDON over and palm leaves under, following broad oval outline; small marks, consecutively: WS; Britannia; lion's head erased; a coffeepot.

Angel, Philemon: (*fl*. *c*. 1685–1700) London
Marks included: figure of an angel over LONDON with a wreath under, in round outline; four small marks, i.e. shields, containing, consecutively: P (italic); A (italic); angel figure; lion rampant.

Annison, William Glover: (recorded 1742) London
Marks used: shield per pale, with an animal, and two stars over an open book, with W^M GLOVER over, and ANNISON under, in rounded cartouche; label, ANNISON / CROOKED LANE / LONDON in three lines, in wavy outline.

Bache, Richard: (*fl.* 1779–1805) London
Mark used: figure of standing angel between columns, with RICHARD above and BACHE below, in near rectangular outline.

Bacon, George: (*fl. c.* 1745–1771) London
Marks used: a pig in a circle, with GEORGE curving above, and BACON below, in oval outline; a rectangular label IN THE STRAND/LONDON in two lines.

Bacon, Thomas: (*fl. c.* 1725 onward) London
Marks used: pig with FECIT over, in oval, with THOMAS above and BACON below, in broad oval outline; crowned rose over LONDON in circular outline.

Bancks, James: (*fl.* first half 18th century) Wigan, Lancashire
Marks included: label with ·IAMES·/BANCKS in two lines, curved; crowned rose between palm leaves, in oval outline; four small marks, consecutively: IB; bird; fleur-de-lis; lion rampant; in block outline.

Barber, Nathaniel: (*fl. c.* 1777–1788) London
Marks used include: shield divided per pale, with NATHANIEL over and BARBER below, in broad oval outline; four small marks, consecutively: SS; Britannia; crowned rose; griffin's head (?) erased; curved label with LONDON/SUPERFINE in two lines; SNOW-HILL/LONDON in two lines in cartouche outline.

Barlow, John: (*fl.* end 17th century) London
Marks included: lily rising from plough-share (?) with JOHN above and BAR-LOW under, in curved outline; crowned rose with palm leaves under LONDON in circular outline; four small marks, i.e. shields, which include: lion rampant; griffin's head erased; and IB.

Barton, Daniel: (*fl. c.* 1670–1699) London
Marks included: helmet between palm leaves, with DA·BARTON over, in rounded triangular outline; four small marks: D.B in shield; helmet in lozenge; lion passant in rectangle; fleur-de-lis in lozenge.

Belson, John: (*fl. c.* 1745–1783) London
Marks included: bell over sun in splendour, between columns, with LONDON in curve over, and BELSON below, in rectangular outline with curved top; crowned rose between columns, with FISH curved over, and STREET HILL under, in similar outline; a bell in a circle, with LONDON in outer ring, and JOHN BELSON above outside, in circular scalloped outline; small marks, consecutively, in shields: TB; a bell; lion's head.

Benson, John: (*fl.* mid 18th century) London
Marks included: two-headed eagle displayed, with IOHN over and BENSON below, in broad oval outline; small marks (rectangular) with, consecutively: lion passant; crown; I; and B (the initials as Gothic caps); as a label, I·BENSON/IN LONDON in two lines, in plain rectangle.

Bentley, C.: (*fl.* 1840s) London
Marks included: circle surrounded by C·BENTLEY WOODSTOCK Sᵀ in circular outline; small marks included in small rectangles: CB; lion rampant; rosette.

Blackwell, Benjamin: (*fl.* 1740s) London
Marks included: a bell, with BENIA-MIN over, and BLACKWELL under, in curved outline; crowned rose with leaf sprays under, and LONDON over, in curved outline; small marks, four rectangles, each with lion passant, to right.

Bonvile, John: (*fl.* 1679–1686) London
Marks included: crown over five stars between palm leaves, with IOHN over and BONVILE below, in shaped outline; crowned rose between palm leaves, with LONDON over, in rounded triangular outline; four small marks: I·B; globe; three stars; lion passant.

Bridges, Stephen: (recorded 1692) London
Marks included: full name in oval outline, dotted; crowned rose between palm leaves; large X between initials SB in wreath-bordered circular outline; small shield marks include: lion passant; lion's head; label with S·BRIDGES in rectangle with wavy edges.

Broadhurst, Jonathan: (*fl. c.* 1719–1738) London

Mark used: stag between columns, with **IONATHAN** curved above, and **BRODHVRST** under, in shaped outline.

Brooker, Joseph: (*fl.* later 18th century) London
Mark used: demi-unicorn between palm leaves, with **IOSEPH** above and **BROOKER** below, in curved outline.

Brown(e), A.: (*fl.* early 18th century) Edinburgh, Midlothian
Mark used: thee-towered castle between initials A B, found over a date, all in triangular outline.

Browne & Swanson: (*fl.* 1760s) London
Mark used: an animal (? dog) with **BROWNE** over and **& SWANSON** in shaped outline.

Bryce, David: (recorded 1660) Edinburgh, Midlothian
Mark used: castle between initials D B found over a date (e.g. 1654) in rectangle of cross form.

Burford & Green: (*fl. c.* 1748–1780) London
Marks included: two shields (one with three stags on it) with **BURFORD** over and **& GREEN** under, in shaped outline; crowned rose, with **MADE IN** over, and **LONDON** under, in shaped outline; four small marks, i.e. shields, with consecutively: B & G; lion passant; figure of Britannia; crowned lion's head; curved label with **IN·Y·POULTRY** over **LONDON**.

Butcher, James, Jr: (before *c.* 1720) Bridgewater, Somerset
Marks included: rose and crown over with **IAMES·BUTCHER** around, in broad oval outline; four small marks, consecutively: IB; lion rampant; harp; rose and crown.

Carpenter, John: (*fl. c.* 1710–1747) London
Marks included: compasses enclosing globe between scrolled outline with **IOHN** over and **CARPENTER** below, in shaped outline; four small marks, i.e. rectangles with, consecutively, IC; lion passant; globe.

Carpenter & Hamberger: (*fl. c.* 1798–1805) London

Marks included: compasses enclosing globe, with **CARPENTER** over and **HAMBERGER** under, in shaped outline; crowned rose over **LONDON**.

Carter, A.: (*fl.* mid 18th century) London
Marks included: two lions rampant affronté with small crescent over, with crest above, and Latin motto under, in shaped outline; crowned rose, over **LONDON**, in broad oval outline.

Cartwright, Thomas: (*fl. c.* 1712–1743) London
Marks included: a bird (sometimes resembling a hoopoe) with **THOMAS** over and **CARTWRIGHT** under, in broad oval or circular outline; curved label with **SUPERFINE** over **HARD METAL**.

Chamberlain, Johnson: (*fl. c.* 1734) London
Marks included: crown over Prince-of-Wales feathers, with **IOHNSON** over and **CHAMBERLAIN** under; rectangular label with **CHAMBERLAIN**.

Chamberlain, Thomas: (*fl.* 1730s–1806) London
Mark used: crown over Prince-of-Wales feathers, with **THOMAS** over and **CHAMBERLAIN** under

Cleeve, Alexander: (*fl.* 1688–1739) London
Marks included: hand holding a rose between initials A C in a dotted circle; crowned rose over **LONDON** in shaped outline; small marks (shield or rectangle) with e.g. lion's head; or AC; curved label with **MADE·IN** over **LONDON**.

Cleeve, Alexander: (*fl. c.* 1715–1748) London
Marks included: hand holding Tudor rose with buds, with **ALEX** over, and **CLEEVE** under, in broad oval outline; shield, quartered, with **ALEX CLEEVE** running round over, in dotted circle; **LONDON** over crowned rose between palm leaves, in dotted oval; hand holding Tudor rose, between columns, with **ALEX** and **CLEEVE**; crowned rose between columns, with **MADE IN** over, and **LONDON** under; four small marks, shield-shaped, with e.g. lion's head; lion rampant; RW.

Cleeve, Bourchier: (*fl. c.* 1736–1757) London
Marks included: large Tudor rose in hand, between columns, with BOUR-CHIER over and CLEEVE under, in rectangular outline with curved top; crowned rose between columns, with MADE IN over in curve, and LONDON under, in similar outline.

Cleeve, Bourchier & Richard: (*c.* 1754) London
Marks included: hand holding Tudor rose, between columns, with BOURᴿ & RICHᴰ over, and CLEEVE; crowned rose between columns, with MADE IN over and LONDON below.

Coats, Archibald and William: (recorded 1799) Glasgow, Lanarkshire
Marks included: sailing ship with ARCHᴰ/ WILLᴹ/ COATS/ LONDON on four sides of square outline containing the touch; crown and rose between I F in oval outline.

Cocks, Samuel: (*fl.* early 19th century) London
Marks included: two cocks facing, with COCKS over and LONDON under, in wide oval outline; crowned Tudor rose with MADE IN over and LONDON under, in shaped outline.

Compton, Thomas: (*fl.* 1775–1817) London
Marks included: COMPTON, with or without LONDON under, in oval outline; crowned Tudor rose with MADE IN over and LONDON under; rectangular label with COMPTON/LONDON in two lines; shaped label with SUPERFINE/HARD METAL in two lines.

Compton, Thomas & Townsend: (*fl.* 1810–1815) London
Marks included: dove flying over animal (? a horse) surrounded by the three names following the oval outline; crowned Tudor rose with MADE IN over and LONDON below; four small marks (rectangular) with a chevron, lion passant, T & C.

Cotton, Jonathan: (*fl.* 1704–1740) London
Mark used: bird with rose and crescent, circled by IONATHAN COTTON in large oval outline.

Cotton, Jonathan: (*fl.* 1735–1760) London
Mark used: eagle and stalked rose over bird in oval, surrounded by IONA-THAN COTTON in broad oval outline.

Cotton, Jonathan & Thomas: (*fl. c.* 1750) London
Marks included: eagle, flowers, and bird, with IONATHAN/& THOMAS in two curving lines over, and COTTON curving below, in shaped outline; small marks included: eagle; lion's head crowned; X; bird; label with LONDON/BRIDGE in two lines in rectangle with wavy edge.

Cutlove, Thomas: (*fl.* before 1680) London
Mark used: three fleur-de-lis among three stars, between palm leaves, with T·CUTLOVE curved over, all in oval outline.

Donne, John: (*fl.* 1692–1730) London
Marks included: hand with a bell (?) between two palm leaves, with IOHN over, and DONNE under, in shaped outline; crowned Tudor rose between palm leaves, with LONDON over and the date MDCXCII under, in rounded outline; label MADE IN/LONDON in two curving lines.

Durand, Jonas: (*fl. c.* 1692–1735) London
Mark used: E SONNANT over 1699 over a rose, between palm leaves, with IONAS over, and DURAND below.

Durand, Jonas: (*fl.* 1732–1775) London
Mark used similar to that of earlier Jonas Durand.

Dyer, Lawrence: (*fl. c.* 1645–1675) London
Marks included: shield bearing three anchors, with palms below, and LONDON over L. DYER above; crowned Tudor rose and palm leaves, with LONDON over; initials L D among three anchors in rounded shield outline; small marks in shields: lion passant; lion's head; three anchors; LD.

Dyer, Lawrence: (*fl.* early 18th century) London
Mark used: three anchors on a shield between palm leaves, with LAW over and DYER below, in shaped outline.

Eddon, William: (*fl. c.* 1689–1737) London
Marks included: emblem between initials W E in dotted circular outline; small marks of oval outline with lion's head; circle; lion passant; WE.

Edwards, J.: (*fl. c.* 1800) London
Mark used: crescent surrounded by EDWARDS WILDERNESS ROAD in circle with wavy edge.

Elderton, John: (*fl. c.* 1693–*c.* 1731) London
Marks included: three tuns, with IOHN over and ELDERTON below, in cartouche outline; small marks, shield shape, with, consecutively: three tuns; IE; lion passant; crowned leopard's head.

Elliott, Bartholomew: (*fl.* 1738–1746) London
Mark used: fancy figure, surrounded by BARTHOLOMEW ELLIOTT in wide oval.

Ellis, Samuel: (*fl. c.* 1720–1773) London
Marks included: fleece, with SAMUEL over and ELLIS below, in broad oval outline; crowned Tudor rose between palms, with LONDON over; small marks in rough ovals: fleece; lion's head erased, Britannia; SE; curving label with S:ELLIS/LONDON in two lines.

Fleming, William: (recorded 1717) Edinburgh, Midlothian
Marks included: bust (man in wig) with MAY TRADE FLOURISH arranged around it, in cartouche; crown over rose with FLEMING curved under, all in shaped outline.

Fletcher, Richard: (*fl. c.* 1678–1701) London
Marks included: windmill between the initials R F; crowned Tudor rose date 169–; small marks: lion passant; barred circle; lion's head; RI.

Fly, Martha: (*fl.* later 17th century) London
Mark used: fly between palm leaves, and MARTHA·FLY curving above, in shaped outline.

Fly, Timothy: (*fl. c.* 1710–1739) London
Marks included: a fly with TIM FLY curving over, in cartouche outline;

crowned rose with palm leaves, and LONDON above, in similar outline; small marks: lion passant; lion's head crowned; fly; TF; labels, TIM·FLY/IN LONDON in two curving lines; MADE·IN/·LONDON in two lines in rectangle.

Fly, William: (*fl. c.* 1680–1700) London
Marks included: a fly between palm leaves, with WILL FLY over in shaped outline; crowned rose with LON DON cutting across horizontally, in shaped outline; small marks: lion passant; lion's head crowned; fly; WF over fly (?).

Fly & Thompson: (*fl.* 1730s) London
Mark used: a fly surrounded by FLY AND THOMPSON in rounded outline.

Foster, Benjamin: (*fl.* 1730s onward) London
Marks included: oval "shield" with label over chevron and three emblems, with BEN. FOSTER curving above, and LONDON below, in cartouche outline; labels with SUPERFINE/HARD METTLE in two curving lines, or LONDON in rectangle with beaded border.

Gerardin & Watson: (*fl.* early 19th century) London
Marks included: GERARDIN with WATSON in circle round & in circular outline; WATSON * GERARDIN around numeral (2) in circular outline.

Giffin, Thomas: (*fl.* 1713–1764) London
Mark used: heart under coronet, with THOMAS · GIFFIN around, in broad oval outline.

Giffin, Thomas: (*fl. c.* 1760–1777) London
Marks included: crown over heart over spear, between columns, with THOMAS above and GIFFIN below, in shaped outline; crowned Tudor rose between columns, with MADE IN above and LONDON below; small marks: lion rampant; lion's head erased; coronet over sword; TG with two pellets over; all in small shields; label with THO GIFFIN/IN LONDON in two curving lines.

Gisburne, James: (*fl.* early 18th century) London

Mark used: lion rampant against a shield, in oval, with IAMES curving above and ·GISBURNE below, in shaped outline.

Gray & King: (recorded 1718) London
Marks included: pelican in her piety, with IO·GRAY over, and IA·KING below, in shaped outline; crowned Tudor rose, in shaped outline; label with MADE IN/LONDON in two lines in rectangle with scalloped edges.

Green, William Sandys: (*fl. c.* 1725–1737) London
Marks included: a griffin crest, with WᴹSANDYS over and GREEN below, in cartouche outline; crowned Tudor rose between two flowers, with WᴹSANDYS over and GREEN below.

Gregory, Edward: (recorded between 1705 and not later than 1733) Bristol, Somerset
Marks included: double-headed eagle displayed, between columns, with EDWARD GREGORY in two curves above, in shaped outline; four small marks, consecutively: EG; Britannia; griffin's head erased; double-headed eagle.

Hammerton, Henry: (*fl. c.* 1705–1741) London
Marks included: crown over tun, between initials H H; crown over tun between palm leaves, with HENRY HAMMERTON curving round above, and date 1707 below; crowned Tudor rose with palm leaves, in shaped outline.

Harton & Sons: (*fl. c.* 1860–1890) London
Marks included: sword between TRADE MARK with H&S over, and LONDON below; crowned X; small marks: crown; H; sword; S; rose; SUPERFINE HARD METAL in two lines.

Hitchman, James: (*fl.* early 18th century) London
Marks included: lion holding key, with ·I·HITCHMAN curving over, in dotted oval outline; IH alongside lion with key, in round outline; crowned rose over LONDON in dotted broad oval outline; small marks (shields): IH; anchor; fleur-de-lis (?); and lion's head; labels with HITCHMAN over LONDON forming semicircle, in semicircular out-

line; or I·HITCHMAN/MADE·IN·LONDON in two lines, in shaped rectangular outline.

Hitchman, Robert: (*fl.* 1737–1761) London
Marks included: animal between columns, with R·HITCHMAN below, or similar with ROBERT above and HITCHMAN below, in shaped outline; small marks (shields): RH; lion passant; Britannia; and anchor; label with R·HITCHMAN/IN LONDON in two curving lines.

Holmes, George: (recorded 1742) London
Marks included: four fleur-de-lis with GEORGE above and HOLMES below; labels with LONDON or SUPERFINE/HARD METAL in two curved lines.

Home, John: (*fl. c.* 1749–1771) London
Marks included: shield device with six partlets on one side, with IOHN above and HOME below, in shaped outline; labels with SNOWHILL/LONDON in two curving lines, or LONDON/SUPERFINE the same; small marks: S·S; Britannia; crowned lion's head; lion's head erased.

Howard, William: (*fl.* late 17th century) London
Marks included: crown over shield bearing fleur-de-lis, between palm leaves, with WILLIAM over and HOWARD below; crowned rose between palm leaves, with DRURY LANE over and LONDON below, both touches in similar broad oval outline; crowned rose between palms, over LONDON in rounded shaped outline; small marks: WH; lion's head crowned; fleur-de-lis; lion passant; also: lion passant; lion's head; FF in italics; WH with two pellets above and one below.

Hulls, John: (*fl. c.* 1676–1709) London
Mark used: Prince of Wales feathers between palm leaves, with IOHN·HVLLS curved over, and LONDINI (or LONDON) below.

Hulls, Ralph: (*fl. c.* 1660–1682) London
Marks included: initials RH over a grasshopper, in dotted circular outline.

Hunton, Nicholas: (*fl. c.* 1660–1670) London

113

Marks included: initials NH over a talbot (dog) with a date between its legs (1662), in dotted circular outline; half-animal holding a stag's head, between palm leaves, with crown over NICH·HUN-TON above, the whole in a shaped outline.

Iles, Robert: (*fl.* 1691–1735) London Marks included: acorn sprig between initials RI in beaded circular outline; crown over rose between palm leaves with LONDON curved over, in near-oval outline; small marks: four lozenges each with lion rampant; four with, consecutively' R; I (both italics); lion passant; acorn sprig; each in small rectangle.

Ingles, Jonathan: (*fl.* 1669–1702) London Marks included: initials II over clasped hands over date (1670) all in beaded circular outline; clasped hands under date (1671) with star below, between palm leaves, with IO·INGLES curving over, in dotted oval outline; small marks: oval with initials II.

Jackman, Nicholas: (*fl.* 1699–1736) London Marks included: figure with stand (?) surrounded by NICHOLAS IACK-MAN in dotted round outline; small marks, consecutively: NI; anchor; eagle; and lion passant; label MADE·IN/ LONDON in two curved lines.

Jackson, John: (*fl.* 1689–1716) London Marks included: leaf (?) between palm leaves with I·IACKSON above; crown and rose between palm leaves, with LONDON over; four small marks, consecutively: NI; anchor; bird; lion passant; label LONDON in rectangle with serrated edges.

de Jersey, William: (*fl.* 1732–1785) London Marks included: eagle surrounded by WILLIAM DE·IERSEY, in shaped outline; crowned rose in circle.

Jones, Charles: (*fl.* 1786–1795) London Marks included: Paschal lamb between columns with C·JONES curved above and LONDON below, in shaped rectangular outline; paschal lamb with MADE IN above and LONDON below, in square outline; label with C·JONES.

Jones, John: (*fl.* 1727–1750) London Marks included: bull with open book over, with IOHN above and IONES below, in shaped outline; crown and rose between palm leaves with LONDON over, in shaped outline; open book between initials II over bull with date (1700) below, in dotted circular outline; label with IN LONDON in curved line.

Joseph, Henry: (*fl.* 1736–1771) London Marks included: escallop shell with HENRY over and IOSEPH curved below, in cartouche outline; labels with various inscriptions, e.g. NEW·STREET/ STBRIDES/LONDON in three lines; MADE·IN / LONDON in two lines in rectangular outline; and SUPER· FINE/ HARD·METAL in two lines in rectangular outline.

Joseph, Henry and Richard: (*fl. c.* 1780) London Marks included: escallop shell with HY & RD over and IOSEPH below, in cartouche outline; escallop shell with HENRY &/RICHARD curved over in two lines, and IOSEPH below, in cartouche outline.

Jupe, John: (*fl.* 1735–1781) London Marks included: fleur-de-lis and rose with IOHN over and IUPE below, in cartouche outline; crown and rose with MADE IN over and LONDON below, in cartouche outline; small marks with consecutively: lion rampant; lion's head; bird; I·I; labels with: SUPERFINE/ FRENCH/METAL; SUPERFINE/ HARD METAL in decorative outline; QUEEN/STREET/LONDON in three lines in shaped outline.

Jupe, Robert: (*fl.* 1697–1738) London Marks included: fleur-de-lis over rose, with ROBERT over, and IUPE below, in cartouche outline; crown and rose with LONDON over and date below (1698); label MADE·IN/LONDON in shaped rectangular outline with wavy bottom edge.

Jupe, Robert: (recorded 1776) London Marks included: fleur-de-lis over rose between palm leaves, with ROBERT over and JUPE below, in cartouche outline; label with R·IUPE·IN/LON-DON in shaped outline.

Kelk, Nicholas: (*fl. c.* 1640–1687) London
Marks included: hand holding flower
spray between initials N K in dotted circular outline; crown over rose in shield.

Kenton, John: (*fl.* 1677–1717) London
Marks included: initials I K with star
above and below, with IOHN·KEN-
TON curved above, and palm leaves
around below, in shaped outline; crown
over rose between palm leaves with
LONDON above in shaped outline;
four small marks: IH; star; lion's head;
lion passant.

King, Richard: (*fl. c.* 1745–1798) London
Marks included: bird between columns
with KING below, or with RICHARD
over in addition; crown and rose between
columns, with GRACIOUS/STREET
below, or with GRACIOUS above and
STREET below; labels with: RD·
KING/IN:LONDON in rectangle;
SUPERFINE/HARD·METAL in
dotted rectangle; and LONDON in
plain rectangle.

Langford, John: (*fl. c.* 1719–1757) London
Marks included: a tun with a hand over
holding a hammer, between leaf sprays,
with JOHN over and LANGFORD
below, in broad oval outline; crown over
rose in shaped outline.

Langford, John: (recorded 1780) London
Marks included: hand with hammer held
near the horizontal over a tun, with
JOHN over, and LANGFORD under
in cartouche outline; labels with LON-
DON in scalloped rectangle, or SUPER·
FINE/HARD·METAL in two curved
lines; four small marks: I·L; hand holding hammer; tun; lion rampant (to R).

Lawrence, Stephen: (*fl. c.* 1667–1689)
London
Marks included: crown over initials SL
with double quatrefoil between palm
leaves, in oval outline; the same, but
without the crown or leaves, in dotted
circular outline; LAWRENCE with
crown above and SL below between palm
leaves, in broad oval outline; small shield
marks: SL.·' lion passant; globe.

Lawrence, Stephen: (recorded 1708)
London
Marks included: trefoil between SL
under a crown, between palm leaves, with
STEPHEN over and LAWRENCE

below, in cartouche outline; crowned rose
between palm leaves, with LONDON
below, in shaped outline; small marks in
shield form: lion passant; globe; S:L.

Leach, Jonathan: (*fl. c.* 1740–1769)
London
Marks included: shield quartered with
swords, rose, etc., with IONATHAN
above and LEACH below, in cartouche
outline; small marks in shield form: I·L;
rider (?); lion passant; lion's head.

Leapidge, Edward: (*fl. c.* 1699–1724)
London
Marks included: unicorn (on right) facing a wheatsheaf, between palm leaves,
with EDW·LEAPIDGE/LONDON
curving above, in oval outline; crown and
rose between palm leaves with LON-
DON in curve over, in shaped outline;
small marks: EL; wheatsheaf; lion's
head, globe.

Leapidge, Edward: (recorded 1728)
London
Marks included: small animal emblem
between columns with EDWARD over
and LEAPIDGE below, in square
panel; crown and rose between columns
with MADE·IN above and LONDON
below, also in square panel; small marks
in shield form: EL; wheatsheaf (?); lion's
head; globe.

Leapidge, Thomas: (recorded 1691)
London
Marks included: animal facing wheatsheaf (?), between palm leaves, with
THO·LEAPIDGE/LONDON curv-
ing over, in broad oval outline; crown
and rose between palm leaves, in oval
outline.

Little, Henry: (*fl.* 1734–1764) London
Marks included: crown over cock, between columns, with HENRY curving
over, and LITTLE below, in shaped
outline; crown over rose, over LON-
DON in shaped outline; small marks in
shield form: lion rampant (?); lion's head
crowned; lion passant; H·L; label with
·H·LITTLE·/IN·LONDON· in two
curved lines.

Lovell, John: (*fl.* 1725–1742) Bristol,
Somerset
Marks included: crowned rose between
initials IL, in cartouche with dotted
border; small marks, in shield form: I·L;

crownea X; lion rampant; lion's head; label of wavy outline with IOHN·LOVELL.

Marten, Robert: (*fl. c.* 1645–1674) London
Marks included: R M over a bird (marten) in beaded circular outline; small marks: lion's head; globe; S A; also lion passant, and R H over a bird.

Maxwell, Stephen: (*fl.* 1780s) Glasgow, Lanarkshire
Marks included: sailing ship surrounded by SUCCESS · TO / Y · BRITISH / COLONIES and S MAXWELL to side of square outline with serrated edges; sailing ship surrounded by MAY· Y · UNITED/STATES · OF /AMERICA FLOURISH, arranged around sides of rectangular shape.

Moir, Alexander: (recorded 1675) Edinburgh, Midlothian
Mark used: castle between initials A M over a date (1672).

Munday, Thomas: (*fl.* 1754–1774) London
Marks included: bust of man in wig, with THOMAS curved above, and MUNDAY below, in cartouche outline; small marks with: T·M; bust; lion's head; Britannia.

Munden & Grove: (*fl.* 1760–1773) London
Mark used: stalk with rose on left and thistle (?) on right, with WM above and EG below, the initials arranged in the corners of the square outline (the corners being canted).

Nash, Edward: (*fl.* 1717–1738) London
Marks included: three fleurs-de-lis with EDWARD curved above and NASH below, in shaped outline; crown over rose between palms, in shaped outline; labels with: ED·NASH/IN LONDON in two curved lines, and LONDON in rectangle with serrated edges.

Newham, John: (*fl.* 1699–1731) London
Marks included: globe between palm leaves with lion passant over, surmounted by IOH·NEWHAM in oval outline; globe between I N with lion passant over, in circular outline; small marks: lion passant; Britannia; globe; I.N.

Newman, Richard: (recorded 1747; d. 1789) London
Mark used: mitre between two columns, with RICHARD curved over, and NEWMAN below, in rectangle with curved top.

Nicholson, Robert: (*fl.* 1690–1731) London
Marks included; goose (?) flying on a globe, with ROBERT over and NICHOLSON below; crown and rose over LONDON in cartouche outline; label, NICHOLSON.

Norfolk, Richard: (*fl. c.* 1735–1783) London
Marks included: three fleurs-de-lis with lion, with RD·NORFOLK curved above, and IN·LONDON below, in shaped outline; LONDON over crown and rose; small marks: crown over R·N; Britannia; lion passant; lion's head crowned; labels with: MADE·IN/LONDON in two curved lines, or SUPERFINE/HARD METTLE in two curved lines.

Oliver, John: (*fl.* later 17th century) London
Mark used: seven-branched candlestick, surrounded by IOHN·OLIVER·LONDON in dotted oval outline.

Parr, Norton: (*fl. c.* 1742; d. 1773) Cork, Ireland
Mark used: swan between columns, with NORTON curved above, and PARR below.

Parr, Robert: (recorded *c.* 1681) London
Marks included: bust of man in ruff, with OLD THO PARR curved over, and AGED 152 below, in cartouche outline; label with: ROBT PARR in curved line.

Patience, Robert: (*fl. c.* 1735–1777) London
Marks included: draped figure with ROBERT curved over, and PATIENCE below, in cartouche outline; crown and rose between palm leaves, with LONDON curved over, in broad oval outline.

Pedder, Joseph: (*fl. c.* 1727) London
Mark used: cock over crossed keys, with IOSEPH curved above and PEDDER below, in oval outline.

Perchard, Hellier: (*fl. c.* 1710–1740) London
Marks included: anchor with date (1709) about it, and HELLARY curved over, and PERCHARD below, in cartouche outline; small marks: bird (?); lion passant; JW; also: lion passant; lion's head crowned; fleur-de-lis; I·H.

Pettitt, John: (*fl. c.* 1685–1713) London
Marks included: unicorn passant, with IOHN curved above, and PETTIT below, in cartouche outline; crown and rose with initials I P in shaped outline small marks: lion passant; B; lion's head crowned; I·P; label, FREE·OF· LONDON.

Piggott, Francis: (*fl. c.* 1736–1760) London
Marks included: crescent over flower spray with FRANCIS curved over, and PIGGOTT under, in cartouche outline; crown and rose with MADE IN over and LONDON below, in cartouche outline; small marks: Britannia; lion's head erased; others indecipherable; label with NEWGATE/STREET/LONDON.

Pitt & Dadley: (recorded *c.* 1781) London
Marks included: hare passant with PITT over and & DADLEY below, in oval cartouche outline; PITT and DADLEY forming circle about & in circular outline; small marks: lion passant; lion's head; cross (?); R·P.

Pitt & Floyd: (recorded *c.* 1769) London
Mark used: hare passant, with PITT over, and & FLOYD below, in cartouche outline.

Pitts, Richard: (*fl. c.* 1747–1792) London
Marks included: hare passant with RICHARD over and PITTS below, in flattened oval outline, or cartouche outline; small marks: lion passant; lion's head; cross (?) R·P.

Porteus, Robert: (*fl. c.* 1760–1790)
Marks included: ostrich with ROBERT over and PORTEOUS below, in shaped outline; crown and rose with MADE IN curved over, and LONDON below, in shaped outline; label with GRACE-CHURCH/STREET·LONDON in decorative panel.

Porteus, Robert and Thomas: (recorded 1762) London

Marks included: ostrich with ROB:& THO curved over, and PORTEUS below, in shaped outline; crown and rose with SUCCESSORS·TO above and RICHD·KING below, in shaped outline; label with: GRACECHURCH/ STREET·LONDON in decorative outline.

Priddle, Samuel: (*fl. c.* 1773–1800)
Mark used: crescent over flower spray with SAMUEL curved over, and PRIDDLE below, in cartouche outline.

Raper, Christopher: (*fl. c.* 1670–1694) London
Mark used: sword among three castles, between palm leaves, with CHRIS* RAPER over, in broad oval outline.

Rawlinson, John: (*fl. c.* 1674) London
Mark used: mitre between palm leaves, with IOHN/LONDINI curved over, and RAWLINSON below, in cartouche qutline.

Rhodes, Thomas: (*fl. c.* 1721–1746) London
Marks included: dove under sunrays, between columns, with THOMAS over and RHODES below, in square-shaped outline; dove between initials TR in circular outline; crowned X over rose, in shaped outline.

Ridding, Thomas: (*fl. c.* 1674–1697) London
Mark used: pelican in her piety on a shield, between palm leaves, with THOMAS/RIDDING curved over, in broad oval outline.

Ridding, Thomas: (recorded 1699) London
Marks included: pelican in her piety between palm leaves, with THOMAS over and RIDDING below, in shaped outline; small marks: TR; sun (?); globe; lion rampant.

Righton, Samuel: (*fl. c.* 1732–1743) London
Marks included: cock over olive branches, with SAMUEL·RIGHTON curving over, in oval outline; small marks: lion passant; Britannia; cock; S·R.

Rudsby, Andrew: (*fl. c.* 1712–1730) London

Marks included: dove flying over wheatsheaf (?), between columns, with ANDREW in semicircle above, and RUDSBY below, in shaped outline; small marks: A·R; wheatsheaf; lion rampant.

de St Croix, John: (*fl. c.* 1730) London
Marks included: three lions passant, surrounded by IOHN DE ST CROIX in shaped outline; initials IDSX with six-point star above and below, in rough circle; the initials XSID arranged as a cross, in a circle; small marks include: IW; Britannia; lion's head erased; label with MADE IN/LONDON in two lines, curving.

Sandys, William: (*fl. c.* 1692–1703) London
Marks included: griffin rampant, with WILLIAM curved over and SANDYS below, in cartouche outline; griffin rampant, among six fleurs-de-lis, with WILLIAM over and SANDYS below, in cartouche outline.

Scattergood, Thomas: (*fl. c.* 1700–1732) London
Mark used: rosette over two hands holding mallets, between palms, with THOMAS over and SCATTERGOOD below, in circular outline.

Scattergood, Thomas: (*fl. c.* 1736–1775) London
Mark used, hand over rounded shield with three hands (?) upon it, with THOMAS over and SCATTERGOOD below, in cartouche outline.

Shorey, John, Jr: (*fl. c.* 1708–1725) London
Marks included: bird on rose, between palm leaves, with IOH SHOREY curving over, in oval outline; crown and rose between palm leaves, with LONDON over, in cartouche outline; crown and rose with LONDON over, and GOD PROTECT under, in cartouche outline; small marks: lion passant; lion's head; wheatsheaf (?); IS; also lion passant; cock; lion's head crowned; IS in italic caps; labels with I·SHOREY/LONDON in two curved lines, or LONDON plain.

Smith, Richard: (*fl. c.* 1677–1705) London
Marks included: name running round inside beaded circle; with date (1677); small marks: lion passant; lion's head crowned; rose; RS.

Smith, Samuel: (recorded 1728) London
Marks included: paschal lamb between columns, with SAMUEL curved above, and SMITH below; in shaped outline; hare and wheatsheaf (?) between columns, with SAMUEL over, and SMITH below, in rectangular outline; crown and rose between columns, with MADE·IN over, and LONDON below, in rectangular outline; labels with: MADE· ON / SNOW HILL / LONDON in three curved lines, or MADE·IN·/ ·LONDON.

Smith & Leapidge: (*fl. c.* 1728) London
Mark used: hare and wheatsheaf between columns, with SMITH & over, and LEAPIDGE below, in rectangular outline.

Spackman, James: (*fl. c.* 1704–1758) London
Mark used: fleur-de-lis between Maltese crosses over coronet and palm leaves, with IAMES curving over, and SPACKMAN under, in cartouche outline.

Spackman, Joseph: (*fl. c.* 1749–c. 1764) London
Marks included: fleur-de-lis and stars (?) over coronet and palm leaves, with IOSEPH curved over, and SPACKMAN below, in cartouche outline; crown and rose, with MADE IN over and LONDON below, in shaped outline; small marks: fleur-de-lis; lion's head crowned; labels with: SPACKMAN/ FENCHURCH / STREET / LONDON or CORNHILL/LONDON in curved lines.

Spackman, Joseph, & Co: (*fl. c.* 1785) London
Marks included: Royal coat-of-arms, surrounded by: HIS·MAJESTY'S· PATENT, in flattened oval outline; fleur-de-lis, coronet, palm leaves, with IOSEPH curved over, and SPACKMAN & CO under, in shaped outline; labels with: SPACKMAN/CORNHILL / LONDON, or PATENT/ OVAL, each in flattened oval outline.

Spackman, Joseph & James: (*fl. c.* 1782) London
Marks included: fleur-de-lis and coronet among crosses, over palm leaves, with

JOSH & JAS curved over, and SPACK-MAN below, in cartouche outline; crown and rose, with MADE·IN curved over, and LONDON below, in cartouche outline; label with CORNHILL/LONDON in curved lines.

Spackman & Grant: (*fl. c.* 1709) London
Marks included: fleur-de-lis over coronet with crosses, between palm leaves, and SPACKMAN curved over and & GRANT below, in cartouche outline; crown and rose between palm leaves, with LONDON over, in dotted oval outline; crown and rose over LONDON in shaped outline; small marks: lion passant; lion's head crowned; globe; IS; label: MADE IN/LONDON in rectangle with wavy edges.

Stanton, James: (*fl. c.* 1815–1835) London
Marks included: escallop with STANTON curved over and SHOE LANE below, in broken oval outline; escallop with STANTON over, and LITTLE/BRITAIN under, in near-oval outline; small marks: lion passant; Britannia; lion's head erased; three escallops.

Stanton, Robert: (*fl. c.* 1810–1842) London
Marks included: Royal standard, with R STANTON 97 BLACKMAN ST BORO round it, in beaded upright broad oval outline; small marks: RS; lion passant; three fleurs-de-lis (?); Britannia.

Swanson, Thomas: (*fl. c.* 1753–1783) London
Marks included: a talbot (dog) with THOMAS curving above, and SWANSON below, in shaped outline; a fleece with THOMAS above and SWANSON below, in broad oval outline; crown and rose with MADE IN curving above and LONDON below; small marks: fleece; lion's head erased; Britannia; SE; label with SUCCESSOR/TO·S·ELLIS/LONDON in curved lines.

Templeman, Thomas: (*fl. c.* 1670–1697) London
Marks included: crown over temple between columns, with T·TEMPLEMAN over and LONDON below, in oval outline; crown and rose between palm leaves; temple over palm leaves, with

THOMAS TEMPLEMAN around above, in broad oval outline; label: TEMPLEMAN.

Tisoe, James: (*fl. c.* 1733–1771) London
Marks included: portcullis, with IAMES above and TISOE below, in cartouche outline; crown and rose, with WEST-MINSTER above and LONDON below, in cartouche outline; small marks: I·T; lion's head; two mullets with sword (?); lion passant.

Townsend, John: (*fl. c.* 1748–1801) London
Marks included: dove and lamb, with JOHN over, and TOWNSEND below, in cartouche outline; dove and lamb with TOWNSEND below in oval outline; hand holding flower spray, between columns, with MADE·IN curving over, and LONDON below, in shaped outline; small marks: lamb and dove; lion's head; Britannia; IT; labels with: MADE IN/LONDON, or FENCHURCH/STREET LONDON, in shaped rectangles, or SUPERFINE/HARD METAL in two curved lines.

Townsend & Compton: (*fl. c.* 1785–1805) London
Marks included: dove and lamb, with TOWNSEND & COMPTON around, in cartouche outline; crown and rose with MADE·IN over and LONDON below, in shaped outline; small marks: lion rampant; sword: T&C; labels with: SUPER FINE / HARD METAL or FEN CHURCH / STREET LONDON in decorative rectangles.

Vaughan, John: (*fl. c.* 1753–1807) London
Marks included: Paschal lamb on a field, between columns, with IOHN curving above, and VAUGHAN below, in shaped outline; Paschal lamb with MADE IN above and LONDON below; small marks: I·V; lion's head crowned; lion passant; lion's head; label with: I·VAUGHAN.

Walmsley, John: (*fl.* early 18th century) Gainsborough, Lincs.
Mark used: crown over heart, between palm leaves, with IOHN over and WALMSLEY under, in cartouche outline.

Watts, John: (*fl. c.* 1725–1760) London
Marks included: globe on stand, resting on INO WATTS, in shaped outline; crown and rose on LONDON, in shaped outline; small marks recorded include: IV; globe on stand; lion passant to right; lion's head; also I V; globe on stand; Britannia; lion passant to right; and lion rampant; lion's head; bird: LR.

Whittle, Francis: (*fl. c.* 1715–1738) London
Marks included: dove on tree, with FRANCIS above and WHITTLE below, in cartouche outline; small marks: FW; Britannia; lion or griffin's head erased; dove; label with SUPER FINE/ HARD METAL in two curved lines.

Withers, Benjamin: (*fl. c.* 1719–1730) London
Marks included: crown over a cock, with BENIAMIN curving over, and WITHERS below, in cartouche outline; crown and rose between palms, over LONDON; small marks: cock; lion's head crowned; lion passant; BW; labels with: LONDON in rectangle with serrated edges, or B·WITHERS/IN· LONDON in decorative rectangle.

American Silversmiths' marks

American silversmiths at first followed English usage, i.e. enclosing personal initials in punches of various forms or outlines. By the 18th century, American silversmiths used either initials, or the surname in full, in a square or oblong panel with plain or serrated edges; this was the normal custom. The use of the surname differs from the English custom, for in England, by decree, the use of initials only was allowed.

AB	**Adrien Bancker** (1703–1772) New York, N.Y. (oval punch)
AB	**Abel Buel** (1742–1825) New Haven, Conn. (elongated oval punch)
AB	**A. Billing** (recorded 1780) Troy, N.Y. (square punch)
AC	**Alexander Camman** (*fl.* early 19th century) Albany, N.Y. (oblong punch)
AC	**Aaron Cleveland** (recorded 1820) Norwich, Conn. (oblong punch with canted corners)
AC	**Arnold Collins** (*fl.* late 17th century) Newport, R.I. (scutcheon, heart-shape, or small oblong punch)
AC	**Albert Cole** (*fl.* early 19th century) New York, N.Y. (A over C, in diamond-shape punch)
AC	**Abraham Carlisle** (*fl.* 1790s) Philadelphia, Pa. (square punch)
AD	**Amos Doolittle** (1754–1832) New Haven, Conn. (oval punch)
AD	**Abraham Dubois** (*fl. c.* 1778) Philadelphia, Pa. (oval punch)
A·E·W	**Andrew E. Warner** (1786–1870) Baltimore, Maryland. (oblong punch with serrated ends; also AEW in interlaced italic caps, in plain oblong punch)
A.F *or* **A.F.** *or* **AGF**	**Abraham G. Forbes** (*fl. c.* 1770) New York, N.Y. (oblong punch)
A & G.W.	**A. & G. Welles** (*fl.* early 19th century) Boston, Mass. (oblong punch)
AH	**Ahasuerus Hendricks** (*fl. c.* 1675) New York, N.Y. (oval punch)
A·J·&·C⁰.	**A. Jacobs & Co** (*fl. c.* 1820) Philadelphia, Pa. (oblong punch)

AL   **Aaron Lane** (*fl. c.* 1780) Elizabeth, N.J.
(oblong punch)

AL   **Adam Lynn** (*fl.* late 18th century) D.C.
(oblong punch)

AP   **Abraham Poutreau** (*fl. c.* 1725) New York, N.Y.
(heart-shape punch)

A&R   **Andras & Richard** (*fl.* 1790s) New York, N.Y.
(oblong punch)

A.S.   **Anthony Simmons** (*fl.* late 18th century) Philadelphia, Pa.
(oblong punch)

AT   **Andrew Tyler** (1692–1741) Boston, Mass.
(oblong or heart-shape punch; also AT sometimes
crowned, in shaped punch)

AU   **Andrew Underhill** (*fl.* 1780s) New York, N.Y.
(oblong punch)

AW   **Antipas Woodward** (*fl.* 1790s) Middletown, Conn.
(oblong punch)

BB   **Benjamin Bussey** (1757–1842) Dedham, Mass.
(oblong punch)

BB   **Benjamin Brenton** (1695–1749) Newport, R.I.
(oblong punch)

BB   **Benjamin Benjamin** (*fl. c.* 1825) New York, N.Y.
(incised, or in oblong punch with canted corners)

B&D   **Barrington & Davenport** (*fl. c.* 1805) Philadelphia, Pa.
(oblong punch with serrated edges)

B.G   **Baldwin Gardiner** (*fl. c.* 1814) Philadelphia, Pa.
(oblong punch)

B.G.&CO   **B. Gardiner & Co** (*fl. c.* 1836) New York, N.Y.
(oblong punch)

BH   **Benjamin Hurd** (1739–1781) Boston, Mass.
(oblong punch)

BH   **Benjamin Hiller** (b. 1687) Boston, Mass.
(heart-shape punch or oblong with waved top and bottom edges)

B&I *or* B&J   **Boyce & Jones** (*fl. c.* 1825) New York, N.Y.
(each in oblong punch)

BL   **Benjamin Lamar** (*fl. c.* 1785) Philadelphia, Pa.
(oval punch)

B&M   **Bradley & Merriman** (*fl. c.* 1825) New Haven, Conn.
(oblong punch, or shaped to include star)

B.P   **Benjamin Pierpont** (1730–1797) Boston, Mass.
(square or heart-shape punch)

BR Bartholomew Le Roux (recorded 1688) New York, N.Y.
(oblong punch with curved ends)

BR Bartholomew Le Roux (recorded 1713) New York, N.Y.
(shaped punch)

B&R Brower & Rusher (recorded 1834) New York, N.Y.
(oblong punch)

B&R Burnet & Ryder (*fl.* late 18th century) Philadelphia, Pa.
(oblong punch)

BS Benjamin Sanderson (1649–1678) Boston, Mass.
(oblong, or near-oblong punch)

BS Bartholomew Schaats (1683–1758) New York, N.Y.
(heart-shape or oblong punch)

B&S Beach & Sanford (1785–1788) Hartford, Conn.
(oblong punch)

BT&B Ball, Tompkins & Black (*fl. c.* 1839) New York, N.Y.
(oblong punch)

BW Barnard Wenman (recorded 1789) New York, N.Y.
(oblong punch)

BW Billious Ward (1729–1777) Guilford, Conn.
(shaped or oval punch)

B.W Bancroft Woodcock (recorded 1754) Wilmington, Delaware.
(oval punch)

BW&C⁰ Butler, Wise & Co (recorded 1845) Philadelphia, Pa.
(oblong with rounded end)

B&W Beach & Ward (1789–1795) Hartford, Conn.
(oblong punch with rounded ends)

C.A.B. Charles A. Burnett (recorded 1793) Alexandria, Va.
(oblong punch)

C.B C. Brigden (recorded 1770) Boston, Mass.
(oblong punch)

CB Clement Beecher (1778–1869), Berlin, Conn.
(oblong or rounded punch, both serrated)

CC Charles Candell (recorded 1795) New York, N.Y.
(oblong punch)

CC Christian Cornelius (recorded 1810) Philadelphia, Pa.
(oblong punch)

CC&D Charters, Cann & Dunn (recorded 1850) New York, N.Y.
(oblong punch)

C.C.&S. Curtis, Candee & Stiles (recorded 1840) Woodbury, Conn.
(oblong punch)

CG   Cesar Ghiselin (recorded 1695) Philadelphia, Pa.
(oblong or inverted heart-shape punch)

C.H   Charles Hequembourg, Jr. (1760–1851) New Haven, Conn.
(shaped punch)

C.H   Christopher Hughes (1744–1824) Baltimore, Maryland.
(oblong punch)

CK   Cornelius Kierstede (1675–1757) New Haven, Conn.
(oblong or oval punch)

CL   Charles Leach (1765–1814) Boston, Mass.
(oblong punch with waved edges)

C.L.B   Charles L. Boehme (1774–1868) Baltimore, Maryland.
(oblong punch)

C&M   Coit & Mansfield (recorded 1816) Norwich, Conn.
(oblong punch, sometimes with rounded corners)

C.O.B.   Charles Oliver Bruff (*fl. c.* 1763) New York, N.Y.
(oblong punch)

C&P   Cleveland & Post (*fl. c.* 1815) Norwich, Conn.
(oblong punch, sometimes with serrated edges)

C&P   Curry & Preston (recorded 1831) Philadelphia, Pa.
(oblong punch)

CR   Charles Le Roux (1689–1745) New York, N.Y.
(oval punch)

CR   Christopher Robert (1708–1783) New York, N.Y.
(oval punch)

C.S.   Caleb Shields (recorded 1773) Baltimore, Maryland.
(oval or oblong punch)

CVB   Cornelius Vanderburgh (1653–1699) New York, N.Y.
(CV over B in heart-shape punch)

CVGF
or **C.V.G.F.**   Collins V. G. Forbes (recorded 1816) New York, N.Y.
(oblong punch)

CW   Charles Whiting (1725–1765) Norwich, Conn.
(oval or shaped punch)

C.W   Christian Wiltberger (1770–1851) Philadelphia, Pa.
(oblong punch)

DB   Daniel Boyer (1726–1779) Boston, Mass.
(oblong punch or shaped punch)

DB&AD   Bayley & Douglas (recorded 1789) New York, N.Y.
(oblong punch)

D.C   Daniel B. Coan (recorded 1789) New York, N.Y.
(oblong punch)

DCF **Daniel C. Fueter** (recorded 1756) New York, N.Y.
(oblong punch with rounded ends)

DD **Daniel Deshon** (1697–1781) New London, Conn.
(shaped punch)

D:D *or* DD **Daniel Dupuy** (1719–1807) Philadelphia, Pa.
(shaped, oval, or oblong punch)

DDD **Dupuy & Sons** (recorded 1784) Philadelphia, Pa.
(shaped punch)

DF **Daniel C. Fueter** (recorded 1756) New York, N.Y.
(oblong punch)

DH **Daniel Henchman** (1730–1775) Boston, Mass.
(oblong punch)

DH **David Hall** (1760–1779) Philadelphia, Pa.
(shaped punch)

D.I **David Jesse** (1670–1705) Boston, Mass.
(oval punch)

DI **David Jackson** (*fl. c.* 1782) New York, N.Y.
(shaped punches)

DM **David Mygatt** (1777–1822) Danbury, Conn.
(oblong punch)

DM **David Moseley** (1753–1812) Boston, Mass.
(oblong punch)

DN **David I. Northee** (d. 1788) Salem, Mass.
(oblong punch)

D&P **Downing & Phelps** (recorded 1810) New York, N.Y.
(oblong punch)

D.R *or* DR **Daniel Rogers** (d. 1792) Newport, R.I.
(oblong punch)

DR **Daniel Russel** (*fl. c.* 1720) Newport, R.I.
(shaped oval punch)

DS **David Smith** (*fl.* later 18th century) Philadelphia, Pa.
(oblong punch)

DT **David Tyler** (1760–1804) Boston, Mass.
(flattened oval punch)

D.T.G. **D. T. Goodhue** (*fl.* 1840s) Boston, Mass.
(oblong punch)

D.V **Daniel Vinton** (*fl. c.* 1790) Providence, R.I.
(oblong punch)

DV *or* D.V.
or DVV **Daniel Van Voorhis** (*fl. c.* 1770) New York, N.Y.
(oblong punch)

D&W   Davis & Watson (*fl. c.* 1815) Boston, Mass.
(italic caps in oblong punch)

DY   Daniel You (*fl.* 1740s) Charleston, South Carolina.
(rounded oval punch)

EA   Ebenezer Austin (*fl.* 1780s) Hartford, Conn.
(oblong punch)

EB   E.Baker (1740–1790) New York, N.Y.
(oblong punch)

EB   Elias Boudinot (1706–1770) Philadelphia, Pa.
(oblong or close oval punch)

EB   Everardus Bogardus (*fl.* late 17th century) New York, N.Y.
(oblong punch)

EB   Ezekiel Burr (1764–1846) Providence, R.I.
(oblong punch; also EB in italic caps, in shaped or oval punch)

EB   Ephraim Brasher (recorded 1760s) New York, N.Y.
(oblong or tight oval punch)

EB&CO   Erastus Barton & Co (*fl.* 1820s) New York, N.Y.
(oblong punch)

E·C   Elias Camp (recorded 1825) Bridgeport, Conn.
(oblong punch with serrated edges)

EC   Ebenezer Chittenden (1726–1812) New Haven, Conn.
(oblong or oval punch)

ED   E. Davis (recorded 1775) Newburyport, Mass.
(oblong punch with rounded corners)

EH
or **E·H**   Eliakim Hitchcock (1726–1788) New Haven, Conn.
(oblong punch)

EH   Eliphaz Hart (1789–1866) Norwich, Conn.
(oblong punch)

EL   Edward Lang (1742–1830) Salem, Mass.
(oblong punch)

EM   Edmund Milne (recorded 1757) Philadelphia, Pa.
(oblong punch)

EME   Edgar M. Eoff (1785–1858) New York, N.Y.
(oblong punch)

EP.   Edward Pear (*fl.* 1830s) Boston, Mass.
(oblong punch with serrated edges)

EP   Elias Pelletreau (1726–1810) Southampton, N.Y.
(oblong punch)

EPL   Edward P. Lescure (*fl.* 1820s) Philadelphia, Pa.
(italic caps in oblong punch)

E&P Eoff & Phyfe (recorded 1844) New York, N.Y.
(oblong punch, rounded end at P)

E&S Easton & Sanford (recorded 1816) Nantucket, Mass.
(oblong punch)

EW Edward Webb (early 18th century) Boston, Mass.
(oblong punch)

EW Edward Winslow (1669–1753) Boston, Mass.
(oblong or shaped punch)

F.&G. Fletcher & Gardiner (recorded 1812) Philadelphia, Pa.
(oblong punch)

F&H Farrington & Hunnewell (*fl.* 1830s) Boston, Mass.
(oblong punch)

F.M Frederick Marquand (*fl.* 1820s) New York, N.Y.
(oblong punch; also F·M)

F&M Frost & Munford (recorded 1810) Providence, R.I.
(oblong punch with serrated edges)

FR Francis Richardson (d. 1729) Philadelphia, Pa.
(heart-shape punch; also FR crowned, in closely-shaped punch)

FW Freeman Woods (*fl.* late 18th century) New York, N.Y.
(italic caps in oblong punch)

F.W.C Francis W. Cooper (*fl.* 1840s) New York, N.Y.
(FWC over NY in tight oblong punch)

G.B George Bardick (recorded 1790) Philadelphia, Pa.
(oblong punch)

GB Geradus Boyce (recorded 1814) New York, N.Y.
or **G.B** (oblong punch)

B Gerrit Onkelbag (1670–1732) New York, N.Y.
GO (close-shaped trefoil punch)

GC George Canon (early 19th century) Warwick, R.I.
(oblong punch)

GD George Drewry (*fl.* 1760s) Philadelphia, Pa.
(oval punch, indented upper edge, between G and D)

GD George Dowig (*fl.* 1770s) Philadelphia, Pa.
(oblong or oval punch; also G·D in oval punch)

G&D Goodwin & Dodd (*fl. c.* 1813) Hartford, Conn.
(oblong punch)

GF George Fielding (*fl.* 1730s) New York, N.Y.
(oval punch)

GH	George Hutton (recorded 1799) Albany, N.Y. (oval punch)
G.H	George Hanners (1697–1740) Boston, Mass. (oblong punch; also crowned G.H in scutcheon-shape punch)
G&H	Gale & Hayden (*fl.* 1840s) New York, N.Y. (oblong punch with canted corners)
GL	Gabriel Lewin (recorded 1771) Baltimore, Maryland. (oblong punch)
G&M	Gale & Moseley (recorded 1830) New York, N.Y. (oblong punch, plain or with serrated edges)
GR	George Ridout (recorded 1745) New York, N.Y. (oblong punch with canted corners)
GRD	G. R. Downing (*fl. c.* 1810) New York, N.Y. (oblong punch)
GS	George Stephens (recorded 1790) New York, N.Y. (flattened oval punch; also G.S. in concave oblong punch with serrated end)
G&S	Gale & Stickler (*fl.* 1820s) New York, N.Y. (oblong punch)
GT	George Tyler (1740–1785) Boston, Mass. (oblong punch)
G.W.&H	Gale, Wood & Hughes (recorded 1835) New York, N.Y.
H.B	Henry Bailey (recorded 1780) Boston, Mass. (oblong punch)
HB	Henricus Boelen (1684–1755) New York, N.Y. (apparently crowned HB in close-shaped oval punch)
H&B	Hart & Brewer (first years 19th century) Middletown, Conn. (oblong punch)
HH	Henry Hurst (1665–1717) Boston, Mass. (oblong or flattened scutcheon punch)
H&H	Hall & Hewson (recorded 1819) Albany, N.Y. (oblong punch)
H&I	Heydorn & Imlay (*fl. c.* 1810) Hartford, Conn. (oblong punch with waved edges)
H.L	Harvey Lewis (recorded 1811) Philadelphia, Pa. (oblong punch)
H.L.W. & CO	Henry L. Webster & Co (*fl.* 1840s) Providence, R.I. (oblong punch)
H&M	Hays & Myers (*fl.* 1770s) New York, N.Y. (oblong punch)

H&M   **Hall & Merriman** (recorded *c.* 1826) New Haven, Conn.
(incised)

H&N   **Hyde & Nevins** (recorded *c.* 1798) New York, N.Y.
(oblong punch)

HP   **Henry Pitkin** (*fl.* 1830s) East Hartford, Conn.
(flattened octagonal punch)

HRT   **Henry R. Truax** (recorded 1815) Albany, N.Y.
(italic caps in oblong punch with serrated edges; also plain HRT in plain oblong punch)

HS   **Hezekiah Silliman** (1739–1804) New Haven, Conn.
(oblong punch)

H&S   **Hart & Smith** (recorded *c.* 1815) Baltimore, Maryland.
(oblong punch; also H&S incised)

H&S   **Hotchkiss & Shreuder** (mid 19th century) Syracuse, N.Y.
(H in round punch, & in diamond-shape punch, S in round punch)

H&W   **Hart & Wilcox** (early 19th century) Norwich, Conn.
(oblong punch)

IA   **I. Adam** (*fl. c.* 1800) Alexandria, Va.
(italic caps in oval punch)

IA   **John Allen** (1691–1760) Boston, Mass.
(quatrefoil, oval, or knobbed oval punch)

IA   **Isaac Anthony** (*fl.* early 18th century) Newport, R.I.
(oval punch)

IA   **Joseph Anthony** (recorded 1783) Philadelphia, Pa.
(italic caps in oblong punch)

IA   **John Avery** (1732–1794) Preston, Conn.
(oblong punch)

I.A   **Josiah Austin** (1718–1780) Charlestown, Mass.
(oblong punch)

I.A   **Minott & Austin** (*fl.* 1765–1769) Boston, Mass.
(oblong punch, with "Minott" in separate oblong punch)

IA
IE   **Allen & Edwards** (early 18th century) Boston, Mass.
(in two separate shaped punches)

I·B   **John Benjamin** (1731–1796) Stratford, Conn.
(oblong punch)

IB
or **I·B**   **Jacob Boelen** (recorded 1773) New York, N.Y.
(oval or oblong punch)

I·B   **John Burger** (recorded 1786) New York, N.Y.
(oblong punch)

IB   **Jacob Boelen** (1659–1729) New York, N.Y.
(rounded scutcheon punch, with shaped top)

IB   **John Burt** (1691–1745) Boston, Mass.
(with crown above and dot below, in shaped punch; also
I:B in oblong punch; also crowned I:B in shaped scutcheon punch)

IBL   **John Burt Lyng** (recorded 1761) New York, N.Y.
(oblong punch)

IBV   **John Brevoort** (1715–1775) New York, N.Y.
(flattened oval, or trefoil punch)

IC   **John Carman** (recorded 1771) Philadelphia, Pa.
(oblong punch with canted corners)

I·C   **John Champlin** (1745–1800) New London, Conn.
(oblong punch)

I.C   **Jonathan Clarke** (recorded 1734) Newport, R.I.
(also IC, in oblong punch; also IC in oval punch)

I·C   **Joseph Carpenter** (1747–1804) Norwich, Conn.
(oblong punch)

I.C
or IC   **John Coburn** (1725–1803) Boston, Mass.
(square punch)

IC   **John Coddington** (1690–1743) Newport, R.I.
(oval punch, with top and tail resembling a turnip)

IC   **John Coney** (1655–1722) Boston, Mass.
(oval or oblong punch; also IC over four-point star, in
cartouche-shape punch; also crowned IC over animal in scutcheon)

ID   **Jeremiah Dummer** (1645–1718) Boston, Mass.
(oblong punch; also ID over star in scutcheon or cartouche punch)

ID   **John David** (1736–1794) Philadelphia, Pa.
(oval punch)

ID   **John Dixwell** (1680–1725)
(almost circular punch)

IE   **John Edwards** (recorded 1700) Boston, Mass.
(crowned, with star under, in scutcheon punch)

IE
or I·E   **Joseph Edwards** (1707–1777) Boston, Mass.
(oblong punch)

IG   **John Gardiner** (1734–1776) New London, Conn.
(rounded oblong punch)

IG   **Joseph Goldthwaite** (1706–1780) Boston, Mass.
(crowned, in plain scutcheon punch)

IG   **John Gray** (1692–1720) New London, Conn.
(flattened oval punch)

I.G   **John D. Germon** (recorded 1782) Philadelphia, Pa.
(oblong punch)

IGL   **Jacob G. Lansing** (*fl.* 1730s) Albany, N.Y.
(oblong punch, the G being a very small letter)

IH   **John Hastier** (recorded 1726) New York, N.Y.
or I·H   (oblong, oval, scutcheon, or heart-shaped punch)

IH   **John Hull** (1624–1683) Boston, Mass.
(in heart-shaped punch; also IH with star above, in shaped oblong punch)

I·H   **Jacob Hurd** (1702–1758) Boston, Mass.
(shaped oval punch)

I.H   **John Hutton** (*fl. c.* 1721) New York, N.Y.
or IH   (oblong punch; also as I·H)

IH   **Hull & Sanderson** (recorded *c.* 1652) Boston, Mass.
with RS   (RS with star above, in shaped punch; IH as for John Hull)

IHL   **Josiah H. Lownes** (d. 1822) Philadelphia, Pa.
(oblong punch; also JHL in oblong punch)

IHM   **John H. Merkler** (recorded *c.* 1780) New York, N.Y.
(oblong punch)

IHR   **John H. Russell** (*fl.* 1790s) New York, N.Y.
(oblong punch with serrated edges)

I·I   **Jacob Jennings** (1739–1817) Norwalk, Conn.
(oblong punch)

I·J   **John Jenkins** (recorded 1777) Philadelphia, Pa.
(square punch)

IK   **Joseph Keeler** (1786–1824) Norwalk, Conn.
(oblong punch, with plain, or serrated, edges)

I·L   **Jeffery Lang** (1708–1758) Salem, Mass.
(oblong punch)

IL   **John Leacock** (recorded 1751) Philadelphia, Pa.
(oval or square punch; also I·L in oblong punch)

IL   **John Lynch** (1761–1848) Baltimore, Maryland.
or I·L   (square punch)

I·L·T   **John Le Telier** (recorded 1770) Philadelphia, Pa.
(oblong punch)

I·M   **John McMullin** (recorded *c.* 1790) Philadelphia, Pa.
(oblong punch; also IM incised)

IM   **Jacob Marius Groen** (*fl.* early 18th century) New York, N.Y.
(oblong punch)

I:M   **John Moulinar** (recorded 1744) New York, N.Y.
or I·M   (oblong punch)

I.M.   **James Murdock** (*fl. c.* 1779) Philadelphia, Pa.
(oblong punch)

IN   **Joseph Noyes** (d. 1719) Philadelphia, Pa.
(flattened oval punch)

IN   **Johannis Nys** (*fl.* late 17th century) Philadelphia, Pa.
(heart-shape punch; also IN in oblong punch)

I·NR   **Joseph & Nathaniel Richardson** (*fl.* 1785) Philadelphia, Pa.
(oblong punch, or incised)

I·O   **Jonathan Otis** (1723–1791) Newport, R.I.
(oblong punch)

IP   **Job Prince** (1680–1704) Milford, Conn.
(rough oval punch)

I·P   **Jacob Perkins** (1766–1849) Newburyport, Mass.
(shaped punch; also crowned IP in shaped scutcheon punch)

IP   **John Pearson** (*fl.* 1790s) New York, N.Y.
(oblong punch)

I·P   **John Potwine** (recorded 1737) Boston, Mass.
(oblong punch)

I.P.T. & SON   **John P. Trott & Son** (*fl.* 1820s) New London, Conn.
(oblong punch)

I&PT   **John & Peter Targee** (*fl.* early 19th century) New York, N.Y.
(oblong punch)

IR   **John Le Roux** (recorded 1723) New York, N.Y.
(oval punch)

I.R   **Joseph Richardson** (1711–1784) Philadelphia, Pa.
(oblong punch)

I·R   **Joseph Rogers** (recorded 1808) Newport, R.I.
(flattened oval punch)

I.R   **Joseph Richardson, Jr.** (recorded 1786) Philadelphia, Pa.
(oblong punch with softened corners)

IR&S   **Isaac Reed & Son** (*fl. c.* 1810) Stamford, Conn.
(oblong punch)

I&R   **Johnson & Riley** (*fl.* 1780s) Baltimore, Maryland.
(italic caps in oblong punch with rounded ends)

I·S   **John Stuart** (d. 1737) Providence, R.I.
(square punch; also IS in square punch)

I·S   **I. Smith** (1742–1789) Boston, Mass.
(oblong punch)

IT   **John Tanner** (*fl. c.* 1740) Newport, R.I.
(oval heart-shaped punch)

I.T.   **John Targee** (recorded 1799) New York, N.Y.
(oblong punch)

IT   **John Touzell** (recorded 1756) Salem, Mass.
(square punch)

I.T	**James Turner** (d. 1759) Boston, Mass. (oval punch)
ITE	**Jacob Ten Eyck** (1704–1793) Albany, N.Y. (the TE conjoined; in oblong or shaped punch)
IV	**J. Vanderhan** (*fl. c.* 1740) Philadelphia, Pa. (italic caps in shaped punch)
I·V	**John Vernon** (*fl.* 1790s) New York, N.Y. (oblong or shaped oval punch)
I·V *with* **TU**	**Underhill & Vernon** (recorded 1787) New York, N.Y. (IV in shaped oval punch, with TU in square punch)
S **I V**	**Jacobus Van de Spiegel** (1668–1708) New York, N.Y. (in trefoil punch; also IVS in oblong punch with serrated edges; also IVS in flattened oval or rough oblong)
IVK	**John Van Newkirke** (recorded *c.* 1716) New York, N.Y. (the IV conjoined; oblong punch)
IW	**Joshua Weaver** (*fl. c.* 1815) West Chester, Pa. (shaped oval punch)
IW *or* **I·W**	**John Waite** (*fl. c.* 1770) Kingstown, R.I. (oblong punch)
IWF	**John W. Forbes** (recorded 1805) New York, N.Y. (found over NY in oblong punch)
I.W.G	**John Ward Gilman** (recorded 1792) New York, N.Y. (incised)
JA *or* **J.A**	**Jeromimus Alstyne** (*fl. c.* 1766) New York, N.Y. (oblong punch, plain or with serrated edges)
J&A.S	**J. & A. Simmons** (*fl.* early 19th century) New York, N.Y. (oblong punch)
J.B	**John Boyce** (recorded *c.* 1800) New York, N.Y. (oblong punch; found accompanied by NY in separate oblong punch)
J.B	**James Black** (recorded 1811) Philadelphia, Pa. (oblong punch)
J.B	**James Butler** (recorded 1734) Boston, Mass. (oval punch)
JC	**Joseph Clark** (recorded 1791) Danbury, Conn. (oblong punch)
JC	**Jonathan Crosby** (1743–1769) Boston, Mass. (rounded oval punch)
J.C.M	**John C. Moore** (*fl.* 1840s) New York, N.Y. (oblong punch)
JD *or* **J:D**	**John Denise** (recorded *c.* 1797) New York, N.Y. (oblong punch)

JD   **John David, Jr.** (recorded 1792) Philadelphia, Pa.
or **J.D**   (oblong, oval, or flattened oval punch)

J.F   **Foster & Richards** (recorded *c.* 1815) New York, N.Y.
(oblong punch)

JG   **John Gardiner** (1734–1776) New London, Conn.
(dented circle punch)

J.G   **John Gibbs** (recorded 1798) Providence, R.I.
(shaped punch)

JG   **James Gough** (*fl.* later 18th century) New York, N.Y.
(oblong punch)

J.H.C   **John H. Connor** (*fl.* 1830s) New York, N.Y.
(oblong punch)

J.J.S.   **John J. Staples, Jr.** (*fl.* 1780s) New York, N.Y.
(oblong punch)

JL   **John Lynch** (*fl.* late 18th century) Baltimore, Maryland.
(oblong punch)

J.L   **Joseph Loring** (recorded 1788) Boston, Mass.
(rounded oblong punch)

J.L.W   **John L. Westervell** (recorded 1845) Newburgh, N.Y.
(oblong punch)

J.M   **Joseph Moulton** (*fl.* early 18th century) Newburyport, Mass.
(oblong punch)

JM   **J. Merchant** (*fl.* late 19th century) New York, N.Y.
(oval punch)

J.M'F.   **John McFarlane** (recorded *c.* 1796) Boston, Mass.
(oblong punch)

J.P.T   **John Proctor Trott** (recorded 1799) New London, Conn.
(oblong punch)

J.P.W   **Joseph P. Warner** (1811–1862) Baltimore, Maryland.
(oblong punch)

JR   **Joseph Richardson, Jr.** (*fl.* 1770s) Philadelphia, Pa.
(oblong punch; also JR incised)

J.R   **Joseph Richardson** (1711–1784) Philadelphia, Pa.
(oblong punch)

J.S   **Joseph Shoemaker** (recorded 1798) Philadelphia, Pa.
(oval punch)

JS   **Joel Sayre** (1778–1818) New York, N.Y.
(oblong punch)

J.S.B   **John Starr Blackman** (1777–1851) Danbury, Conn.
(oblong or flattened oval punch)

J.&T.D   John & Tunis Denise (*fl.* 1770s) South Kingston, R.I.
(oblong punch)

J.W   John Waite (recorded *c.* 1798) New York, N.Y.
(shaped punch)

J.W   John Wendover (*fl. c.* 1695) New York, N.Y.
(shaped oblong punch)

J.W   Joseph Wyatt (recorded 1797) Philadelphia, Pa.
(oblong punch)

JW   James Ward (1768–1856) Hartford, Conn.
(oval punch)

J.W.B   Joseph W. Boyd (*fl. c.* 1820) New York, N.Y.
(oblong punch)

J.W.F.   John W. Faulkner (*fl. c.* 1835) New York, N.Y.
(oblong punch)

J&W   Jones & Ward (mid 19th century) Boston, Mass.
(oval punch)

K.C.&J.   Kidney, Cann & Johnson (mid 19th century) New York, N.Y.
(oblong punch)

K&D   Kidney & Dunn (*fl.* 1840s) New York, N.Y.
(oblong punch, plain or with serrated edges)

KL   Knight Leverett (recorded 1736) Boston, Mass.
(flattened oval, or shaped oval punch)

K.&S.   Kirk & Smith (*fl. c.* 1815) Baltimore, Maryland.
(oblong punch)

KE   Koenraet Ten Eyck (1678–1753) New York, N.Y.
(oblong punch)

L.B   Luther Bradley (1772–1830) New Haven, Conn.
(oblong punch)

L.B   Loring Bailey (recorded 1780) Hingham, Mass.
(oblong punch)

LF   Lewis Fueter (*fl.* 1770s) New York, N.Y.
(italic caps in oblong punch)

L&G   Lincoln & Green (recorded *c.* 1810) Boston, Mass.
(oblong punch)

LH   Ludwig Heck (*fl. c.* 1760) Lancaster, Pa.
(oblong punch)

LH   Littleton Holland (1770–1847) Baltimore, Maryland.
(italic caps in oblong punch)

LW   Lemuel Wells (recorded 1791) New York, N.Y.
(oblong punch)

L.W.&Co	**Lemuel Wells & Co** (recorded 1790s) New York, N.Y. (oblong punch)
L&W	**Leonard & Wilson** (recorded 1847) Philadelphia, Pa. (oblong punch with serrated edges)
MB	**Miles Beach** (1743–1828) Litchfield, Conn. (rounded oval punch; also M·B in oblong punch)
M&B	**Merriman & Bradley** (recorded 1817) New Haven, Conn. (oblong punch, plain or with serrated edges)
M.G *or* **MG**	**Miles Gorham** (1757–1847) New Haven, Conn. (oblong punch)
MH	**Marquette Hastier** (*fl. c.* 1770) New York, N.Y. (oblong punch)
M.J *or* **MJ**	**Munson Jarvis** (1742–1824) Stamford, Conn. (oblong punch)
MM	**Marcus Merriman** (1762–1850) New Haven, Conn. (oblong punch with serrated edges; also M in square punch; also M·M in oblong punch; also MM in segmental punch)
MM	**Myers Myers** (1723–1795) New York, N.Y. (oblong punch; also italic caps in oval punch)
M.M&Co	**Marcus Merriman & Co** (recorded 1817) New Haven, Conn. (oblong punch with serrated edges)
MP *or* **M·P**	**Matthew Petit** (recorded 1811) New York, N.Y. (oblong punch)
MR	**Moody Russel** (recorded 1694) Barnstable, Mass. (oval or shaped oblong punch)
M&R	**McFee & Reeder** (recorded 1796) Philadelphia, Pa. (oblong punch)
N·A	**Nathaniel Austin** (1734–1818) Boston, Mass. (oblong punch)
NB	**Nathaniel Burr** (1698–1784) Fairfield, Conn. (oblong punch)
N·B	**Nathaniel Bartlett** (recorded 1760) Concord, Mass. (oblong punch)
NC	**Nathaniel Coleman** (*fl. c.* 1775) Burlington, New Jersey. (oval punch)
NH	**Nathaniel Helme** (1761–1789) South Kingston, R.I. (oblong punch)
NH	**Nicholas Hutchins** (1777–1845) Baltimore, Maryland. (flattened oval punch)

N.H&CO   **N. Harding & Co** (*fl. c.* 1830) Boston, Mass.
(oblong punch)

NM   **Nathaniel Morse** (*fl.* early 18th century) Boston, Mass.
(oblong punch; also crowned NM in shaped punch)

NN   **Nehemiah Norcross** (recorded *c.* 1796) Boston, Mass.
(oblong punch)

N·R   **Nicholas Roosevelt** (1715–1769) New York, N.Y.
(oblong or flattened oval punch)

NS   **Nathaniel Shipman** (1764–1853) Norwich, Conn.
(oblong punch)

NV   **Nathaniel Vernon** (1777–1843) Charleston, South Carolina.
(oblong punch)

OP   **Otto Paul De Parisien** (*fl.* 1760s) New York, N.Y.
(oval punch: also OPDP in oblong punch with rounded ends)

O&S   **Oakes & Spencer** (*fl. c.* 1814) Hartford, Conn.
(oblong punch)

PA   **Pygan Adams** (1712–1776) New London, Conn.
(oblong punch, sometimes with slightly rounded corners)

PB   **Phineas Bradley** (1745–1797) New Haven, Conn.
(oblong punch)

P.D   **Phillip Dally** (recorded *c.* 1779) New York, N.Y.
(oblong punch)

PD   **Peter David** (1707–1755) Philadelphia, Pa.
(oval punch)

PDR   **Peter De Riemer** (1736–1814) Philadelphia, Pa.
(oblong punch, sometimes with rounded ends)

PG   **Philip Goelet** (recorded 1731) New York, N.Y.
(oblong or oval punch)

PH   **Philip Hurlbeart** (recorded *c.* 1761) Philadelphia, Pa.
(irregular shaped punch)

PH   **Philip Huntington** (recorded 1796) Norwich, Conn.
(oblong punch)

P.L   **Peter Lupp** (1797–1827) New Brunswick, New Jersey.
(oval punch)

P.L.K   **Peter L. Krider** (mid 19th century) Philadelphia, Pa.
(oblong punch)

P.M   **P. Mood** (recorded 1806) Charleston, South Carolina.
(oblong punch)

P&M   **Parry & Musgrave** (recorded 1793) Philadelphia, Pa.
(oblong punch)

PO   Peter Oliver *(fl. c.* 1710*)* Boston, Mass.
(heart-shape punch)

P.O   Peter Olivier (recorded 1797) Philadelphia, Pa.
(oblong punch with serrated edges)

PP   Peter Perreau (recorded 1797) Philadelphia, Pa.
(oblong punch; also P·P in shaped punch)

P.Q   Peter Quintard (1699–1762) New York, N.Y.
(oblong punch; also PQ in rounded punch, and P⊄ in oblong punch)

PR   Paul Revere (1702–1754) Boston, Mass.
(in crowned scutcheon punch)

PR   Paul Revere II (1735–1818) Boston, Mass.
(oblong punch; also PR in italic caps in circle or oblong punch)

PS   Philip Syng (1676–1739) Philadelphia, Pa.
(oblong punch)

P.S   Philip Sadtler (1771–1860) Baltimore, Maryland.
(shaped oblong punch)

PS   Philip Syng II (1702–1789) Philadelphia, Pa.
(oblong or heart-shape punch)

P&U   Pelletreau & Upson (recorded 1818) New York, N.Y.
(oblong punch)

PV   Peter Vergereau (1700–1755) New York, N.Y.
(oblong punch with rounded end; also P.V in shaped oblong punch)

PVB   Peter Van Beuren (recorded 1798) New York, N.Y.
(italic caps in plain oblong punch or shaped punch)

P.VB   Peter Van Inburgh (1689–1740) New York, N.Y.
(oblong punch, the VB as monogram)

PVD
or P.V.D   Peter Van Dyke (1684–1750) New York, N.Y.
(flattened oval punch; also shaped punch)

R.&A.C.   R. & A. Campbell (recorded 1853) Baltimore, Maryland.
(oblong punch)

RB   Roswell Bartholomew (1781–1830) Hartford, Conn.
(oblong punch with serrated edges)

RB   Robert Brookhouse (mid 18th century) Salem, Mass.
(italic caps in rounded oblong punch)

RC   Robert Campbell (recorded 1834) Baltimore, Maryland.
(oblong punch)

RD   Robert Douglas (recorded 1776) New London, Conn.
(oblong punch)

RD   Richard Van Dyke (1717–1770) New York, N.Y.
(rounded oval punch)

RE or R·E	**Robert Evans** (d. 1812) Boston, Mass. (oblong punch)
RF	**Rufus Farnam** (recorded 1796) Boston, Mass. (oblong punch)
RF	**Robert Fairchild** (1703–1794) Durham, Conn. (oval or shaped oval punch)
R·G	**Rufus Greene** (1707–1777) Boston, Mass. (oblong punch with serrated edges or shaped round punch; also RG in plain oblong punch)
RG	**Rene Grignon** (d. 1715) Norwich, Conn. (in crowned curved punch)
R&G	**Riggs & Griffith** (recorded 1816) Baltimore, Maryland. (oblong punch)
RH	**Richard Humphreys** (*fl.* 1770s) Philadelphia, Pa. (oblong punch; also R·H in flattened oval punch; also RH in italic caps, rounded punch)
R&L	**Roberts & Lee** (recorded 1775) Boston, Mass. (oblong punch with serrated edges)
R·M	**Reuben Merriman** (1783–1866) Litchfield, Conn. (oblong punch with serrated edges)
RR	**Richard Riggs** (d. 1819) Philadelphia, Pa. (shaped oval oblong punch)
RS	**Robert Sanderson** (d. 1693) Boston, Mass. (with star over RS in trefoil-shape punch)
RVD	**Richard Van Dyke** (1717–1770) New York, N.Y. (oblong punch with rounded ends; also RD in heart-shape punch)
RW or R·W	**Robert Wilson** (recorded 1816) New York, N.Y. (oval punch)
R&WW	**R. & W. Wilson** (*fl.* 1820s) Philadelphia, Pa. (oblong punch)
SA	**Samuel Avery** (1760–1836) Preston, Conn. (oblong punch; also found with SA in italic caps)
S·A	**Samuel Alexander** (*fl.* early 19th century) Philadelphia, Pa. (oblong punch)
SB or S·B	**Samuel Burt** (1724–1754) Boston, Mass. (oblong punch)
SB or S·B	**Stephen Bourdett** (recorded 1730) New York, N.Y. (rounded oblong punch)
SB	**Standish Barry** ((1763–1844) Baltimore, Maryland. (oblong punch)

SB	**Samuel Buel** (1742–1819) Middletown, Conn. (rounded oval punch; also S·B in oblong punch)
SB	**Samuel Burill** (recorded 1733) Boston, Mass. (flattened oval punch; also "sb" over a star in heart-shape punch)
S&B	**Shepherd & Boyd** (recorded 1810) Albany, N.Y. (oblong punch)
S·C	**Samuel Casey** (1724–1773) South Kingston, R.I. (rounded oval punch)
SC&Co	**Simon Chaudrons & Co** (recorded 1807) Philadelphia, Pa. (oblong punch)
S&C	**Storrs & Cooley** (*fl. c.* 1830) New York, N.Y. (shaped punch)
S*D	**Samuel Drowne** (1749–1815) Portsmouth, New Hampshire. (flattened oval punch)
SE	**Samuel Edwards** (1705–1762) Boston, Mass. (crowned SE over small star, in scutcheon punch)
S.E	**Stephen Emery** (1725–1801) Boston, Mass. (oblong punch with rounded ends; also SE in rounded punch)
SF	**Samuel Ford** (recorded 1797) Philadelphia, Pa. (oblong punch)
SG	**Samuel Gilbert** (*fl. c.* 1798) Hebron, Conn. (oblong punch)
SG	**Samuel Gray** (1684–1713) New London, Conn. (heart-shape punch)
S:H	**Stephen Hopkins** (1721–1796) Waterbury, Conn. (oblong punch)
SH *or* **S·H**	**Stephen Hardy** (1781–1843) Portsmouth, New Hampshire. (oblong punch)
SH	**Samuel Haugh** (1675–1717) Boston, Mass. (squat letters in oblong punch)
S.J	**Samuel Johnson** (*fl. c.* 1780) New York, N.Y. (oblong punch)
S.K	**Samuel Kirk** (1792–1872) Baltimore, Maryland. (oblong punch, plain, or with serrated edges)
S.L *or* **S·L**	**Samuel Leach** (*fl.* 1740s) Philadelphia, Pa. (oblong punch)
S·M	**Samuel Merriman** (1769–1805) New Haven, Conn. (oblong punch)
SM	**Sylvester Morris** (1709–1783) New York, N.Y. (flattened oval punch)

S&M   **Sibley & Marble** (*fl.* 1801–1806) New Haven, Conn.
(oblong punch)

SP   **Samuel Parmelee** (1737–1803) Guilford, Conn.
(oblong or oval punch)

SR   **Samuel R. Richards, Jr.** (recorded 1793) Philadelphia, Pa.
(flattened oval punch)

S&R   **Sayre & Richards** (recorded 1802) New York, N.Y.
(oblong or flattened oval punch)

SS   **Simeon Soumain** (1685–1750) New York, N.Y.
(oblong punch)

SS   **Silas Sawin** (recorded 1823) Boston, Mass.
(square punch)

SS   **Samuel Soumaien** (*fl. c.* 1754) Philadelphia, Pa.
(square or oval punch)

ST   **Samuel Tingley** (*fl. c.* 1767) New York, N.Y.
(oblong punch; also italic caps in shaped or square punch)

SV   **Samuel Vernon** (1683–1735) Newport, R.I.
(over star, in heart-shape punch)

SW   **Samuel Warner** (*fl.* late 18th century) Philadelphia, Pa.
(oblong punch)

S·W   **Samuel Waters** (recorded 1790) Philadelphia, Pa.
(oblong punch)

S·W   **Samuel Williamson** (recorded 1794) Philadelphia, Pa.
(oblong punch; also SW in flattened oval punch)

S W   **Silas White** (recorded 1792) New York, N.Y.
(each initial in separate, square punch; also SW in oblong punch)

SWL   **S. W. Lee** (*fl.* early 18th century) Providence, R.I.
(oblong punch)

TA   **Thomas Arnold** (1739–1828) Newport, R.I.
(Roman or italic caps in oblong punch)

TB   **Thauvet Besley** (recorded 1727) New York, N.Y.
(crowned monogram, incised)

TB   **Timothy Brigden** (recorded 1813) Albany, N.Y.
(oblong punch with serrated edges)

T·B   **Thomas Burger** (*fl. c.* 1805) New York, N.Y.
(oblong punch)

TB.   **Timothy Bontecou** (1693–1784) New Haven, Conn.
(incised)

T·B   **Timothy Bontecou, Jr.** (1723–1789) New Haven, Conn.
(soft oblong punch; also TB in oval punch)

T&B **Trott & Brooks** (recorded 1798) New London, Conn.
(oblong punch)

TC **Thomas Carson** (*fl. c.* 1815) Albany, N.Y.
(shaped punch)

T.C.C. **Thomas Chester Coit** (*fl. c.* 1812) Norwich, Conn.
(oblong punch)

T.C&H **Thomas Carson & Hall** (recorded 1818) Albany, N.Y.
(oblong punch)

T&C **Trott & Cleveland** (*fl.* 1790s) New London, Conn.
(oblong punch)

TD **Timothy Dwight** (1645–1691) Boston, Mass.
(heart-shape punch)

T·D·D **Tunis D. Dubois** (recorded 1799) New York, N.Y.
(oblong punch)

T.E **Thomas Knox Emery** (1781–1815) Boston, Mass.
(oblong punch)

TE **Thomas Edwards** (1701–1755) Boston, Mass.
(crowned, in shaped square punch; also T.E. in oblong punch)

T.E.S **T. E. Stebbins** (recorded 1810) New York, N.Y.
(oblong punch)

TH **Thomas Hammersley** (1722–1781) New York, N.Y.
or T·H (oblong punch with rounded ends, or shaped punch; also TH in
italic caps in square punch)

T&H **Taylor & Hinsdale** (recorded 1801) New York, N.Y.
(oblong punch)

T·K **Thomas Kinne** (1786–1824) Norwich, Conn.
(oblong punch with serrated edges; also TK and T.K. in
oblong punches)

T.K **Thaddeus Keeler** (recorded 1805) New York, N.Y.
(oblong punch)

TM **Thomas Millner** (1690–1745) Boston, Mass.
or T·M (flattened oval punch)

TN **Thomas Norton** (recorded 1796–1806) Farmington, Conn.
(oblong punch)

TR **Thomas Revere** (recorded 1789) Boston, Mass.
(oval punch)

TS **Thomas Savage** (recorded 1689) Boston, Mass.
(heart-shape punch)

T·S **Thomas Shields** (*fl. c.* 1771) Philadelphia, Pa.
(also TS, in oblong punch)

TS **Thomas Skinner** (1712–1761) New York, N.Y.
(flattened oval punch)

TSB   **Tobias Stoutenburgh** (1700–1759) New York, N.Y.
(flattened oval punch)

T·T   **Thomas Trott** (1701–1777) Boston, Mass.
(oblong punch; also T.T in shaped punch)

T.U   **Thomas Underhill** (recorded 1779) New York, N.Y.
(oblong punch)

T.W   **Thomas H. Warner** (1780–1828) Baltimore, Maryland.
(shaped oval punch)

T·U   **Underhill and Vernon** (recorded 1787) New York, N.Y.
with I·V   (the TU in oblong punch, the IV in shaped oval punch)

T·W   **Thomas Whartenby** (recorded 1811) Philadelphia, Pa.
(oblong punch)

T·Y   **Thomas You** (*fl. c.* 1756) Charleston, South Carolina.
(oval punch)

U&B   **Ufford & Burdick** (*fl. c.* 1814) New Haven, Conn.
(oblong punch)

V&C   **Van Voorhis & Cooley** (recorded 1786) New York, N.Y.
(oblong punch)

V.V&S   **Van Voorhis & Schanck** (recorded 1791) New York, N.Y.
(oblong punch)

V&W   **Van Ness & Waterman** (recorded 1835) New York, N.Y.
(oblong punch)

WA   **William Anderson** (recorded 1746) New York, N.Y.
(oblong punch)

W&B   **Ward & Bartholomew** (recorded 1804) Hartford, Conn.
(oblong punch)

WB   **William Ball** (*fl. c.* 1752) Philadelphia, Pa.
(oblong punch with rounded ends; also W.B in italic caps
in shaped punch)

WB   **William Breed** (*fl. c.* 1750) Boston, Mass.
(oval punch; also WB as monogram in near heart-shape punch)

W.B.N   **William B. North** (1787–1838) New York, N.Y.
(oblong punch)

W&B   **Ward & Bartholomew** (recorded 1804) Hartford, Conn.
(oblong punch, plain, or with serrated edges)

WC   **William Clark** (*fl. c.* 1774) New Milford, Conn.
(oval punch)

WC   **William Cross** (*fl. c.* 1712) Boston, Mass.
(rough oblong punch)

W·C   **William Cleveland** (1770–1837) New London, Conn.
(oblong punch; also WC in oblong punch with serrated edges)

WC   **William Cowell** (1682–1736) Boston, Mass.
(scutcheon, flattened oval, or shaped punch; also W.C in shaped punch)

W·F   **William Forbes** (recorded 1830) New York, N.Y.
(oblong punch)

WG   **William Gale** (recorded 1816) New York, N.Y.
(oblong punch)

WG   **William Ghiselin** (*fl. c.* 1751) Philadelphia, Pa.
(in almost square punch)

WG   **William Grant, Jr.** (recorded 1785) Philadelphia, Pa.
(oval punch)

W.G   **William Gurley** (*fl.* early 19th century) Norwich, Conn.
(oblong punch)

W&G   **Woodward & Grosjean** (recorded 1847) Boston, Mass.
(oblong punch with rounded ends)

W.G&S   **William Gale & Son** (recorded 1823) New York, N.Y.
(oblong punch)

WH   **William Haverstick** (*fl. c.* 1781) Philadelphia, Pa.
(oblong punch)

W·H   **William Hollingshead** (recorded 1770) Philadelphia, Pa.
(oblong punch; also WH in italic caps in shaped punch)

WH   **William Heurtin** (recorded 1731) New York, N.Y.
(oblong punch)

W.H   **William Homes, Jr.** (1742–1835) New York, N.Y.
(oblong punch; also WH)

W.H   **William Homes** (recorded 1733) Boston, Mass.
(oblong punch; also WH in oblong or oval punch)

W&H   **Wood & Hughes** (recorded 1846) New York, N.Y.
(oblong punch)

W·I   **William Jones** (1694–1730) Marblehead, Mass.
(oblong punch)

WJ   **William B. Johonnot** (1766–1849) Middletown, Conn.
(oblong punch)

WK   **William Kimberly** (*fl. c.* 1795) New York, N.Y.
(oblong punch)

W.K
B   **Benjamin Wynkoop** (1675–1751) New York, N.Y.
(initials arranged thus in heart-shape punch)

WK
B   **Cornelius Wynкoop** (recorded 1724) New York, N.Y.
(WK over B in heart-shape punch)

WL	**William Little** (*fl. c.* 1775) Newburyport, Mass. (oblong punch)
WM	**William Moulton** (*fl. c.* 1807) Newburyport, Mass. (oblong punch)
W.P	**William Pollard** (*fl.* early 18th century) Boston, Mass. (flattened oval punch)
W·R	**William Roe** (*fl.* early 19th century) Kingston, N.Y. (oblong punch)
WR	**William Rouse** (1639–1705) Boston, Mass. (oval punch; also WR with star above and below, in shaped punch)
W·S	**William Simes** (1773–1824) Portsmouth, New Hampshire. (oblong punch with rounded ends)
W·S *with* **Minott**	**Minott & Simpkins** (*fl.* 1770s) Boston, Mass. (each in oblong punch)
W·S·N	**William S. Nichol** (1785–1871) Newport, R.I. (oblong punch)
W.S.P. *with* **TR**	**Pelletreau & Richards** (*fl. c.* 1825) New York, N.Y. (in separate oblong punches)
W.S.P.	**William Smith Pelletreau** (1786–1842) Southampton, Long Island, N.Y. (oblong punch with serrated edges)
WT	**Walter Thomas** (recorded 1769) (shaped punch)
WV	**William Vilant** (*fl. c.* 1725) Philadelphia, Pa. (heart-shape punch)
W.V.B	**William Van Beuren** (recorded 1790) New York, N.Y. (shaped oval punch)
W.W	**William Whetcroft** (1735–1799) Baltimore, Maryland. (oblong punch)
W.W	**William Ward** (1742–1828) Litchfield, Conn. (oblong punch)
WWG	**W. W. Gaskins** (*fl.* 1830s) Providence, R.I. (oblong punch)
ZB *or* **Z·B**	**Zachariah Brigden** (1734–1787) Boston, Mass. (nearly square punch)
ZS	**Zebulon Smith** (1786–1865) Maine.

American Pewterers' Marks

Early makers of pewter in the U S.A. used "touches" (the correct term for a mark on pewter) that could be easily recognised by means of the distinction of the device employed. Unfortunately today such marks are all too often somewhat unrecognisable due to wear, or indeed by having been somewhat hastily applied in the first instance. Three periods of fashion in marking may be distinguished. At first (pre-Revolutionary) English customs strongly influenced American usage. The rose and crown, and the lion rampant, were favourite devices, very often found associated with a number of other marks (in square or shield punches) of no real significance. The middle period (during or after the War of Independence) the American eagle was commonly used, sometimes with more or less stars in allusion to the current number of States in the Union. The later period (from *c.* 1825 onward) displays the common practice of using the individual pewterer's name with place of origin, either enclosed in a rectangular label, or merely incised.

Archer, Ellis S.: (*fl. c.* 1845) Philadelphia.
Mark recorded:
ARCHER'S PATENT PHILAD^
in three lines, over JUNE 18th 1842,
arranged in large flattened oval.

Archer & Janney: (*fl. c.* 1847) St Louis, Mo.
Mark recorded:
ARCHER & N. E. JANNEY. ST. LOUIS in a long narrow panel.

Armitages & Standish: (*fl. c.* 1840)
Mark recorded:
ARMITAGES
& STANDISH

Austin, Nathaniel: (1741–1816) Charlestown, Mass.
Marks recorded include:
Lion rampant enclosed between two columns with NATHL (above) and AUSTIN (below); N. AUSTIN in a circle, or in a label with CHARLES-TOWN; the American eagle between columns.

Austin, Richard: (*fl.* 1792–1817) Boston, Mass.
Marks recorded include:
R.A.BOSTON plain, or in an oblong panel; RICHARD AUSTIN as curved oval panel, associated with emblems of a bird and animal.

Babbitt, Crossman & Co.: (*fl.* 1826/28) Taunton, Mass.
Mark recorded: full name in oblong panel.

Babbitt & Crossman: (1814–1826) Taunton, Mass.
Mark recorded: name in oblong panel.

Badger, Thomas, Jr: (1764–1826) Boston, Mass.
Mark recorded: American eagle with THOMAS (above) and BADGER (below), in square panel with curved top edge.

Bailey & Putnam: (*c.* 1830–1835) Malden, Mass.
Mark recorded: BAILEY in punch with serrated edges, over & in round punch, over PUTNAM in punch with serrated edges.

Barns, Blakslee: (*fl. c.* 1805–1810) Berlin, Conn. Also at Philadelphia, Pa. (1812–1817).
Marks recorded include: B. BARNS over PHILADA in a square panel; B. BARNES over PHILADIA in a square panel; BB under a bird, in a round or oval punch with a serrated edge; B BARNS over an eagle, in a round punch.

Barns, Stephen: (*fl. c.* 1795) Conn.

Mark recorded: American eagle with stars above in upright oval panel, with STEPHEN (above) and BARNS (below) outside.

Bartholdt, William: (*fl.* 1850–1854) Williamsburg, N.Y.
Mark recorded: WM BARTHOLDT incised.

Bassett, Francis, II: (*fl.* 1754, d. 1800) New York, N.Y.
Marks recorded include: FB with a star over, in an oval punch; animal over FB, in round punch; cartouche enclosing F. BASSETT over a fleur-de-lys between two stars, a coronet and palm leaves under.

Bassett, Frederick: (*fl.* 1761–1780, and 1785–1800) New York, N.Y. Also at Hartford, Conn. (1781–1785).
Marks recorded include: FB with a fleur-de-lys above and below, in an oval; also FREDERICK BASSET surrounding a crown over NY over a rose, in a cartouche.

Bassett, John: (*fl.* 1720–1761) New York, N.Y.
Mark recorded: I.B with fleur-de-lys above and below, in oval punch.

Belcher, Joseph, Jr: (*fl.* 1776–1784) Newport, R.I. Also at New London, Conn. (after 1784).
Mark recorded; J:B in an oval; the name BELCHER apparently part of a cartouche, may be his.

Billings, William: (*fl.* 1791–1806) Providence, R.I.
Marks recorded include: anchor between W.B in upright oval panel; W. BILLINGS in curved label.

Boardman, Henry S.: (recorded 1841) Hartford, Conn. Also at Philadelphia, Pa. (*c.* 1844–1861).
Mark recorded: BOARDMAN over PHILADᴬ.

Boardman, Luther: (recorded 1836) South Reading, Mass. Also at Chester, Conn. (*fl.* 1837–*c.* 1842).
Marks recorded include: L.B in oblong panel; eagle with stars, surrounded by L. BOARDMAN WARRANTED, in circular panel.

Boardman, Thomas D.: (*fl.* 1804–1850) Hartford, Conn.
Marks recorded include: cartouche enclosing name and American eagle; T.D.B. in oblong with serrated edges; T. D. BOARDMAN in long oblong label, over HARTFORD in oblong serrated panel.

Boardman, T. D. & S.: (*fl. c.* 1810–1850) Hartford, Conn.
Mark recorded: eagle, facing left, in circle, surrounded by BOARDMAN WARRANTED, circular punch; TD & SB in oblong panel; imputed marks include: American eagle in wide oval; American eagle, facing right, in cartouche; also BOARDMAN with animal over, in shaped cartouche.

Boardman, Timothy, & Co: (*fl.* 1822–1825) New York, N.Y. Merchant trading for T. D. & S. Boardman.
Used the mark TB & Cº in oblong panel with serrated edges.

Boardman & Co: (*fl.* 1825–1837) New York, N.Y.
Said to have traded for T. Boardman & Co.
Mark recorded: American eagle surrounded by BOARDMAN & CO NEW YORK in upright or horizontal oval panel.

Boardman & Hall: (*fl. c.* 1845) Philadelphia, Pa.
Connected with Boardman & Co (supra).
Mark recorded: BOARDMAN over & HALL in shaped rectangle with PHILADᴬ in oblong panel.

Boardman & Hart: (*fl.* 1827–1850) New York, N.Y.
Connected with Boardman & Co (supra).
Marks recorded include: BOARDMAN over & HART in shaped rectangle, associated with N. YORK in oblong punch; also N. YORK surrounded by BOARDMAN & HART in large oval with serrated edges.

Boyd, Parks: (*fl.* 1797–1819) Philadelphia, Pa.
Marks recorded include the words P. BOYD. PHILA with or without an eagle in the punch.

Boyle, Robert: (*fl.* 1753–1758) New York, N.Y.

Mark recorded: a device between two columns, with ROBERT (above) and BOYLE (below); NEW-YORK in oblong.

Bradford, Cornelius: (*fl.* 1752) New York, N.Y. Also (*fl.* 1758–1770) at Philadelphia, Pa.; New York again until 1770.
Marks recorded include: crowned rose between columns with CORNELIUS (above) and BRADFORD (below); also C. BRADFORD with PHILADELPHIA.

Brook Farm: (*c.* 1845) West Roxbury, Mass.
Mark recorded: BROOK FARM in curved label.

Brunstrom, John A.: (*fl.* 1783–1793) Philadelphia, Pa.
Mark recorded: IAB in rectangular punch.

Buckley, Townsend M.: (*fl. c.* 1855) Troy, N.Y.
Mark recorded: T. M. BUCKLEY incised.

Byles, Thomas: (*fl.* 1738–1771) Philadelphia, Pa.
Mark recorded: crowned rose between columns over T. BY (incomplete).

Cahill, J. W. & Co: (*fl. c.* 1835)
Provenance not determined.
Mark recorded: J. W. CAHILL & CO in curved label with serrated edges.

Calder, William: (*fl. c.* 1817–1856) Providence, R. I.
Mark recorded: American eagle with CALDER (above) and PROVIDENCE (below) in cartouche; also CALDER in oblong panel with serrated edges.

Capen, Ephraim: (*fl. c.* 1848) New York, N.Y.
Mark recorded: E· CAPEN· incised.

Capen & Molineux: (*fl.* 1848–1854) New York, N.Y.
Mark recorded: NY in oblong panel with CAPEN & in curved label (above) and MOLINEUX in curved label (below).

Carnes, John: (1698–1760) Boston, Mass.
Mark ascribed: crowned shield between BOSTON on left and (presumably) own name on right, in cartouche.

Coldwell, George: (*fl. c.* 1789–1810) New York, N.Y.
Mark recorded: G. COLDWELL in oblong panel with wavy edges.

Colton, Oren: (*fl. c.* 1835) Philadelphia, Pa.
Mark recorded: O. COLTON incised.

Copeland, Joseph: (*fl. c.* 1675–1691) Chuckatuck and Jamestown, Va.
Mark recorded: heart surrounded by CHUCKATUCK in a circle, with 1675. JOSEPH·COPELAND· forming outer circle in circular punch.

Cox, William: (*fl.* 1715–1721) Philadelphia, Pa.
Mark recorded: animal head with WILLIAM over and COX under, forming oval design.

Crossman, West & Leonard: (*fl.* 1828–1830) Taunton, Mass.
Mark recorded CROSSMAN over WEST & LEONARD incised.

Curtis, Lemuel J.: (*fl.* 1836–1849) Meriden, Conn.
Mark recorded: L. J. CURTISS in oblong panel.

Curtiss, Daniel: (*fl.* 1822–1850) Albany, N.Y.
Marks recorded include: D CURTISS in swirling label; D. CURTISS over an urn in an (incomplete) oval.

Curtiss, I.: (*c.* 1820)
Provenance not determined.
Marks recorded include I·CURTISS or I·CURTIS in oblong panel; heraldic eagle (rather crude).

Cutler, David: (1703–1772) Boston, Mass.
Mark ascribed: UTLER (incomplete).

Danforth, Edward: (*fl. c.* 1788) Middletown, Conn. Also (*c.* 1790) Hartford, Conn.
Marks recorded include: lion rampant with EDWARD (above) and DANFORTH (below) in cartouche; lion rampant between initials E D with rim of pellets, in cartouche; E.D in a flattened shield.

Danforth, John: (*fl.* 1773–1793) Norwich, Conn.
Marks recorded include: lion rampant

between columns with JOHN (above) and DANFORTH (below) surmounted by NORWICH with effect of a cartouche; lion rampant between initials J.D in round punch; initials JD in an oblong punch.

Danforth, Joseph: (*fl.* 1782–1788) Middletown, Conn.
Marks recorded include: lion rampant between columns with JOSEPH (above) in curved label and DANFORTH (below) in oblong label, all forming cartouche; initials I · D in oblong punch, or JD in flattened shield punch.

Danforth, Joseph Jr: (*fl. c.* 1807–*c.* 1812) Richmond, Va.
Marks recorded include: American eagle with JD and stars forming circle round it; eagle with JD at feet and stars scattered around its head associated with RICHMOND over WARRANTED in shaped rectangle.

Danforth, Josiah: (*fl. c.* 1825–1837) Middletown, Conn.
Marks recorded include: American eagle with DANFORTH and MIDD.CI around in round panel with serrated edge; J. DANFORTH in oblong panel.

Danforth, Samuel: (*fl.* 1793–1803) Norwich, Conn.
Mark recorded: SAMl DANFORTH in oblong panel; mark ascribed includes the eagle (apparently) with NORWICH in curved panel, presumably as cartouche.

Danforth, Samuel: (*fl.* 1795–1816) Hartford, Conn.
Marks recorded include: American eagle with stars and SAMUEL (above) and DANFORTH (below) curving as cartouche; American eagle perched on SD and ringed with 19 stars, in oval; American eagle between initials S D in upright oval with plain or serrated edge; S.D in small oval punch.

Danforth, Thomas: (*fl.* 1727–1733) Taunton, Mass. Also (1733–1773) Norwich, Conn.
No marks recorded yet.

Danforth, Thomas II: (*fl.* 1755–1782) Middletown, Conn.
Marks recorded include: lion rampant between columns with THOMAS in curved label attached over, supported on DANFORTH in oblong label forming a cartouche; lion rampant between initials T D in curved cartouche with beaded rim; initials T · D in flattened shield.

Danforth, Thomas III: (*fl.* 1777–*c.* 1808) Rocky Hill, Conn. Also (1807–1813) at Philadelphia, Pa.
Marks recorded include: American eagle with T D above or below, in oval punch; initials T.D in oblong punch, or in upright oblong with canted corners; T. DANFORTH over PHILADA in shaped rectangle.

Danforth, Thomas IV: (1792–1836) Philadelphia, Pa.
No marks recorded as yet.

Danforth, William: (*fl.* 1792–1820) Middletown, Conn.
Mark recorded: American eagle with stars with WILLIAM (above) and DANFORTH (below) in shaped panel.

Day, Benjamin: (1706–1757) Newport, R.I.
Mark recorded: initials BD in flattened octagonal punch.

Derby, Thomas S.: (*fl. c.* 1818–1850) Middletown, Conn.
Mark ascribed: bust surrounded with palm leaves (below) and GEN. JACKSON (above) in circular panel.

Derby, Thomas S., Jr: (*fl. c.* 1840–1850) Middletown, Conn.
Mark recorded T. S. DERBY. in oblong panel.

De Riemer, Cornelius B. & Co: (*fl. c.* 1835) Auburn, N.Y.
Mark recorded: C. B. DE RIEMER & C⁰ over AUBURN, all incised.

Dunham, E.: (after 1825)
Provenance not determined.
Mark recorded E. DUNHAM in oblong panel.

Dunham, Rufus: (*fl.* 1837–1861) Westbrooke, Me.
Marks recorded include: R. DUNHAM in oblong panel with serrated edges, or incised.

Dunham, R. & Sons: (*fl.* 1861–1882) Portland, Me.

Mark recorded: coffee pot over PORT-LAND ME with R. DUNHAM & SONS forming semicircle above.

Edgell, Simon: (*fl.* 1713–1742) Philadelphia, Pa.
Marks recorded include: S·EDGELL in oblong panel; SIMON EDGELL making a semicircle to a bird or such device.

Eggleston, Jacob: (*fl.* 1796–1807) Middletown, Conn. Also (1807–1813) at Fayetteville, N. Carolina.
Marks recorded include: American eagle among stars with J.E (above) in oval; American eagle with stars round its head in upright oval over EGGLESTON.

Elsworth, Williams J.: (*fl.* 1767–1798) New York, N.Y.
Marks recorded include: W.E in oblong punch with canted corners; W·E in oblong panel with serrated edges; lamb with pennant with WILLIAM in curved label (above) and ELSWORTH in curved label (below); mark ascribed, WE conjoined, with a pellet above and below, in an oval.

Endicott, Edmund: (*fl.* 1846–1853) New York, N.Y.
Mark recorded: E. ENDICOTT incised.

Endicott & Sumner: (*fl.* 1846–1851) New York, N.Y.
Mark recorded: ENDICOTT over SUMNER in rectangle with serrated edges, with N.Y. in small oblong punch.

Everett, James: (*fl. c.* 1716) Philadelphia, Pa.
Mark recorded: device resembling a crown between initials I E supported by a hand (?) in oval panel.

Fenn, Gaius & Jason: (*fl.* 1831–1843) New York, N.Y.
Mark recorded: FENN *** NEW* YORK *** forming circular label.

Flagg & Homan: (*fl.* 1842–1854) Cincinnati, Ohio.
Mark recorded; FLAGG & HOMAN in an oval panel.

Fuller & Smith: (mid 19th century) New London, Conn.
Mark recorded: firm's name forming a semicircle, incised.

Gardner: (mid 19th century)
Provenance not determined.
Mark recorded: first part incomplete, Y & GARDNER in oblong panel.

Gerhardt & Co: (mid 19th century)
Provenance not determined.
Mark recorded: GERHARDT over & CO incised.

Gleason, Roswell: (*fl.* 1822–1871) Dorchester, Mass.
Marks recorded include: eagle over stars with R. GLEASON above, in oval panel; ROSWELL GLEASON incised.

Graves, Henry H.: (mid 19th century) Middletown, Conn.
Mark recorded: H. H. GRAVES in oblong panel.

Graves, Joshua B.: (*fl. c.* 1844) Middletown, Conn.
Mark recorded: J. B. GRAVES in oblong panel with serrated edges.

Green, Samuel: (*fl. c.* 1778–*c.* 1830) Boston, Mass.
Mark recorded: S. G·BOSTON in curved label.

Griswold, Ashbil: (*fl.* 1807–1842) Meriden, Conn.
Marks recorded include: American eagle with stars above (*c.* 14) and GRISWOLD below, in oval; American eagle with GRISWOLD above in circle with serrated edge; American eagle in circle with ASHBIL in curved label attached (above) and GRISWOLD in curved label attached (below); initials A.G in small oblong.

Griswold, Sylvester: (*fl. c.* 1820) Baltimore, Md.
Mark recorded: S. GRISWOLD BALTIMORE forming circle round eagle (?), in circular panel with serrated edge.

Hall & Boardman: (*fl.* 1849–1857) Philadelphia, Pa.
Mark recorded: HALL over BOARDMAN in shield effect, over PHILA in oblong label attached.

Hall & Cotton: (mid 19th century)
Provenance not determined.

Mark recorded HALL & COTTON in oblong label with serrated edges.

Hamlin, Samuel: (*fl. c.* 1771–1801) Providence, R.I.
Marks recorded include: SAMUEL and HAMLIN in attached curved labels; eagle and stars over HAMLIN in rough circular panel; star (?) in cartouche between initials S H; SH in small square punch with canted corners.

Hamlin, Samuel E.: (*fl.* 1801–1856) Providence, R.I.
Marks recorded include: American eagle in cartouche over HAMLIN; eagle with shield (bearing anchor?) with HAMLIN over, in circle with serrated edge; HAMLIN in oblong panel with serrated edges.

Harbeson, Benjamin: (*fl.* early 19th century) Philadelphia, Pa.
Mark recorded: HARBESON PHILA forming circle in circular panel.

Hera, C. & J.: (*fl.* 1800–1812) Philadelphia, Pa.
Mark recorded: C. & I. HERA in curved label with serrated edges attached to PHILADELPHIA in plain curved label, over small escutcheon.

Heyne, Johann C.: (*fl.* 1754–1780) Lancaster, Pa.
Marks recorded include: crown, over I·C·H in oblong; initials I.C.H in shaped oblong panel.

Hinsdale, John & Daniel: (*fl. c.* 1815) Traded at Middletown, Conn. using as mark: J. & D. HINSDALE over eagle, in flattened oval panel.

Holmes, Robert, & Sons: (*fl. c.* 1853) Baltimore, Md.
Mark recorded: HOLMES & SONS over BALTIMORE in rectangle.

Holt, Thomas R.: (*fl.* 1845–1849) Meriden, Conn.
Mark recorded: T. R. HOLT, incised, or in oblong panel.

Homan, Henry: (*fl.* mid 19th century) Cincinnati, Ohio.
Mark recorded: H. HOMAN.

Homan & Co.: (mid 19th century) Cincinnati, Ohio.
Mark recorded: HOMAN & CO over CINCINNATI.

Hopper, Henry: (*fl.* 1842–1847) New York, N.Y.
Mark recorded: H. HOPPER in oblong panel with serrated edges.

Horan, Johann C.: (*fl.* 1754–1785) Philadelphia, Pa.
Mark recorded: ICH in a shield.

Horsford, E. N.: (*fl.* after 1830)
Provenance not determined.
Mark recorded: E. N. HORSFORD'S over PATENT.

Houghton & Wallace: (*fl.* mid 19th century) Philadelphia, Pa.
Mark recorded: HOUGHTON & WALLACE.

Humiston, Willis: (*fl. c.* 1840) Troy, N.Y.
Mark recorded: W. HUMISTON in curved label attached over TROY NY in oblong panel.

Hunt, S.: (*fl.* after 1830)
Provenance not determined.
Mark recorded: S HUNT.

Hyde, Martin: (*fl. c.* 1857) New York, N.Y.
Mark recorded: M. HYDE.

Johnson, Jehiel: (*fl.* 1815–1825) Middletown, Conn. Also (*c.* 1818) at Fayetteville, N. Carolina.
Marks recorded include: American eagle perhaps with stars, and with initials J J in circular panel.

Jones, Edward: (*fl.* 1837–1850) New York, N.Y.
Mark recorded: not fully decipherable, name surrounding a device, as circular panel.

Jones, Gershom: (*fl.* 1774–1809) Providence, R.I.
Marks recorded include: lion rampant between columns, with GERSHOM in curved label attached (above) and JONES in oblong as support (below); American eagle with stars, surrounded by PROVIDENCE BY G JONES in oval upright panel; initials GJ in square or rectangular punch, associated with an anchor in separate punch; shield bearing an anchor, surrounded by letters; mark ascribed (partly indecipherable): rose with MADE BY .... PROVIDENCE ..

Keene, Josiah: (*fl.* 1801–*c.* 1817) Providence, R.I.
Mark recorded: initials I·K in circle surrounded by scalloped border.

Kilbourn, Samuel: (*fl.* 1814–1830) Baltimore, Md.
Mark recorded: eagle with KILBURN (above) and BALTIMORE (below) in circle.

Kimberly, De Witt: (*fl.* 1845–1849) Meriden, Conn.
Mark recorded: D.W.K in oblong label with serrated border.

Kirby, Peter: (*fl. c.* 1736–*c.* 1776) New York, N.Y.
Mark recorded: initials P K with star between, in circular punch with beaded border.

Kirby, William: (*fl. c.* 1760–1794) New York, N.Y.
Marks recorded include: WM:KIRBY in curved label, forming circle with NEW YORK in curved label, surrounding a device (indecipherable); initials W·K in oblong punch, or circular punch with beaded border, also in square punch with canted corners, associated with a number of emblems, joined.

Kirk, Elisha: (*fl.* later 18th century) York, Pa.
Mark recorded: ELISHA KIRK in oblong label over YORKTOWN in similar label.

Knight, W. W. & Co: (*fl. c.* 1840) Philadelphia, Pa.
Traded using mark: W. W. KNIGHT & CO.

Kruiger, Lewis: (*fl.* 1833) Philadelphia, Pa.
Mark recorded: L. KRUIGER PHILAD forming an open oval.

Lafetra, Moses: (*fl.* 1811–1816) New York, N.Y.
Mark recorded: shield device with M·L (remainder indecipherable) surrounding it, in circular panel.

Leddell, Joseph, Sr: (*fl. c.* 1711–1753) New York, N.Y.
Marks ascribed to him: similar to those used by Joseph Leddell, Jr.

Leddell, Joseph, Jr: (*fl. c.* 1740–1754) New York, N.Y.
Marks recorded include: I·LEDDELL in curved label; initials IL in circular punch.

Lee, Richard: worked variously, as follows: (1788–1790) Grafton, N. H.; (1791–1793) at Ashfield, Mass.; (1794–1802) at Lanesborough, Mass.; (1802–1825) at Springfield, Va.
Marks recorded include: R:LEE in stepped oblong label; RICHARD·LEE in oblong panel with serrated edges; initials R·L in oval with serrated edges.

Lee, Richard, Jr: (*fl. c.* 1795–*c.* 1815) Springfield, Va.
Marks recorded include: fleur-de-lys between initials R L; RICHARD· LEE in oblong label with serrated edges.

Leonard, Reed & Barton: (*fl.* 1835–1840) Taunton, Mass.
Mark recorded: LEONARD REED & BARTON.

Lewis, Isaac C.: (*fl.* 1834–1852) Meriden, Conn.
Mark recorded: I. C. LEWIS.

Lewis, I. C. & Co: (*fl.* 1839–1852) Meriden, Conn.
Mark recorded: ICL & CO.

Lewis & Cowles: (*fl.* 1834–1836) East Meriden, Conn.
Mark recorded: MERIDEN surrounded by LEWIS & COWLES forming open diamond.

Lightner, George: (*fl. c.* 1806–1815) Baltimore, Md.
Marks recorded include: American eagle surrounded by G. LIGHTNER BALTIMORE in large oval with serrated edge; American eagle with stars in large oval with G. LIGHTNER in curved label attached (above) and BALTIMORE in curved label attached (below).

Locke, J. D.: (*fl.* 1835–*c.* 1860) New York, N.Y.
Mark recorded: J. D. LOCKE over NEW YORK all in rectangle, with serrated edges.

Love, I.: (*fl.* after 1840) Baltimore, Md.
Mark recorded: I·LOVE incised.

Lowe, I.: (*fl.* after 1800)
Provenance not determined.
Mark recorded: I·LOWE in curved label.

Lyman, William W.: (*fl.* 1844–1852) Meriden, Conn.
Mark recorded: LYMAN in oblong label.

Manning, E. B.: (*fl. c.* 1850–*c.* 1865) Middletown, Conn.
Mark recorded: E. B. MANNING forming a crescent over PATENT all incised.

Manning, Bowman & Co: (*fl. c.* 1866) Middletown, Conn.
Mark recorded: MANNING BOWMAN & CO.

Marston: (*fl.* after 1830) Baltimore, Md.
Mark recorded: MARSTON over BALTIMORE in shaped rectangle.

McEuen, Malcolm & Duncan: (*fl.* 1793–1798) New York, N.Y.
Mark ascribed: American eagle with stars in broad upright oval, surrounded by band of lettering N. YORK (inscription incomplete).

McQuilkin, William: (*fl.* 1845–1853) Philadelphia, Pa.
Mark recorded: Wᴹ MᶜQUILKIN in oblong label.

Melville, David: (*fl.* 1755–1793) Newport, R.I.
Marks recorded include: DM or D:M in small rectangle; anchor between the initials D M; an anchor on a shield, with stars above and NEWPORT; shield with (incomplete) ADE IN NEW and BY D: MEL over.

Melville, S. & T.: (*fl. c.* 1793–1800) Newport, R.I.
Marks recorded include: anchor on a shield, with stars and curved label S & T·MEL (incomplete) over; S & over T in small rectangle with serrated edges and M in square also serrated.

Melville, Thomas, Jr: (*fl.* 1796–1824) Newport, R.I.
Marks recorded include: initials T and M in small separate rectangles; shield with stars over and NEWPORT.

Meriden Britannia Co: (*fl.* from 1852) Meriden, Conn.
Mark recorded:
MERIDEN
BRITANNIA
CO

Morey & Ober: (*fl.* 1852–1855) Boston, Mass.
Mark recorded: American eagle over MOREY & OBER and BOSTON in curved labels forming an oval.

Morey & Smith: (*fl.* 1857–1885) Boston, Mass.
Mark recorded: American eagle over MOREY & SMITH in curved label over WARRANTED BOSTON in shaped rectangle attached, all with serrated edges.

Munson, John: (*fl.* 1846–1852) Yalesville, Conn.
Mark recorded: J. MUNSON in oblong with serrated edges.

Neal, I.: (*fl. c.* 1842)
Provenance not determined.
Mark recorded: in a circle the words I. NEAL'S PATENT and date MAY 4th 1842.

Nott, William: (*fl.* 1813–1817) Middletown. Also (1817–1825) at Fayetteville, N. Carolina.
Mark recorded: American eagle ringed with stars, over W NOTT, in large oval panel.

Olcott, J. W.: (*fl. c.* 1800) Baltimore, Md.
Mark recorded: American eagle with OLCOTT over, and BALTIMORE under, in circular panel.

Ostrander, Charles: (*fl.* 1848–1854) New York, N.Y.
Mark recorded: OSTRANDER incised.

Ostrander & Norris: (*fl.* 1848–1850) New York, N.Y.
Mark recorded: OSTRANDER in curved label over & NORRIS in curved label, together forming oval.

Palethorp, John H.: (*fl.* 1820–1845) Philadelphia, Pa.

Marks recorded include: J. H. PALE-THORP in oblong, over PHILAD^A in oblong; PALETHORP'S over PHI-LAD^A in shaped oblong with serrated edges; PALETHORP'S in oblong panel with serrated edges.

Palethorp, Robert, Jr: (*fl.* 1817–1822) Philadelphia, Pa.
Marks recorded include: American eagle in flattened horizontal oval, surrounded by R. PALETHORP PHILA (incomplete); R. PALETHORP J^R over PHI-LAD^A in shaped rectangle.

Palethorp, R. & J. H.: (*fl.* 1820–1826) Philadelphia, Pa.
Mark ascribed: eagle in oval (incomplete).

Palethorp & Connell: (*fl.* 1839–1841) Philadelphia, Pa.
Mark recorded: PALETHORP over & CONNELL over PHILAD^A each in separate oblong panel.

Parker, Charles, & Co: (*fl.* mid 19th century) Meriden, Conn.
Mark recorded: C. PARKER & CO in oblong panel.

Parker, J. G.: (*fl. c.* 1840) Rochester, N.Y.
Mark recorded: N.Y. in small rectangle with J. G. PARKER in curved label over and ROCHESTER in curved label under, together forming oval.

Parkin, W.: (*fl.* after 1830)
Provenance not determined.
Mark recorded: W. PARKIN incised.

Parmenter, W. H.: (*fl.* after 1840)
Provenance not determined.
Mark recorded: the words GEO. CARR'S PATENT MADE by W. H. PARMENTER arranged in a circular panel.

Pierce, Samuel: (*fl. c.* 1792–*c.* 1831) Greenfield, Mass.
Marks recorded include: eagle with SAMUEL over and PIERCE below, in shaped panel; initials S. P. over cross, in circle.

Plumly & Bidgood: (*fl. c.* 1825) Philadelphia, Pa.
Mark recorded: PLUMLY & BID-GOOD in rectangle.

Porter, Allen: (*fl.* 1830–1840) Westbrook, Me.
Mark recorded: A. PORTER in oblong with serrated edges.

Porter, Freeman: (*fl.* 1835–*c.* 1860) Westbrook, Me.
Mark recorded: F. PORTER WEST-BROOK in circular panel.

Porter, James: (*fl. c.* 1795–*c.* 1803) Baltimore, Md.
Mark recorded: American eagle, with JAMES above and PORTER below, in rectangle shaped like cartouche.

Potter, W.: (*fl. c.* 1835)
Provenance not determined.
Mark recorded: W. POTTER in oblong.

Putnam, James H.: (*fl.* 1830–1855) Malden, Mass.
Mark recorded: PUTNAM in oblong with serrated edges.

Reed & Barton: (*fl.* from 1840 onwards) Taunton, Mass.
Mark recorded: REED & BARTON.

Reich, John P.: (*fl. c.* 1820–1830) Salem, N. Carolina.
Mark recorded: P. REICH SALEM. N.C. forming circle in circular panel.

Renton & Co: (*fl.* after 1830) New York, N.Y.
Mark recorded: RENTON & CO over NEW YORK.

Richardson, B. & Son: (*fl. c.* 1839) Philadelphia, Pa.
Mark recorded: B. RICHARDSON & SON over PHILADELPHIA.

Richardson, George: (*fl. c.* 1818–1845) Boston, Mass. Also at Cranston, R.I.
Marks recorded include: G. RICHARD-SON in oblong alone, or with BOSTON under; G. LENNORE C^O in curved label with serrated edges and CRANS-TON. R.I. in curved label with serrated edges, both forming an oval about an eagle in a small circle.

Rogers, Smith & Co: (*fl. c.* 1850) Hartford, Conn.
Mark recorded: ROGERS, SMITH & CO·HARTFORD, CT. inside round circle with beaded edge.

Rust, Samuel: (*fl.* 1837–1845) New York, N.Y.
Mark recorded: S. RUSTS PATENT over NEW YORK.

Sage, Timothy: (*fl. c.* 1848) St Louis, Mo.
Mark recorded: T. SAGE in oblong, over ST. LOUIS, MO.

Sage & Beebe: (*fl.* after 1840)
Provenance not determined.
Mark recorded: SAGE & BEEBE.

Savage & Graham: (*fl. c.* 1837) Middletown, Conn.
Mark recorded: MIDD.CT. surrounded by SAVAGE (above) GRAHAM (below) forming circle.

Savage, William H.: (*fl.* 1837–1840) Middletown, Conn.
Mark recorded: SAVAGE MIDD.CT. form oval.

Sellew & Co: (*fl.* 1830–*c.* 1860) Cincinnati, Ohio.
Marks recorded include: eagle surrounded by SELLEW & CO CINCINNATI in oval panel; SELLEW & CO over CINCINNATI.

"Semper Eadem": (*c.* 1760–*c.* 1780) Boston, Mass.
Mark recorded: crowned rose between columns, with SEMPER above and EADEM under, forming a sort of cartouche.

Sheldon & Feltman: (*fl.* 1847–1848) Albany, N.Y.
Marks recorded include: SHELDON & FELTMAN ALBANY arranged in three lines; the same arranged to form a triangle.

Shoff, I.: (*fl. c.* 1785) provenance thought to be Pennsylvania.
Mark recorded: I·SHOFF in oblong.

Sickel & Shaw: (*fl.* mid 19th century) Philadelphia, Pa.
Mark recorded: PHILADᴬ with SICKEL & SHAW arranged above in curve.

Simpkins, Thomas: (1702–1756) Boston, Mass.
Mark recorded: four-petalled flower, crowned, in oval, with name (incomplete) ·SIMPKINS· surrounding it, in a broad oval panel.

Simpson, Samuel: (*fl.* 1837–1852) Yalesville, Conn. Also at New York, N.Y.
Mark recorded: S. SIMPSON in oblong.

Simpson & Benham: (*fl.* 1845–1847) New York, N.Y.
Mark recorded: SIMPSON & BENHAM in three lines.

Skinner, John: (*fl. c.* 1760–1790) Boston, Mass.
Marks recorded include: lion rampant between columns with (?) JOHN above (indecipherable) over SKINNER at foot; I:SKINNER over BOSTON in double label; initials IS in a shield.

Smith, Eben: (*fl.* 1841–1856) Beverly, Mass.
Mark recorded: E. SMITH in oblong.

Smith & Co: (*fl.* 1853–1856) Albany, N.Y.
Mark recorded: SMITH & CO in curved label.

Smith & Feltman: (*fl. c.* 1849–1852) Albany, N.Y.
Mark recorded: SMITH & FELTMAN ALBANY arranged in two lines.

Smith & Morey: (*fl. c.* 1841) Boston, Mass.
Mark recorded: SMITH & MOREY in oblong label.

Southmayd, Ebenezer: (*fl.* 1802–*c.* 1830) Castleton, Vt.
Marks recorded include: sailing ship (incomplete) over name THMAYD (incomplete); sailing ship over initials E·S·

Stafford, Spencer: (*fl.* 1794–1827) Albany, N.Y.
Marks recorded include: S. STAFFORD in oblong label over ALBANY; crowned rose in rectangle.

Stafford, S. & Co: (*fl.* 1817–1824) Albany, N.Y.
Mark recorded: emblem surrounded by S. STAFFORD & CO ALBANY.

Stalkamp, J. H. & Co: (*fl.* mid 19th century) Cincinnati, Ohio.

Mark recorded: J. H. STALKAMP & CO in curved label, over CINCINNATI in smaller curved label.

Standish, Alexander: (*fl.* after 1835) Provenance not determined.
Mark recorded: ALEX^R STANDISH.

Starr, William H.: (*fl.* 1843–1846) New York, N.Y.
Mark recorded: W. H. STARR in curved label with serrated edges, over N.Y. in rough oval label with serrated edges.

Stedman, S.: (*fl.* after 1800) provenance not determined.
Mark recorded: S. STEDMAN.

Taunton Britannia Mfg Co: (*fl.* 1830–1835) Taunton, Mass.
Marks recorded include: T. B. M. CO.; TAUNTON BRIT^A over MANF^G CO.

Tomlinson: (*fl. c.* 1843)
Provenance not determined.
Mark recorded: TOMLINSON'S PATENT, 1843 in three lines.

Trask, Israel: (*fl. c.* 1825–*c.* 1856) Beverly, Mass.
Mark recorded: I·TRASK in oblong label with canted corners.

Trask, Oliver: (*fl. c.* 1825–*c.* 1839) Beverly, Mass.
Mark recorded: O·TRASK in oblong label with serrated edges.

Treadway, Amos: (*fl. c.* 1785) Middletown, Conn.
Mark recorded: emblem resembling coffeepot on stand, between columns, with AMOS in curved label attached (above) and TREADWAY similarly below; a mark resembling a fleur-de-lys with DDELTOWN in curved label above (incomplete) is ascribed to him.

Vose & Co: (*fl.* after *c.* 1840) Albany, N.Y.
Mark recorded: VOSE & CO over ALBANY.

Wallace, R. & Co: (from 1855) Wallingford, Conn.
Mark recorded: R. WALLACE & CO. in oblong label.

Ward, H. B. & Co: (*fl. c.* 1849) Wallingford, Conn.
Mark recorded: H. B. WARD in plain oblong label.

Warren: (*fl.* after 1830)
Provenance not determined.
Mark recorded: WARREN'S HARD METAL in two lines.

Wayne, C. P. & Son: (*fl. c.* 1835) Philadelphia, Pa.
Mark recorded: C. P. WAYNE & SON in plain oblong label over PHILAD^A in oblong label.

Weekes, James: (*fl.* from *c.* 1820) New York, N.Y. Also at Poughkeepsie, N.Y. (from *c.* 1835)
Marks recorded include: J. WEEKES N Y in oblong label: J. WEEKES alone, or over BROOKLYN.

Weekes, J. & Co: (*fl.* 1833–1835) Poughkeepsie, N.Y.
Mark recorded: WEEKES & CO (incomplete) in oblong label with serrated edges.

Whitcomb, A. G.: (after 1820) Boston, Mass.
Mark recorded: A. G. WHITCOMB. BOSTON arranged around inside edge of circular panel.

Whitehouse, E.: (after 1800)
Provenance not determined.
Marks recorded include: WHITEHOUSE in oblong label with serrated edges; WHITEHOUSE over WARRANTED.

Whitfield, G. & J.: (*fl.* 1836–1865) New York, N.Y.
Mark recorded: G. &. J. WHITFIELD.

Whitlock, John H.: (*fl.* 1836–1844) Troy, N.Y.
Marks recorded include: crouching animal in lobed panel with WHITLOCK over TROY N Y together in oblong label; WHITLOCK over TROY N.Y. in oblong label with shaped ends.

Whitmore, Jacob: (*fl. c.* 1758–*c.* 1790) Middletown, Conn.
Marks recorded include: crowned rose encircled by JACOB over and WHITMORE below, in separate curved labels; double (quasi-Tudor) rose in circular panel with beaded edge.

Wildes, Thomas: (*fl.* 1833–1840) New York, N.Y.
Marks recorded include: T. WILDES in plain oblong label, or in curved label with serrated edges.

Will, George: (*fl.* 1798–1807) Philadelphia, Pa.
Mark recorded: GW in cursive capitals in oval surrounded by LONG LIVE THE PRESIDENT in circular panel.

Will, Henry: (*fl.* 1761–1775; 1783–*c*.1793) New York, N.Y. Also at Albany, N.Y. (*fl.* 1775–1783).
Marks recorded include: HENRY. WILL over line of pellets over NEW YORK all in rectangular panel; shield between columns with HENRY WILL in curved label (over) attached and NEW YORK in oblong panel (below) attached; crowned rose in cartouche formed of HENRY WILL curved over with NEW YORK curved below; HENRY WILL in slightly-curved label close over NEW YORK similar; crowned rose in rectangle. Other marks ascribed to him are incomplete; sometimes found associated with very small rectangle containing a lion rampant.

Will, John: (*fl. c.* 1752–*c.* 1763) New York, N.Y.
Marks recorded include: initials I.W in circle with serrated edges; I W with a pellet above and below in circle with serrated edges; sailing ship between columns (upper part incomplete) with NEW YORK in oblong attached below; lion rampant in curved cartouche.

Will, William: (*fl. c.* 1770; d. 1798) Philadelphia, Pa.
Marks recorded include: W·W with fleur-de-lys over, in shaped oval; WᴹWILL over PHILADELPHIA in two linked curved labels; Wᴹ WILL in oblong label with serrated edges; W. WILL over PHILA· over DELPHIA with small emblem (? a castle) over in shaped rectangle with beaded edges; Wᴹ WILL/PHILADEL/PHIA in three attached labels slightly curved with rounded edges, forming one panel; some incomplete marks also ascribed show an animal or bird in an oval, perhaps surrounded by PHILA WILLI.

Williams, Lorenzo L.: (*fl.* 1835–1842) Philadelphia, Pa.

Mark recorded: L. L. WILLIAMS over PHILADᴬ

Williams, Otis: (*fl. c.* 1826–1830) Buffalo, N.Y.
Mark recorded: eagle surrounded by O.WILLIAMS BUFFALO in upright oval with beaded edge.

Williams & Simpson: (*fl.* 1837) Yalesville, Conn.
Mark recorded: W & S in oblong label.

Woodbury, J. B.: (*fl.* 1835) Philadelphia, Pa.
Marks recorded include: American eagle surrounded by stars (above) and J. B. WOODBURY (below) in circular panel; American eagle surrounded by J. B. WOODBURY (above) and sprinkle of stars (below); J. B. WOODBURY over PHILADᴬ each in oblong label with serrated edges; J. B. WOODBURY in plain oblong label.

Woodbury & Colton: (*fl. c.* 1835) Philadelphia, Pa.
Mark recorded: WOODBURY & COLTON in plain oblong label.

Woodman, Cook & Co: (*fl.* after 1830) Portland, Me.
Mark recorded: WOODMAN, COOK & CO.

Yale, Charles: (*fl. c.* 1818–1835) Wallingford, Conn.
Mark recorded: CHARLES YALE & CO in curved label over WALLINGFORD in curved label, together forming oval shape; the word BRITANNIA may be found associated in plain oblong label.

Yale, Hiram: (*fl.* 1822–1831) Wallingford, Conn.
Mark recorded: bird's head (? eagle) encircled by H. YALE (above) and WALLINGFORD (below) in near-circular panel.

Yale, Hiram, & Co: (*fl.* 1824–1835) Yalesville, Conn.
Mark recorded: H·YALE and WALLINGFORD curved to form horizontal oval about & CO.

Yale, W. & S.: (*fl. c.* 1810–1820) Meriden, Conn.

Mark recorded: (very indistinct) eagle over W & S in upright broad oval panel.

Yale & Curtis: (*fl.* 1858–1867) New York, N.Y.
Mark recorded: Y A L E & C U R T I S N. Y. in pierced semicircular panel.

Young, Peter: (*fl. c.* 1775) New York, N.Y. Also at Albany, N.Y. (*c.* 1785–*c.* 1800) Marks recorded include: initials P Y in rectangle with serrated edges; P Y in circle with serrated edges; P.Y in oval with serrated edges; crowned rose in rectangle with P and Y in bottom corners; American eagle in curved cartouche with PETER (above), lower part indistinct; P Y in small plain rectangle associated with other small punches, e.g. rampant lion.

Furniture and Tapestry

English Furniture Marks

The names of many English cabinet-makers of the 18th century are recorded (cf. Ambrose Heal "London Furniture Makers", 1953). No trade guild, however, was in being, and therefore no regulations existed such as obtained in France. English cabinet-makers were not in the habit of marking their pieces, except in rare instances.

A Selective List

Chippendale, Thomas: (1718–1779) English maker of furniture, in St Martin's Lane, London. Published "The Gentleman and Cabinet Maker's Director" (1754, 2nd edition 1755, 3rd edition 1762).
Used no marks.

Gillow, Robert, & Co: (*fl.* later 18th century) Lancaster and London
In 1790 were using the mark:
     Robert Gillow and Co.
In 1811 used the mark:

     G & R GILLOW & C⁰
     Merchants
     & cabinetmakers

Ceased soon after this date to be a family firm.

Gumley, John: (*fl. c.* 1694–early 18th century) London
Worked in partnership with James Moore.
Mark recorded:

GUMLEY
Incised

Also recorded:
     John Gumley, 1703

Moore, James: (1670–1726) London
In partnership with John Gumley from 1714 to 1726.
Incised his name on certain gilt gesso pieces of his making.

MOORE

French Furniture Marks

In 1741 it was laid down by the trade guild concerned (known after 1743 as the "Corporation des Menuisiers-Ebénistes") that every master of the craft (maître) should have an iron to stamp his name (more rarely his initials) on each piece of furniture made by him for sale, and also on pieces made by others when repaired by him. This mark was normally put in some inconspicuous place. A committee examined all work done, or in course of being done, and if it reached the required high standard it was stamped accordingly. Privileged craftsmen working for the French Crown were exempt from Guild regulations, and their work therefore was often unstamped. Other craftsmen exempt from Guild regulations were those living in certain anciently privileged quarters of Paris, including a number of foreign craftsmen. After the trade guilds had been dissolved, during the 19th century makers ceased to stamp their furniture; after the Exhibition at Paris in 1882 interest in the old practice revived, with consequent forgery of "signatures" among dealers trading in furniture.
Numbers found on 18th-century pieces may refer to entries in Crown inventories.

Mark used by the Guild

A Selective List of Makers
of Furniture, Clocks, and Bronzes d'Ameublement
with marks

A.V.
Letters recorded (incised) on the bottom tray of a work-table, period Louis XVI; probably for Adam Weisweiler (q.v.).

Baumhauer, Joseph: (d. 1772)
Cabinet-maker, born in Germany, but working in Paris; soon after 1767 he was awarded the rank of "ébéniste privilégé du Roi".
Stamp recorded:
JOSEPH
Between fleurs-de-lis

Beneman, Jean Guillaume: (*fl.* 1784–1804)
Cabinet-maker of German birth, who came to Paris, working as an artisan libre; maître-ébéniste in 1785; worked for the Crown; under the Directoire, and during the Consulate.

G · BENEMAN

Berthoud, Ferdinand: (1727–1807)
Parisian clock- and watch-maker; born in Switzerland; moved to Paris *c.* 1746; elected F.R.S. London.
Stamp recorded:
FERDINAND
BERTHOUD
Inscribed on dial

Boulard, Jean Baptiste: (*c.* 1729–1789)
French cabinet-maker working at Paris; maître-menuisier 1754; working for the Crown from 1777; business carried on by widow, and son Michel Jacques, who received commissions from Napoleon.
Stamp recorded:
J. B. BOULARD
In two varying sizes

Boulle, André Charles: (1642–1732)
French cabinet-maker, gave his name to a particular type of marquetry, using tortoiseshell and brass.
Never signed his works.

Bourbon, Michel: (*fl.* mid 18th century)
Frenchman recorded making sundials at Paris 1753; possibly also made barometers.
Inscription recorded:
BOURBON A PARIS
On dial of cartel barometer

B.V.R.B.
Found on French veneer and marquetry furniture, mostly in rococo style; stamp used by an ébéniste working in the Faubourg Saint-Antoine, Rue Saint-Nicolas, at Paris; little known of him, and name not identified.

Caffiéri, Jacques: (1678–1755)
French fondeur-ciseleur of Italian descent, working at Paris; did much work for the Crown, in the rococo style.
Stamps recorded:

CAFFIERI

A.PARIS

CAFFIERI A.PARIS

CAFFIERI A. PARIS

FAIt PAR CAFFIERI

Caffiéri, Philippe: (1714–1774)
French fondeur-ciseleur, son of Jacques Caffiéri; working at Paris.
Signed his works:
P. CAFFIERI

Carlin, Martin: (d. 1785)
French cabinet-maker working at Paris; maître-ébéniste 1766; worked for Queen Marie Antoinette.
Stamp recorded:
M. CARLIN

M•CARLIN

Coteau, Joseph: (1740–1801)
French peintre-émailleur; noted maker of clock dials, second half of 18th century.
Usually signed:
COTEAU
In the enamel, lower
part of dial
Inscriptions recorded include:
Coteau 1771   10 OCT
Coteau, Thil 1763 ft
Not to be confused with the miniature painter, Jean Coteau (*fl. c.* 1739–1812).

Cozette, Pierre Francois: (*fl.* 18th century)
For *c.* 60 years on staff of the Manufacture Royale des Gobelins at Paris; from 1742 director of the high-warp department; his reproductions of paintings, on tapestry, very fashionable *c.* 1781.
Signed:
Cozette exit

Craemer, M. G.:
Stamp:
M. G. CRAEMER
Recorded on French roll-top desk, originally made for the kings of Sardinia, appearing in the Kraemer Collection sale, at Paris, 1913.

Cressent, Charles: (1685–1768)
French cabinet-maker; worked for Philippe, Duc d'Orléans, Regent of France; an ébéniste who also modelled, cast and gilded the mounts for his own furniture, thus infringing guild regulations. Earlier and best work never stamped.
Stamp recorded:
C. CRESSENT
(of doubtful authenticity)

Cronier, Jean Baptiste: (*fl.* 1781–1793)
Franch clock-maker; became maître-horloger in 1781.
Inscription recorded:
Cronier
A PARIS
(on dial)

Cronier fils: (*fl.* early 19th century)
French clock-makers, the firm incorporated during the First Empire; still working 1825.

Crowned C
Found stamped on French bronze work; said to be a hall-mark used on French bronzes during the period from 5th March 1745 to 4th February 1749; taxes were levied on works made of the various materials, which were stamped to suit, e.g. C for cuivre.

Crowned C T
Found on French furniture in use at the Château de Trianon.
Mark recorded:
Painted: *c.* 1783

Crowned E U
Found on French furniture in use at the Château d'Eu.
Mark recorded:

Crowned F
Found on French furniture in use at the Château de Fontainebleau.
Marks recorded:

Stencilled: on parchment label, 1780s

Stamped: on bronzes d'ameublement, 1780s

Crowned S C
Found on French furniture in use at the Château de Saint-Cloud.
Mark recorded:
Stencilled: 1780s

Crowned T H
Found on French furniture in use at the Palais des Tuileries.
Mark recorded:
Stamped: on bronzes d'ameublement, temp. Louis XVI

Cuvellier, E. J.: (*fl.* 19th century)
French cabinet-maker, whose stamp has been recorded:
E. J. CUVELLIER
Stamped

Daillé, Charles: (*fl. c.* 1722–1760)
Maître-horloger at Paris.
Stamps recorded include:
Daillé A Paris
(the AP conjoined)
and
Daillé
horloger de Madame la dauphine
Inscribed on dial, or
engraved on backplate

David
see Roentgen, David

Delorme, Adrien: (*fl.* later 18th century)
Maître-ébéniste.
Stamp ascribed to him:
DELORME

Delorme, François: (*fl.* first half 18th century)
Cabinet-maker at Paris.
Stamp ascribed to him:
F.D.

Delorme, Jean Louis Faizelot: (*fl. c.* 1763–1780)
Member of family of cabinet-makers working at Paris: maître-ébéniste 1763.
Stamp recorded:

J ∗ L ∗ F ∗ DELORME

Delunésy, Nicolas Pierre: (*fl.* second half 18th century)
Maître-horloger (1764) at Paris.
Inscription recorded:
Delunésy A Paris

Dimier: (? *fl.* 19th century)
Stamp recorded:

DIMIER

DIMIER

This mark, if found on 18th-century pieces, is probably that of a later craftsman doing a repair.

DR
See Roentgen, David

Drouais, François Hubert: (1727–1775)
French portrait painter; name found woven into examples of Gobelins tapestry woven after his paintings:
Drouais pixtr

Dubois, Germain: (*fl. c.* 1757–1789)
French clockmaker at Paris. Maître-horloger 1757.
Inscription recorded:
Gm. Dubois
A PARIS
NB. Many clockmakers of the name Dubois (18th century) are recorded at work, not only in France, but also in Belgium, England and Switzerland.

E.H.B.
Stamp occasionally found on French 18th-century furniture; possibly denoted an owner. Since this stamp has been recorded on a piece belonging to Eugénie Hortense Buonaparte, the initials might stand for her name.

EHB

Erstet, Jean Ulric: (*fl.* 1740–*c.* 1760)
French cabinet-maker, who also sold furniture, at Paris; maître-ébéniste in 1740.
Stamp recorded:

J·U·ERSTET

Fiéffé, Jean Jacques, père: (*fl.* mid 18th century)
French clockmaker working at Paris.
Mark recorded which may be his:
FIÉFFÉ
DE L'OBSERVATOIRE

Fleur-de-lis mark
Found on bronzes d'ameublement; probably indicates origin in Paris.

♣

F.M
Stamp recorded; significance not yet determined; not the mark of a known ébéniste; might be mark of a repairer or of an owner.

FM

Fortier, Alexandre: (*fl. c.* 1725–1760)
Inventor of a certain type of clock movement; known to have collaborated in making the astronomical type of clock.
Inscriptions recorded include:
Inventé par A. Fortier
Alexandre fortier jnvenit Stolle-werck fecit A paris

Foulet or **Foullet, Antoine:** (d. 1775)
French cabinet-maker at Paris; maître-ébéniste in 1749.
Marks recorded include:

ANT FOVLLE

ANT. FOULET

Foullet, Pierre Antoine: (*fl.* 1765–*c.* 1780)
French cabinet-maker at Paris; maître-ébéniste in 1765.
Stamp recorded:

foulet

P A FOULLET
(sometimes seen accompanied by a fleur-de-lis)

Furet, André, l'aîné: (*fl. c.* 1690–1740)
French clockmaker; maître-horloger
1691.
Inscription recorded:
FURET L'AINÉ
A PARIS
Inscribed on dial
NB. Other clockmakers of the name of
Furet are known to have been working
in Paris during the 18th century.

Garnier, Pierre: (*fl. c.* 1720–1800)
French cabinet-maker at Paris; maître-
ébéniste in 1742.
Stamp recorded:

P·GARNIER

Gaudreau, Antoine Robert: (*c.* 1680–1751)
French cabinet-maker to Louis XV from
1726; died before regulations enforced.
No marks.

Gaudron, Pierre: (*fl. c.* 1690–1730 or
later)
Maker of clocks and watches at Paris.
Inscription recorded:
Gaudron AParis
(the AP conjoined)

Gouchon: (? *fl.* later 18th century)
No record of this clockmaker, but some
inscriptions include:
GOUCHON
A PARIS
Painted
Gouchon à Paris
Inscribed

Gourdin, Michel: (*fl.* mid 18th century)
French cabinet-maker at Paris; maître-
ébéniste in 1752; worked for the French
crown in the 1770s.
Stamp used:

M·GOURDIN

Gouthière, Pierre: (1732–*c.* 1813)
French bronze worker; maître-doreur in
1758; celebrated ciseleur; worked for the
Court (*c.* 1769–1777); known work very
rare indeed, and seldom signed.
One example recorded has the words:
PAR GOUTHIERE CIZELEUR ET
DOREUR A PARIS, with the address
QUAY PELLETIER A LA BOUCLE
D'OR 1771.

Guiot: (18th century)
Surname (no Christian names known) of
a number of French clock-makers working at Paris.
Inscription recorded:
Guiot AParis
(the AP conjoined)

Hervé, Jean Baptiste: (*c.* 1700–1780)
French clockmaker; maître-horloger in
1726; some clockcases by Charles Cres-
sent were furnished with movements by
Hervé.
Inscription recorded:
HERVE
A PARIS

Jacob frères: (*fl.* 1796–1803)
Sons of Georges Jacob, French cabinet-
makers at Paris; succeeded by Jacob-
Desmalter.
Stamp used:
JACOB FRÈRES RUE MESLEE

Jacob, Georges: (1739–1814)
French cabinet-maker working at Paris;
under his own name 1765–1796.
Stamp used:

G ◆ I A C O B

with fleur-de-lis (earlier work) between
initial and surname, which later became
a lozenge.
From 1803 Georges Jacob collaborated
with his surviving and younger son
(François Honoré).
Stamp used:
JACOB D. R. MESLEE
NB. Georges Jacob had a house in the
Rue Meslée from *c.* 1789.

Jacob, Henri: (*fl.* second half 18th cen-
tury)
French cabinet-maker at Paris; maître-
ébéniste in 1779.
Stamp used:
H. JACOB

Jacob-Desmalter et Cie: (*fl.* 1803–1813)
French cabinet-makers at Paris; firm
consisting of Georges Jacob (1739–1814)
and his son François Honoré (1779–
1841).
Stamp used:
JACOB D. R. MESLEE

Jaquet-Droz, Pierre: (1721–1790)
Swiss clockmaker working at Basle, Neuchâtel, Geneva, and Madrid.
Inscription recorded:
P. Jaquet Droz à La Chaud de Fonds

Jeanselme, J.: (*fl.* from early 19th century)
Firm trading as Jeanselme Frères from 1829.
Mark recorded:

JEANSELME

Jolly family: (17th and 18th centuries)
Clockmakers working in France, and in England; a number were members of the London Clockmakers' Company.
Inscription recorded:
Jolly AParis
Engraved; the AP conjoined

Joseph
Stamp used by
Baumhauer, Joseph (q.v.)

♥JOSEPH♥

Joubert, Gilles: (1689–1775) also known as Joubert l'aîné.
French cabinet-maker working at Paris; ébéniste du Roi (1763–1774).
Rarely stamped his furniture.

Lacroix, or **Vandercruse, Roger:** (*fl.* second half 18th century)
French cabinet-maker of Flemish descent, maître-ébéniste in 1755.
Stamps used included:
R. LACROIX

The initials R V L C with a lozenge between each.

Le Gaigneur, Louis Constantin: (*fl. c.* 1815)
Frenchman owning the Buhl Manufactury, 19 Queen Street, Edgware Road, London.
Inscriptions recorded include:
Le Gaigneur
Louis Le Gaigneur fecit

Lelarge, Jean Baptiste: (1743–1802)
French furniture maker at Paris; maître-menuisier 1775; used the same stamp as his father.
Stamp recorded:

I×B×LELARGE

Leleu, Jean François: (1729–1807)
French cabinet-maker working at Paris; maître-ébéniste in 1764; in 1780 in partnership with his son-in-law Charles Antoine Stadler (*fl.* 1776–1811)
Stamps used included:
and initials J. F. L.

J·F·LELEU

Le Noir: (18th century)
Surname of several French clockmakers, also of some London clockmakers.
One inscription recorded:
Jean le Noir

Lepaute, Jean André: (1709–*c.* 1787)
French clockmaker at Paris, one of a family of clockmakers.
Inscriptions recorded:
Lepaute
Hgr DU ROY
Lepaute
DE BELLE FONTAINE
A PARIS

Le Roy, Julien: (1686–1759)
French clockmaker at Paris; maître-horloger in 1713.
Inscription recorded:
JULIEN
LE ROY
Inscribed on dial

Levasseur, Etienne: (1721–1798)
French cabinet-maker working at Paris; maître-ébéniste in 1767.
Stamp used:

E◦LEVASSEUR

Lieutaud, Balthazar: (d. 1780)
French cabinet-maker working at Paris; maître-ébéniste in 1749; noted for his fine clockcases.
Stamp used:

B·LIEUTAUD

Linke, F. (*fl.* later 19th century)
Signature noted on a copy (1878) of the
French "Bureau du Roi Louis XV".

MA crowned
Monogram for Marie Antoinette, seen
with GARDE MEUBLE DE LA
REINE making a circle around it.

Marchand, Nicolas Jean: (*fl.* first half
18th century)
French cabinet-maker at Paris; maître-
ébéniste ante 1738; ceased work *c.* 1757.
Stamp used:

MARCHAND

Martinière, Antoine Nicolas: (1706–1784)
French enameller working at Paris.
Mark recorded: surname Martiniere sometimes accompanied by his address (Rue
des Cinq Diamants) and a date.

*Martiniere Emailleur
et pensionare du Roi rue
des 5 diamant a paris*

Martinot family: (*fl.* early 18th century)
French clockmakers at Paris; three were
clockmakers to Louis XIV: Balthazar
(*fl. c.* 1679–1708); Jean Henri (*fl. c.* 1679–
1708); Jérome (*fl.* 1695–1732).
Surname Martinot is recorded.

Mellier & Co: (*fl. c.* 1866–1930s)
London makers of modern reproductions
of French 18th-century furniture.
Stamp recorded:

C·MELLIER & C⁰

C. MELLIER & C⁰
CABINET MAKERS
LONDON W

Michault, J. E.: (*fl.* late 18th century)
French cabinet-maker at Paris.
Stamp recorded:
MICHAULT

Moinet, Louis: (1758–1853)
French author of a treatise on clock-
making.
Mark recorded:
L. MOINET
A PARIS
May indicate a repair by him,
if found on earlier piece

Molitor, Bernard: (*fl. c.* 1773–*post* 1811)
German cabinet-maker working at Paris
from *c.* 1773; maître-ébéniste in 1787.
Stamp used:
B. MOLITOR

Montigny, Philippe Claude: (1734–1800)
French cabinet-maker at Paris; maître-
ébéniste in 1766; specialist in making
furniture in the Boulle style; also a repairer of earlier pieces.
Stamp used:

MONTIGNY

Mynuël: (*fl.* first half 18th century)
Clockmaker, whose name has been found
inscribed:
MYNUEL
Painted on the dial

Oeben, Jean François: (*c.* 1720–1763)
German cabinet-maker, first recorded
working at Paris 1749; made ébéniste du
Roi in 1754.
Stamp used (in later years):
J. F. OEBEN
Pieces made between 1763 and 1767
stamped with his name; these were probably made in his workshop by Riesener
under Veuve Oeben, before their marriage.

Petit, Nicolas: (1732–1791)
French cabinet-maker working at Paris;
maître-ébéniste in 1761.
Stamp used:

N·PETIT
N·PETIT

Piret: (temp. Louis XIV)
Surname found on bronzes d'ameuble-
ment of the period.
Stamped:
PIRET

Richard, Claude and Etienne: (*fl.* second half 18th century)
French (father and son) makers of springs at Paris; surname found on clock springs.
Example:
Richard
May be found with a date

Riesener, Jean Henri: (*fl. c.* 1754–1801)
German-born cabinet-maker working at Paris from post 1754; maître-ébéniste in 1768; ébéniste ordinaire du Roi in 1774.
Stamp used:

J·H·RIE.SENER

Stamp considered a forgery, or false:

Robin, Robert: (1742–1799)
French clockmaker at Paris; horloger to Louis XV and to Marie Antoinette; clockmaker to the Republic in 1795.
Inscription recorded:
Robin

Roentgen, David: (1743–1807)
German-born cabinet-maker later established at Paris (after 1779 onward); made to become maître-ébéniste in 1780.
Stamp used:
DAVID
More frequently he preferred to include his initials in the marquetry decoration of his pieces.

R·V·L·C
Initials with lozenge between.
Stamp used by Roger Vandercruse, also known as Lacroix (q.v.).

R·V·L·C

Schuman, André: (*fl.* 1779–1787)
German-born cabinet-maker working at Paris; maître-ébéniste in 1779.
Stamp used:

A·SCHUMAN

Stollewerck, Michel: (*fl. c.* 1746–1775)
Made the movements for clocks and also for musical boxes; maître-horloger in 1746.
Marks recorded include:
Stollewerck fecit A paris
Stollewerck AParis
The AP conjoined

Thuret, Jacques: (*fl.* 1694–1712)
French clockmaker, appointed to the King (Louis XIV) and to the Observatoire.
Mark recorded:
THURET A PARIS

TW
Found on some bronzes d'ameublement (18th century); thought to be the mark of some repairer (not identified).

Vandercruse, Roger: (*fl.* second half 18th century)
See Lacroix, Roger

Vigier, François: (*fl.* 1744–post 1769)
French clockmaker at Paris; maître-horloger 1744.

Mark ascribed to him:
VIGER
A PARIS
Inscribed on dial
Viger AParis
Engraved on back-plate

Vitel: (*fl.* mid 19th century)
Dealer trading at Paris; surname may be found stamped on 18th-century pieces, perhaps repaired by him:

VITEL.

Weisweiler, Adam: (*fl.* 1778–1810)
German-born cabinet-maker later working at Paris; maître-ébéniste in 1778.
Stamp used:

A·WEISWEILER

Zweiner: (*fl.* later 19th century)
Signature recorded on a 19th-century. copy of the "Bureau du Roi Louis XV"
Zweiner
Paris
1889

Tapestry Marks

In 1528 a regulation was made whereby all Brussels tapestry weavers and dealers in tapestries were required to mark the tapestries. All tapestry weavers in the Low Countries were thereupon required by Charles V to do likewise. Flemish or French weavers emigrating to other countries (e.g. England) naturally continued to follow the same practice. The mark or signature was woven into the selvedge. This unfortunately was often cut away at a later date, so many are now missing.

Representative List of Marks

Antwerp, Flanders
Town mark: two hands on a shield.

Assche, Henri Van: (*fl.* mid 17th century) at Brussels.
Signed his tapestries:

Also: HENDRICK VAN ASSCHE

Baumgarten, William: (established 1893) at Williamsbridge, New York City, N.Y.
Tapestries marked:

Benne, Jacques: (*fl.* mid 16th century) at Oudenarde, Flanders.
Signed his tapestries:

Biest, Hans Van der: (*fl.* early 17th century)
Went from Enghien to Munich (1604–1615).
Marks used included:

Bradshaw: (*fl.* 1760s)
Signature recorded on tapestry made at the Soho factory, London:
BRADSHAW

Brussels, Flanders
Town mark: a red shield, of varying forms, between the initials B B, also of varying styles:

Cammen, Henri Van der: (date not known) at Enghien, Flanders. Marked his tapestries:

Cammen, Jean, or **Jehan, Van der:** (*fl.* later 16th century) at Enghien, Flanders. Signed his tapestries:

Cammen, Philippe Van der: (recorded 1576) at Antwerp, Flanders. Signed his tapestries:

Comans, Alexandre de: (*fl. c.* 1634–1650) Chief tapestry weaver in works at Paris of De Comans & De la Planche. Signed his tapestries:

Comans, Charles de: (d. 1634) Succeeded Marc de Comans at Paris. Signed his tapestries:

Comans, Hippolyté de: (*fl.* later 17th century) at Paris. Signed his tapestries:

Crane, Sir Francis: (d. 1637) at Mortlake factory, Surrey, England. Signed his tapestries:

Crupenn, Remi: (recorded *c.* 1544) at Oudenarde, Flanders. Signed his tapestries:

Delft, Holland
Town mark: a shield between the initials H D:

Demay, Stephen: (*fl.* early 18th century) English tapestry weaver, established *c.* 1700. Mark recorded:

S. D. M.

Dervael, Jean: (recorded *c.* 1544) at Oudenarde, Flanders. Signed his tapestries:

Enghien, Low Countries
Town mark: a shield, gyronny.

Florence, Italy
Town mark: fleur-de-lis associated with the initials of the weaver.

Fulham, London, England
Tapestry works founded by Peter Parisot (*fl.* first half 18th century). Marks not recorded.

Geubels, François: (*fl. c.* 1541–1571) at Brussels.
Signed his tapestries:

Gobelins, Paris, France
Tapestry weaving established here in 1667.
Earlier mark:

Modern mark:

Hatton Garden, London, England
Tapestry made here for some years from 1679, employing some weavers from Mortlake, Surrey.
Mark a variant of the Mortlake shield:

Also recorded: HATTON GARDEN.

Hecke or **Hecque, Leo(n) Van den:** (recorded 1576) at Antwerp, Flanders.
Probably at Brussels.
Marked his tapestries:

Hove, Nicholas Van: (recorded 1576) at Brussels.
Marked his tapestries:

Hyckes or **Hickes, Richard:** (*fl.* later 16th century)
English weaver working in Warwickshire.
Signature recorded:
Ric = Hykes

Karcher, Jehan (?): (*fl.* 16th century)
Flemish weaver working at Ferrara, Italy.
Signed his tapestries:

Karcher, Nicholas: (recorded mid 16th century)
Flemish weaver said to have worked at Florence, Italy.
Marked his tapestries:

Lambeth, London, England
Workshop set up here (*c.* 1670) by William Benood.
Recorded on a tapestry before 1675:
MADE AT LAMBETH

Maecht, Felipe: (*fl.* later 16th century) perhaps working in Spain, and of Flemish or Dutch extraction.
Signature ascribed to him:

Maecht, Philip de: (recorded 1620s)
Master weaver of Dutch or Flemish origin working at Mortlake, Surrey.
Thought to have worked previously with de Comans at Paris.
Signed his tapestries:

Maelsaeck, François Van: (d. 1638) at Brussels.
Marked his tapestries:

Morris, I.: (*fl.* early 18th century)
English tapestry weaver.
Mark recorded (*c.* 1723):

I. MORRIS

Mortlake, Surrey, England
Tapestry weaving established here in 1619, flourishing until *c.* 1703.
Mark: a white shield, of various forms, with the red cross of St George:

Neilson, Jacques: (*fl.* 1749–1788)
Artist of Scottish origin, in charge at the Gobelins tapestry works, Paris.
Signature found:

J. NEILSON

Orley, Michael Van: (*fl.* mid 16th century) probably at Oudenarde, Flanders.
Mark ascribed:

Oudenarde, Flanders
Town mark:

Pannemaker, Wilhelm de: (*fl.* mid 16th century) at Brussels.
Marks used include:

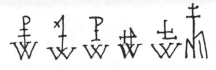

Paris, France
Mark used: a fleur-de-lis and the letter P, accompanied by the initials of the master weaver.

Poyntz, Francis: (d. 1685)
English weaver, connected with Mortlake or Hatton Garden.
Marks included:

FRANCUS POYNTZ
also F P with a shield; or with
HATTON GARDEN.

Raes, Jean: (*fl.* early 18th century) at Brussels.
Marked his tapestries:

Reymbouts, Martin: (recorded 1611–1615) at Brussels.
Marked his tapestries:

Royal Manufactory, Madrid, Spain
Mark recorded:

Santa Barbara factory, Madrid, Spain
Tapestry factory founded here in 1720 by Philip V; closed 1808, reopened 1815.
Mark: a weaver's shuttle.

Saunders, Paul: (*fl.* second half 18th century) at Soho, London, England. Signature recorded (*c.* 1761):
P. SAUNDERS LONDINI

Schrijner, Peter: (*fl.* later 17th century) possibly at Mortlake, Surrey. Monogram ascribed (on Mortlake piece):

NB. This mark might alternatively be that of the weaver Paul Steen.

Segers, Jan: (*fl.* later 17th century) at Brussels and at Paris. Marked his tapestries:

Segers, Wilhelm: (recorded 1688) at Brussels. Marked his tapestries:

Soho, London, England
Tapestry woven here mid 18th century. No special mark recorded.

Spierincx, Armand: (recorded 1555) at Delft, Holland. Marked his tapestries:

Spierincx, François: (recorded 1576 and 1607) at Delft, Holland. Marked his tapestries:

Tayer, Hans: (*fl.* mid 17th century) Master weaver at Paris before 1662. Sometimes called Jean Taye. Marked his tapestries:

Thomson, W. G.: (*fl.* early 20th century) at Edinburgh, Scotland. Mark recorded:

Tournai, Flanders
Town mark: a castle:

Vanderbank, John: (*fl.* later 17th century) at Hatton Garden, London. Recorded between 1689 and *c.* 1727. Marks included: initials J.V.D.B.; name using various spelling.

Vos, Jos de: (recorded 1705) at Brussels. Mark recorded: I. D. VOS.

Vos, Judocus: (*fl.* early 18th century) at Brussels. Signature recorded:
JUDOCUS DE VOS

Wezeler, Georges: (recorded 1534) at Brussels. Goldsmith of Antwerp and noted merchant. Mark:

Ceramics

English and European Marks

Aalmis, Jan: (1714–post 1788)
Ceramic painter, Rotterdam

Abaquesne, Masseot: (d. *c.* 1560)
Faïence potter, Rouen (*fl. c.* 1530–60)
found on drugpots

Absolon, William: (1751–1815)
Pottery decorator, and china and glass
dealer at Yarmouth (*fl.* from *c.* 1790)
Mark, painted in red, occurs on wares
bought from Turner, Wedgwood, Shorthose, and Leeds (impressed with their
marks):

Other marks:

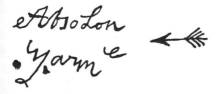

Painted

Abtsbessingem, Thuringia, Germany
Faïence pottery from mid 18th century.
Mark, a fork plus painter's initials:

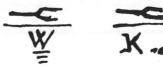

Adams, Benjamin: (1787–1828)
Greengates, Tunstall, Staffordshire.
Managed family business from 1805; sold
out to Meir of Tunstall in 1820. Works
bought back by Adams family in *c.* 1858.
B. ADAMS
Impressed

Adams, J., and Co.: (*fl.* later 19th century)
Styled J. Adams & Co. until 1873, then
known as Adams & Bromley.
Marks, impressed, include:
ADAMS & BROMLEY
J. ADAMS & Co.

Adams, John: (1882–1953)
Pottery manufacturer and designer; joint
founder (1921) and managing director
(1921–49) of Carter, Stabler and Adams,
Poole Pottery. Dorset.

Personal mark

Adams, William: (1746–1805)
Owner of Staffordshire potworks.

ADAMS & Co.
Impressed: on cream-coloured
earthenware
1770–1800
ADAMS & Co.
Impressed: on solid jasper
1780–90

ADAMS
Impressed: on stoneware,
transfer-printed
earthenware, jasper
1787–1805
W. ADAMS & Co.
Impressed: on jasper

Adams, William: (1772–1829)
Potter at Burslem (until 1804), then at
Cliff Bank, Stoke, in partnership with his
sons from 1819; works closed 1864.

ADAMS

Impressed: 1804–64
(except on blue transfer-printed ware)

1810–64
On blue transfer-printed earthenware

Estᵈ 1657
ENGLAND

Impressed: 1820–50
on various wares

W. ADAMS & SONS
STOKE . UPON . TRENT

Printed: 1819–64
on bone china, ironstone china,
enamelled earthenware

W A. & S.

1819–64; on various wares

Adams, William: (1798–1865)
Owned the Greenfield pottery, Staffordshire, from 1834.

ADAMS
Impressed

Ahrenfeldt, Charles: (1807–93)
Factory at Limoges (c. 1886) and at
Carlsbad-Altrohlau (c. 1886); followed
by son Charles (b. 1856).

At Limoges

At Altrohlau

Aire, Pas-de-Calais, France
Faïence made here c. 1730 to 1790.
Reputed marks:

Albissola, northern Italy
Maïolica centre during the 17th and 18th centuries

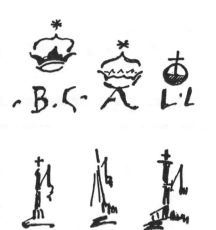

Alcock & Co., Samuel: (*fl.* 1831–59)
The Hill Pottery, Burslem, Staffordshire.
Marks found both impressed and printed:

ALCOCK & CO.
HILL POTTERY   S.A. & Co.
BURSLEM

Sam/Alcock & Co.

Alcora, Valencia, Spain
Faïence made *c.* 1726–*c.* 1780; cream-coloured earthenware from *c.* 1780; hard-paste porcelain from *c.* 1774.
Marks: letter A incised, in colours or in gold, used from 1784. Chaffers mainly gives 19th-century marks.

Transfer-printed in red

Allen, Robert: (1744–1835)
China painter at Lowestoft, Suffolk, 1757–*c.* 1780; set up own enamelling workshop *c.* 1802.

Allen
Lowestoft

The numeral 5 in blue, on inner side of the foot-ring of Lowestoft porcelain, said to be his mark.

Altenburg, Thuringia, Germany
Earthenware, late 18th to early 19th century.

A

Impressed

Alt-Rohlau, Bohemia, Czechoslovakia
Cream-coloured earthenware made by Benedict Hasslacher from 1813 to 1823; taken over by August Nowotny in 1823; said also to have made porcelain.

A.N.   NOWOTNY
       ALTROHLAU

Altwasser, Silesia, Germany
Hard-paste porcelain from 1845 by Tielsch & Co.

Factory mark, pattern number and workmen's marks

Amberg, Bavaria, Germany
Faïence made from 1759 (by Simon Hetzendörfer); cream-coloured earthenware and hard-paste porcelain made from 1790.

The factory continued until 1910.

Amstel, near Amsterdam, Holland
Hard-paste porcelain from 1784 to 1820.

Amstel   *Amstel*

In blue
See also OUDE LOOSDRECHT and WEESP

Andreoli, Giorgio: (*c.* 1465/70–*c.* 1553)
Maïolica painter, working at Gùbbio; especially noted for lustre. Called Maestra Giorgio. Marks occur on pieces dated from 1518 onward:

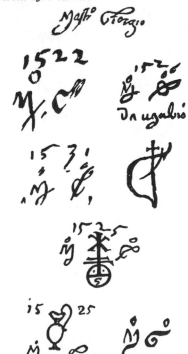

Many variations of his initial "G" occur as follows:

Mark of Vincenzo Andreoli, son of Giorgio, working *c.* 1536 to *c.* 1576:

Also with his father's mark

The mark of Maestro Giorgio has been forged.

Over-neat and careful in rendering: Mark on 19th-century reproduction

Angarano, near Bassano, Italy
Cream-coloured earthenware figure

180

groups, late 18th century. Recorded mark:

Angoulême, Charente, France
Faïence, 1748–c. 1800.

ANGOULEME

Annaburg
Firm of A. Heckmann recorded, with mark, by Chaffers:

Heckmann was a faïence manufacturer.

Annecy, Haute-Savoie, France
White earthenware, 1800–08, marked:

ANNECY

Ansbach, Bavaria, Germany
Hard-paste porcelain, 1758–62; moved to Castle of Bruckberg, 1762–1806; sold 1806; continued to 1860.

In blue

Impressed
on figures

Earthenware, c. 1710 onward. Factory marks uncommon on early productions.

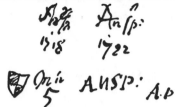

Onolzbach was the old name for Ansbach.

Painters' marks:

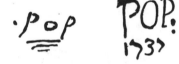

Johann Caspar Ripp: (1710–12)

George Christian Oswald (1711–33)

Johann Georg Christoph Popp (1715–84)

Johann Heinrich Wackenfeld (1716–19)

Johann Valentin Bontemps (c. 1716–29)

Christian Imanuel Kruckenberger
(1718–30)

Johann Leonhard Uz (1723–47)

Johann Wolfgang Meyerhöfer (1724–38)

Joachim Leonhard Wolf (1726–28)

George Nicolaus Hofmann (1732–37)

Johann Leonhard Förster (1733–44)

Johann Julius Popp (1749–92)

Mathias Carl Rosa (1751–68)

Antonibon, Giambattista:
Made earthenware at Le Nove, Italy, from 1728 to 1741, when his son Pasquale took over from him. His monogram occurs on porcelain made *c.* 1762, perhaps in his honour:

Antwerp, Belgium
Maïolica potter Guido Andries, or Guido de Savino, recorded here *c.* 1512; chief centre of manufacture of tin-enamelled pottery until the second half of the 16th century. Other potters identified include Jean Francisco de Bresse (Brescia) in 1513, and Jan Bogaert (1552–71).

On a jug dated 1562

Appel, Johannes Den:
Owner of Delft factory, De Vergulde Boot, from 1759; registered his mark in 1764 as:

Aprey, Haute Marne, France
Faïence factory *c.* 1740 to *c.* 1860.

Artists here included Jacques Jarry, responsible for a certain type of bird painting; mark:

Apt, Vaucluse, France
Earthenware made here from 1728. Factory founded by César Moulind, and eventually in the hands of the widow Claire Arnoux (end of the 18th century).

Impressed

Mark of Claire Arnoux, being the initials VVA for veuve Arnoux.

182

Arbois
Faïence made here from *c.* 1745 to *c.*1800.

Arbois ARBOIS

Arkhangelskoie, near Moscow, Russia
Site of porcelain factory, privately owned
by Prince Nicholas Yussopoff, from 1814
to 1831.

Archangelski Archangelski

Arnhem, Holland
Tin-glazed earthenware made here during
third quarter of 18th century.

Arras, Pas-de-Calais, France
Soft-paste porcelain made here *c.* 1770–86.

AR A R

AR AA

In blue, crimson or purple

Arzberg, Bavaria, Germany
Carl Schumann made general pottery
here from 1880.

Aschach, northern Bavaria, Germany
William Sattler made general pottery
here, 1829–60.

W. S. & S
Impressed

Ashworth, Geo. L., & Bros Ltd
Trading at Hanley from 1862; sold out
1883 to J. H. Goddard, whose descendants continue to present day, using
designs and shapes of C. J. Mason.

ASHWORTHS
REAL
IRONSTONE
CHINA

1870–80
Transfer-printed
and impressed

1870–80
Transfer-printed and impressed

Astbury, Richard Meir: (1765–1834)
Potter and merchant; worked the Foley
Pottery, Lane Delph, Staffordshire, from
1780 until 1797.
Marks recorded:

R.M.A. or ASTBURY

Auffenwerth, Johann: (d. 1728)
Ausgburg goldsmith; signature found on
a cup and saucer painted rather crudely
with tiny emblematic figures (British
Museum):
I. A. W. Augsburg
(Johann Auffen Werth Augsburg)

Augsburg, Swabia, Germany
Important centre for decoration of
Meissen porcelain by outside decorators
(Hausmaler) from *c.* 1725. Hausmaler in-
cluded Johann Auffenwerth (d. 1728)

who produced a small quantity; much attributed to him more likely came from the workshop of Bartolomäus (*c.* 1730–35).

Ault, William: (*fl.* late 19th century)
Made "art" pottery at Swadlincote, near Burton-on-Trent, Staffordshire; some from special designs of Dr Christopher Dresser.

Auxerre, Yonne, France
Faïence factory established here by Claude Boutet in 1785.

Aveiro, Portugal
Faïence made here from *c.* 1780, found marked F.A. (Fabrica Aveiro).

Avisseau, Jean Charles: (1796–1861)
Made pottery in style of Palissy and Henri Deux wares at Tours. Signed in monogram, rarely in full.

Aynsley, Henry & Co.: (*fl. c.* 1870)
Made various earthenwares at Longton, Staffordshire.

Aynsley, John: (1752–1829)
Made cream-coloured earthenware and porcelain at Longton, Staffordshire. Some black transfer-printed wares signed:

Aynsley, Lane End

J. Aynsley, Lane End

Aynsley, John and Sons: (*fl. c.* 1860)
Made bone china at Longton, Staffordshire.

Baddeley, John: (d. 1772)
Made salt-glazed stoneware and cream-coloured earthenware at Shelton, Staffordshire; his family continued the business until *c.* 1802.

Impressed

Baden-Baden, Germany
Zacharias Pfalzer directed a porcelain factory here, 1770–78. Earthenware was made by Antoine Anstett from 1793.

On porcelain

In blue   In colour   On
on porcelain   on faïence   earthenware

Baguley, Isaac: (*fl. c.* 1842–   )
Painter at Derby; bought part of Rockingham works on its closure in 1842 to
decorate china, buying wares from Minton; Brown, Westhead, Moore & Co.,
and others.
Mark:
"Baguley Rockingham Works " with or
without the griffin crest.

Bailey & Batkin: (*c.* 1815–29)
Made lustred pottery at Lane End,
Staffordshire.
Mark recorded:
            Bailey & Batkin,
         SOLE PATENTEES

Baker, Bevans & Irwin: (*fl.* early 19th
century)
Firm working at Swansea, Wales; closed
1838/39.
Marks:
The words BAKER, BEVANS &
IRWIN with SWANSEA forming a
circle round the Prince of Wales's feathers
(impressed); the initials:
            BB & I or BB & Co
            Transfer-printed

Balaam, W.: (*fl.* early 19th century)
Slipware potter at Ipswich.
Mark recorded:
      W. Balaam, Rope Lane Pottery,
            IPSWICH

Ball, Isaac: (*fl.* late 17th century)
Potter at Burslem, Staffordshire.
Mark possibly his:

Initials I. B. on early Staffordshire posset
pots, dated 1696–1700.

Baranovka, Volhynia, Poland
Porcelain factory founded here by the
two Mezer brothers in 1801; continued
until 1917 or later.

Barangówka

In black or brown

Barcella, Stefano:
Venetian maïolica painter; signed a dish
(Victoria and Albert Museum, London):

Barker family: (*fl.* mid 17th/end 19th
century) Staffordshire
Various members potted at different
works, e.g. at Fenton, Lane End, Lane
Delph, etc. (1750–1851). Barker & Hill
recorded at Longton in 1864 and 1875;
Barker Bros recorded in 1889.

Barker, Sutton & Till: (*fl.* 1833–*c.* 1850)
Potters at Burslem, Staffordshire, making
earthenware, lustre ware, and figures. By
1850 Thomas Till sole owner, later taking
sons into partnership.
Marks:
"B.S. & T. Burslem" and TILL impressed

Bassano, Venezia, Italy
Maïolica made here from the 16th to the
mid 18th century.

*Bassano
i 7 i 8*

See under TERCHI

Bates, Elliot & Co.
Bates, Walker & Co.: (*fl.* 19th century)
Potworks at Dalehall, Longport, Staffordshire, passed through various ownerships, from Joseph Stubbs (d. 1836) to last firm, Bates, Walker & Company.
Marks:
BATES WALKER & CO. impressed
or B.W. & CO.

Bayeux, Calvados, France
Factory established here in 1810, making hard-paste porcelain; in 1849 owned by F. Gosse.

Bayreuth, Bavaria, Germany
Faïence factory founded *c.* 1713 by Johann Georg Knöller (d. 1744). Mark, in blue, B.K. for Bayreuth-Knöller. Initials used during succeeding ownerships:

B.F.S. (Bayreuth-Fränkel-Schreck, 1744–47)
B.P.F. (Beyreuth-Pfeiffer-Fränkel, 1747–60)
B.P. (Beyreuth-Pfeiffer, 1760–67)

WEZEL occurs impressed after 1788, when cream-coloured English-type earthenware was exclusively made. These marks often found with initials of painters and decorators:

Bayreu: Büyr

RIP	Johann Kaspar Ripp 1714
C	Johann Clarner 1731–48
G.A.H.	G. A. Hagen 1733–48
In full	Johann Christoph Jucht 1736–63
W.H.P.	Wolfgang Heinrich Parsch 1729–38
POPP	Johann Albrecht Popp 1745–47
O.S.	Johann Martin Anton Oswald 1764
J.M.H.	Johann Markus Hagen (1737–1803) 1760–1803
In full	Johann Heinrich Steinbach (d. 1761) 1760–61

Porcelain made at times during the 18th century. J. C. Schmidt founded a factory in the early 19th century, for making hard-paste porcelain, stoneware, and cream-coloured earthenware; some products were impressed with the "counterfeit mark of Wedgwood."
See under METSCH, Johann Friedrich

Bell, John (d. 1880) and **Matthew P.** (d. 1869):
Founded Glasgow pottery in early 19th century; china and earthenware made from 1842; firm closed down 1891.

Transfer-printed

Belleek, Fermanagh, Ireland
Factory established here in 1857, making china, parian, ironstone, and painted, printed and gilded earthenware, and a curious lustred porcelain.

Given by Jewitt

Bellvue, Meurthe et Moselle, France
Faïence made here from 1758; factory in

control of Charles Bayard and François Boyer in 1771. Bayard and his son started a separate factory a few years later at Toul nearby. English-type earthenware made in the 19th century.

 BELLVUE

Belle Vue Pottery, Hull, England
Established 1802; acquired 1825 by William Bell, making cream-coloured and transfer-printed wares; factory closed 1840.
Marks recorded:

Impressed

Transfer-printed

Berlin, Prussia, Germany
Faïence made from *c*. 1690 through the 18th century by various firms. Hard-paste porcelain made by A. Schumann at Moabit nearby, from 1835, marked:

Berlin, Gotzkowsky's Factory and the Royal Factory
Porcelain made from 1761 onward. The letter G, in underglaze blue, was used in Gotzkowsky's time; from 1763 the sceptre mark was generally used.

> K.P.M. with an orb, in blue or red;
> or with a sceptre impressed
> (1830s)
> KPM accompanied by Prussian Eagle
> (late 1840s)

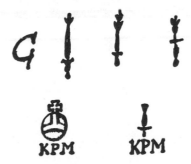

Berlin, Wegely's Porcelain Factory
Hard-paste porcelain made 1752–57.

In blue, or impressed, sometimes with numerals arranged one above the other in two or three tiers. These perhaps indicated mould numbers.

Bettisi, Leonardo di Ascanio, alias Don Pino: (d. *c*. 1589)
Faenza maïolica painter in control of the Camelli workshop in 1570. Mark attributed to him:

Billington, Dora May:
Contemporary English studio potter; decorated industrial pottery made by Meakins.

Incised

Bing & Grondahl:
Established at Copenhagen, Denmark, by
Harold Bing in 1853, making porcelain,
stoneware, and earthenware.

 B & G
CMO   **B&G**

Bingham, Edward: (b. 1829)
Made pseudo-Tudor and 17th-century
pottery at Castle Hedingham, Essex,
c. 1848.

Birch, Edmund John: (*fl. c.* 1796–1814)
Staffordshire pottery firm of Birch &
Whitehead recorded 1796; in 1802 under
Birch only; made black basaltes and
jasper wares in Wedgwood style, marked:
BIRCH or "Birch" (impressed)

Birks, Alboin: (1861–1941)
Artist in pâte-sur-pâte; worked for Mintons Ltd (1876–1937).

ABirks

Blashfield, John Marriott: (*fl.* 1851–)
Produced architectural terra cotta and
statuary, at Stamford, Lincolnshire, from
1858; Stamford Terra Cotta Co. formed
1874; closed 1875. Firm made busts,
statues, and animals (1862 International
Exhibition).
Marks:
J. M. BLASHFIELD (impressed)
BLASHFIELD, STAMFORD

Boch frères, of Keramis, Le Louvière,
Hainault, Belgium
Earthenware factory established 1841;
tiles made at branch factory opened at
Mauberge in France, in 1861.

Bodenbach, Bohemia, Czechoslovakia
Imitation Wedgwood said to have been
made here from c. 1830, using marks:

S & G
Impressed
for Schiller & Gerbing

F. Gerbing   W. Schiller & Sons

WEDGWOOD
Impressed

Bodley & Son: (*fl.* 19th century)
Potters at Burslem, Staffordshire; Edwin
J. D. Bodley sole owner in 1875, continuing until 1890s; made parian, china,
and earthenware.

Boisette, near Melun, Seine-et-Marne,
France
Faïence factory (established c. 1732) also
made porcelain from 1777 until c. 1792.

In blue   The form of the B is variable

Bologna, Italy
Lead-glazed earthenware made from the
15th to the 18th centuries. Some 17th-
century marks:

Maïolica made by Aldovrandi's factory from 1794, and cream-coloured earthenware, with mark CARLO ALDOVRANDI impressed. Imitation Italian Renaissance maïolica made from 1849 by Angelo Minghetti & Son:

Boote, T. & R.: (*fl.* 1842–94)
Founded by Thomas Latham Boote and Richard Boote; made parian statuary and vases at Burslem, Staffordshire.

Bordeaux, Gironde, France
Faïence made from *c.* 1711 onward, at several factories.

David Johnston
1834–45

Impressed
J. Vieillard
1845 onward

Hard-paste porcelain made from 1781 to 1787 by Verneuilh and his nephew.

In gold or underglaze blue
Verneuilh and nephew

Stencilled
Alluaud & Vanier making porcelain, from 1787 to 1790

Latens & Rateau, from 1828

Bornholm Island, Denmark
A German, Johann Spietz, started an earthenware factory here.

Impressed

Bott & Co.: (*fl.* early 19th century)
Made earthenware busts and figures; also silver lustre wares and blue-printed earthenware.

Impressed

Boullemier, Antonin: (1840–1900)
Painted figure subjects on porcelain; worked at Sèvres until 1870, when he worked at Mintons, England.

Boumeester, Cornelis: (*c.* 1650–1733)
Painter of Dutch tin-enamelled pottery:

C:BM

C:BOVMEESTER

Found in blue

Bourg-la-Reine, France
Faïence and porcelain made here from 1774 to 1806 by Jullien and Jacques.

Incised

Bourne, Charles: (*fl.* before 1830)
Made porcelain, Foley pottery, Fenton, Staffordshire.

Bourne & Son: (*fl.* 1812 to present day)
Stoneware manufacturers, first at Belper (1812) and Denby, Derbyshire; from 1834 at Denby only.

Bovey Tracey, Devonshire
Several potworks here in 18th century; Bovey Tracey Pottery Company formed in 1841 to make Staffordshire-type earthenware, continuing until 1956.

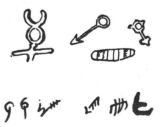

Bow, London
Porcelain made here from *c.* 1750 until 1776.
Numerous factory and workmen's or repairers' marks recorded; most generally recognised Bow marks after 1760 are an anchor and dagger in red or under-glaze blue.

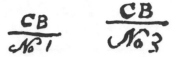

1750

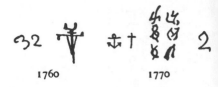

1760   1770

Brain, E. and Company: (*fl.* from 1850)
Founded by Edward Brain at the Foley, Longton, Staffordshire, to make china.

FOLEY
ENGLISH BONE CHINA
PAINTED BY HAND.

Brameld, William: (d. 1813)
Took over Rockingham factory in 1806; succeeded after his death by his three sons; porcelain made from 1820 to 1842.

Painted in red   Impressed

Brampton, near Chesterfield, Derbyshire
Brown stoneware made here from early 18th century, and throughout the 19th century; salt-glazed wares made from *c.* 1838.
Factories recorded with marks include:

S. & H. BRIDDON
(Samuel & Henry Briddon) *c.* 1848

OLDFIELD & CO. MAKERS
(Oldfield, Madin Wright, Hewitt & Company, or John Oldfield)

J. OLDFIELD

OLDFIELD & CO. CHESTERFIELD

Brannan, Charles, Ltd:
Owners of pottery at Barnstaple, Devon, established in the 18th century by one Lovering, later owned by Rendell, and finally by Brannan, continuing today.

190

Breeze, John: (1746–1821)
Made earthenware at Burslem (recorded 1796); the firm's name given in 1805 as John Breeze and Son, Tunstall; the factory to let in 1828, eventually passing to the Adams family.

Bretby Art Pottery, near Burton-on-Trent Established by Henry Tooth at Woodville in 1883.

Brianchon, Jules Joseph Henri:
Took out an English patent in 1857 for an improved method of colouring porcelain, etc.: a mother-of-pearl lustre sheen, popular in later 19th century, and characteristic of Irish Belleek porcelain. Brianchon partner in Gillet & Brianchon, Paris:

Bridgwood, Sampson: (*fl.* early 19th century)
Firm recorded in 1805, making earthenware; later made bone china, now making earthenware again, at Longton.
S. BRIDGWOOD & SON (impressed)

Impressed: 1860   Impressed
               (on fine white earthenware)

Bristol, Gloucestershire, England
Delftware made here *c.* 1650 until late 18th century.
No undisputed factory marks.
Soft-paste porcelain made here from *c.* 1749 until 1752, when the factory amalgated with Worcester.
Hard-paste porcelain made here from 1770 until 1786.

Marks in underglaze blue and blue enamel.

1770   1775

1776

1780

Broom, A.: (*fl.* 19th century)
Figure maker.
Mark recorded:

A. BROOM

Brownfield, William: (d. 1873)
Made earthenware at Cobridge, Staffordshire; took son William Etches into partnership 1871, when bone china was also made; factory closed in 1890.

or: BROWNFIELD & SON
          COBRIDGE STAFFS

upon a scroll enclosing two globes

RAVENNA

W.B.

Brunswick, Germany
Faïence made from 1707; various factories:

Von Hantelmann   Reichard & Behling
1711–49   1749–56

Rudolf Anton Chely
1745–57

Buen Retiro, Madrid, Spain
Porcelain made here from 1759 to 1808, after transference of Royal factory from Capodimonte, Naples. Mark of Bourbon fleur-de-lys used from 1760 to 1804, in various forms:

In blue

given by
Brongniart

given by
Riaño

Impressed
(given by Riaño)

In red   In red
(given by Riaño)   (given by Riaño)

In colour   In red   Impressed
(given by Riaño)

Artists working here, whose marks are recorded, include:
Salvatore Noferi, sculptor (1759–85), transferred from Capodimonte:

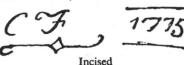

(given by Riaño)
Caetano Fumo, modeller:

Incised

Bullers Ltd: (20th century)
At Milton, Staffordshire, made image toys, decorative pottery, etc. from 1937 until 1955.

BULLERS MADE IN ENGLAND

Incised

Artists:
Anne Potts, figure maker

Agnete Hoy Bohrer, modeller and decorator

     Incised   Painted

Harold Thomas, thrower

James Rushton, decorator

Burmantofts pottery, Leeds, England
Established 1858 making fire-clay wares;
art pottery made 1882–1904; later re-
verted to terra-cotta faïence.

> BURMANTOFTS
> FAÏENCE
> (impressed)

or: BF in monogram

Caduceus mark
Mark found on some Meissen porcelain,
from c. 1723. Thought to represent, not
the caduceus of classic Rome, but perhaps
the tail of the so-called Chinese kite
mark, also found on Meissen ware. It
has been suggested that it was considered
more acceptable to Levantine merchants
dealing in Meissen porcelain than the
crossed-swords mark, which perhaps re-
sembled too nearly the Christian symbol.

Caen, Calvados, France
Hard-paste porcelain made here, c. 1793–
1806, at factory of d'Aigmont-Desmares
and Ducheval.

Stencilled in red

Caffaggiolo, near Florence, Italy
Maïolica made here during the 16th
century. Marks recognised include: the
inscription "in Chafagguolo"; a monogram of the letters SF or SP crossed with
a paraph, with or without a trident.

1514   c. 1513   c. 1515

c. 1510   c. 1515

c. 1540 c. 1545–50 Alessandro Fattorini
c. 1545–50

Campani, Ferdinando Maria: (1702–71)
Maïolica painter working in the istoriato
style of Urbino, known to have worked
at Siena. A dish in the Victoria and
Albert Museum is signed: Ferdinando Ma:
Campani dipinse l'1747 in Siena:

Campolide
Marks found on 19th-century traditional
pottery, made at Lisbon:

Painted in blue   Painted in blue

Cantagalli, Ulysse: (d. 1901)
Proprietor of modern maïolica factory, opened at Florence in 1878.

(A cock is also the mark of the Arnhem factory in Holland.)

Capodimonte, Italy
Soft-paste porcelain factory opened 1743, transferred to Madrid in 1769.

Impressed

On tablewares
(very variable, often smeared)

In gold

Cardew, Michael: (*fl.* 1926–)
Studio potter, making slipware at his Winchcombe Pottery, Gloucestershire, 1926–39; made stoneware at Wenford Bridge, Cornwall, 1939–42, then left for the Gold Coast.

Carey, Thomas: (d. *c.* 1847)
Made earthenware and china at Lane End, Staffordshire; firm listed as Carey and Son in 1818, later as Thomas and John Carey (dissolved 1842).

Carouge, near Geneva, Switzerland
Cream-coloured earthenware made from 1812, notably by Baylon & Co.

BAYLON   BAYLON

Impressed

Carter, Stabler & Adams: (1921–   )
Making tablewares and "fancies" at Poole, Dorset.

Incised on lustre wares produced by Carter before 1921; also Carter & Co.

POOLE
ENGLAND

CARTER
STABLER
ADAMS
POOLE
ENGLAND

Impressed 1921–24.
After 1924, with word "Ltd" added

Impressed after 1921; also in black underglaze

POOLE
ENGLAND

After 1919 in black underglaze

POOLE
ENGLAND

Impressed after 1921

Casa Pirota mark
Conventional representation of a fire wheel or fire bomb (pyrrhus rota, used as a canting device) as a pottery mark by

the leading maïolica workshop at Faenza, the Casa Pirota, worked by the Pirotti family:

16th century
See also FAENZA

Cassel, Hesse-Nassau, Germany
Hard-paste porcelain made here from 1766 until 1788.

Both in underglaze blue

Castel Durante, Urbino, Italy
Made Renaissance maïolica (from c.1508). The factory continued into the 18th century.

A nearly similar inscription
includes the date 1525

Castelli, Abruzzi, Italy
Maïolica made from 16th to 18th centuries. From end of 17th century dominated by the Grue and Gentili families.

Caughley, Shropshire, England
Porcelain made here from 1772 by Thomas Turner; John Rose of Coalport took over the factory 1799; it closed down in 1814. Various marks used, some clearly imitative of English or foreign factories.

Imitation Worcester
Most notable marks, letters S or C in blue, or word "Salopian" in upper or lower case letters, impressed.

In blue

SALOPIAN
Impressed

Chamberlain's factory: (1783–mid 19th century)
Started 1783 by Robert Chamberlain at Worcester, England, making porcelain from 1792; amalgated with the other Worcester factory in 1840; trading as Kerr and Binns in 1852; became the Royal Worcester Porcelain Co. in 1862. Various marks used:

H. Chamberlain
& Sons
Worcester
(incised)

CHAMBERLAIN'S

Chamberlain's
Regent China
Worcester
&155
New Bond Street,
London

Printed in red

195

Chantilly, Oise, France
Soft-paste porcelain made from *c.* 1725 until 1800. Mark, a hunting horn:

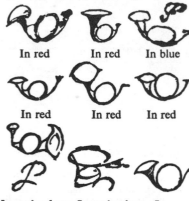

In red	In red	In blue

In red	In red	In red

In underglaze blue	In underglaze blue	In red

Chantilly *Chantilly*

In blue: with the
hunting horn: rare   In blue

villers cotteret

In blue

Early marks usually carefully drawn in red without accompanying sign or initials; later marks in blue more carelessly drawn, smudgy in appearance, and frequently with workman's initials, painted, or incised in the paste. Word "Chantilly" with hunting horn in blue is late 18th-century. The hunting horn in gold occurs only on early "red-dragon" ware.

Chaplet, Ernest: (1835–1909)
French artist-potter.

Chelsea, London, England
Factory established here *c.* 1745, making porcelain, until 1784; under different managements, eventually bought by William Duesbury and John Heath of Derby. The products of the years 1770 to 1784 known as Chelsea-Derby. Closed down 1784. Four clearly defined periods of Chelsea manufacture recognised: Triangle 1745–49; Raised Anchor 1750–53; Red Anchor 1753–58; Gold Anchor 1758–70.

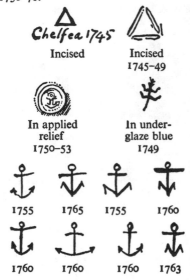

Incised	Incised 1745–49

In applied relief 1750–53	In under-glaze blue 1749

1755	1765	1755	1760
1760	1760	1760	1763

Chemical, Alchemical and Astrological signs
Some of these occur as marks, on Bow, Chelsea, Bristol, and early Worcester porcelain; also on Staffordshire earthenware, e.g. Rogers, of Dale Hall, Burslem.

Aer	A	Air
Terra	▽ ⊕	Earth
Ignis	△	Fire
Aqua	▽	Water
Dies	♂	Day
Nox	☽	Night

Fumus		Smoke
Cineres		Ashes
Sal		Salt
Sol		Gold
Luna		Silver
Jupiter		Tin
Saturn		Lead
Mars		Iron or Steel
Venus		Copper
Mercury		Quicksilver
Antimonium		Antimony
Orichalum		Brass
Faeces Vini		Lees of Wine
Albumen		White of Egg
Arena		Sand
Arsenicum		Arsenic
Atramentum		Ink
Creta		Chalk
Borax		Borax

Chetham family: (*fl.* end 18th century to 1875)
Made earthenware, "pearl" ware, etc., at Longton, Staffordshire, from *c.* 1796; factory eventually controlled by H. Aynsley and Company in 1875.

Chetham & Woolley Lane End, 1798

CHETHAM

Chetwynd, David: (*fl.* 1851–76)
Pottery modeller, 1851–65, at Hanley and Burslem, Staffordshire; partner with Cockson at Cobridge, 1866–76.
Mark, the Royal Arms and the name:

IMPERIAL IRONSTONE CHINA,
COCKSON & CHETWYND.
Given by Jewitt

Child, Smith: (1730–1813)
Established a factory at Tunstall, Staffordshire, in 1763, making transfer-printed and other decorated wares, working until 1783.
Mark:
CHILD
Impressed

Made earthenware with J. H. Clive, 1806 to 1813, as Child & Clive.
Mark also accurs:
CLIVE
Impressed

"Chinese" marks
Marks imitating Chinese characters appear fairly frequently on porcelain made at Bow, Worcester, and Caughley, or by Spode and Mason in north Staffordshire, 18th and early 19th centuries. Also common on red Elers-type ware made in Staffordshire throughout the 18th century.

"Chinese" marks on European porcelain
Examples:

Vienna   Meissen

Choisy-le-Roy, Seine, France
Firm named H. Boulanger et Cie, or Hautin et Boulanger, making porcelain and white earthenware, recorded in 1836 using these marks:

Hard-paste porcelain made late 18th century. Chaffers records:

Cleffius, Lambertus:
Proprietor of De Metale Pot, Delft, 1660–91.

Clementson, Joseph: (1794–1871)
Started in partnership with Jonah Read (Read & Clementson) making earthenware at the Phoenix Works, Shelton, Staffordshire, 1832–39; bought the Bell Works in 1856.

Clerici, Felice:
Maïolica worker at Milan, 1745–80. Probably related to the Clérissys of St Jean du Désert and Moustiers.

Clérissy, Pierre: (1651–1728)
Founded the Moustiers faïence industry in 1679.

See also MOUSTIERS.

Clermont-Ferrand, Puy-de-Dôme, France
Faïence made here at two periods: (1) from c. 1730 to 1743; (2) from 1774 to c. 1784.

Clews (Clewes), Ralph and James:
(fl. 1817 to 1835)
Made blue-printed earthenware at Cobridge, Staffordshire, mainly for the American market; also made ironstone china.

Transfer-printed

Transfer-printed

Clignancourt, Paris
Hard-paste porcelain made here during the later 18th century. Mark of a windmill:

In blue

In gold | Given by Jännicke 1771–75

M, for Monsieur

Stencilled in red initials LSX, for Louis-Stanislas-Xavier, 1775–93

The factory was under the protection of Louis-Stanislas-Xavier, Comte de Provence, also known as "Monsieur", being then the King's brother.

Stencilled in red
1775–93

Clowes, William: (d. *c.* 1815/16)
Made earthenware and black basaltes at Longport, Burslem, Staffordshire, from *c.* 1783; firm styled Henshall, Williamson & Clowes in 1796; and Henshall & Williamson in 1805.
Mark recorded:

W Clowes
Impressed

Coalport or Coalbrookdale, Shropshire, England
Factory established here *c.* 1796 by John Rose, making porcelain, continued by his descendants until 1862. In 1855 owned by a member of the Bruff family; in 1924 sold to Cauldon Potteries Ltd, moving to Staffordshire in 1926.

G Dale
Coalport

1820

JOHN ROSE & C⁰ COALBROOKDALE SHROPSHIRE

Coffee, William: (*fl.* 1794)
Modeller, employed at Derby porcelain factory 1794–95; later made terra cotta. Reputed mark on terra cotta:

W. COFFEE DERBY
Stamped

Coombes, or Combes: (*fl. c.* 1780–1805)
Repairer of china, who re-marked and re-fired pieces, at an address in Queen Street, Bristol, England.

Coombes
Queen St
Bristol

Cooper, Susan Vera, R.D.I.: (*fl.* 1925–   )
Pottery designer: founded Susie Cooper Pottery, Burslem, Staffordshire, 1932.

SUSIE COOPER
PRODUCTION
CROWN WORKS
BURSLEM
ENGLAND

Copenhagen, Denmark
Soft-paste porcelain made here, *c.* 1760 until 1765

Usual mark for Frederick V, 1760–65

Copenhagen, Denmark
Royal Copenhagen Porcelain Manufactory, making hard-paste from 1775.
Mark, three wavy lines in blue, emblems of the three principal Danish waterways into the Baltic, adopted in 1775.

Painted in blue 1775 onwards

Incised

1889   1894

1925   modern

Philip Schou (1838–1922) director in 1884; connected with faïence factory "Aluminia" which worked with the porcelain factory from 1885.

1903   19th century impressed   1929

Copenhagen, Store Kongensgade Factory
Faïence made here during the 18th century.

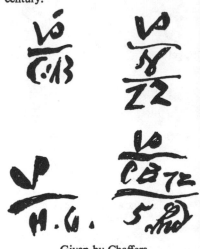

Given by Chaffers

Corn, William and Edward: (*fl.* 19th century)
Began to make earthenware at Burslem, Staffordshire, in 1837; in the 1890s firm gave up making tablewares, and became the Henry Richard Tile Co.

W & EC

Crane, Walter, R. W. S.: (1846–1915)
English general designer, also of pottery and tiles (Wedgwood, 1867–77, Mintons and Pilkingtons); helped to found the Arts and Crafts Society in 1888.
Personal mark:

Creil, Oise, France
English-style earthenware made here from *c.* 1794 to 1895.

!CREIL   CREIL.

Impressed

The transfer-printed mark, in black, of Stone, Coquerel and Le Gros d'Anisy, as a monogram, occurs on white ware printed by these Paris agents, early 19th century:

Creussen, Bavaria
Stoneware made here during the 16th and 17th centuries, the chief potters being the Vest family, who flourished from 1512 onward.

Lorenz Speckner 1618

House marks of the Vest family

Crossed arrows mark
See LA COURTILLE

Crossed L's mark
See SÈVRES.

Crossed swords mark
Taken from the Electoral arms of Saxony, and adopted as the Meissen porcelain factory mark *c.* 1724. On early Meissen the mark is more carefully drawn, with the swords at a wide angle to each other. In the later 18th century, the mark was drawn more freely. For variations see under Meissen.

Some other 18th-century factories were using this mark, often a close imitation, e.g. at Limbach and Volkstedt in Ger-

many, Weesp in Holland, La Courtille, Paris, in France, and Worcester in England.

Limbach, crossed L's with the star similar to Meissen mark of Marcolini period

Volkstedt, rather like 2-pronged forks

Weesp, Holland, crossed swords with 3 dots placed near the blades

La Courtille, Paris, in underglaze blue; crossed flambeaux freely drawn

Worcester

In the 19th century, apart from deliberate forgeries, some firms adopted misleadingly similar signs, e.g. Samson & Co, Paris:

Crossed torches mark
Used by the hard-paste factory of La Courtille, Paris. May be mistaken for a carelessly-drawn Meissen mark. The factory established in 1773, apparently intending to produce imitations of German porcelain.

Cutts, James: (*fl.* 1834–70)
Of Shelton, Staffordshire; designer and engraver of printed earthenware and china, working for most leading firms.

In gold

Cyfflé, Paul Louis: (1724–1806)
Sculptor, working at Lunéville from time to time. Marks on his figures:

All impressed

Cyples family: (*fl.* mid 18th century to mid 19th century)
Potters at Lane End, Staffordshire; Joseph Cyples recorded in 1787; Mary Cyples in 1796; in 1805 Jesse Cyples (d. 1810) was recorded, his sons Richard and William (d. 1865) later working the factory.
Mark given by Chaffers:

I. CYPLES or CYPLES
Incised

CYPLES (impressed) also recorded.

J CYPLES

Dale, John: (*fl.* early 18th century)
Engraver and pottery figure maker, at Burslem, Staffordshire.
Mark recorded:

J.DALE
BURSLEM
Impressed

Dallwitz, Bohemia, Czechoslovakia
Factory founded here 1804 to make earthenware; in 1830 permission was obtained to make porcelain. Various owners included W. W. Lorenz (*c.* 1832), F. Fischer (1850–55), and Franz Urfus (1855–*c.* 1875).

D   DALWITZ

W.W.L.
DALWITZ

FF   FFD   F&U
D
U
DALWITZ

Dalou, Jules: (1838–1912)
French sculptor, who made terracotta figures (various sizes), and also did some work for the Sèvres porcelain factory, between 1879 and 1887.

DALOU

Damm, Aschaffenburg, Germany
Earthenware factory founded here in 1827; became known for reproductions of 18th-century porcelain figures made at Höchst.
The letter D with the old wheel sign of Höchst were used on these.

Dammouse, Pierre-Adolphe: (b. 1817)
Modeller and designer of figures and
ornament at the Sèvres factory from 1852
until 1878, and for Pouyat of Limoges.

Daniell: (*fl.* 19th century)
Dealer whose mark is found on Coalport
and other fine porcelains:

Dannhöfer, Johann Phillipp: (1712–90)
Decorator of pottery and porcelain at the
Vienna factory and elsewhere, e.g.
Höchst, Fulda, and Ludwigsburg.

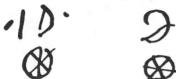

On Höchst faïence

Darte frères: (*fl.* from 1795)
French manufacturers of hard-paste porcelain, in rue de Charonne, Paris.

DARTE
FRERES
A PARIS

Stencilled in red

Davenport family: (*fl.* 1793–1882)
Manufacturers at Longport, Staffordshire; made blue-printed earthenware,
creamware, porcelain, and ironstone
china.

DAVENPORT DAVENPORT
LONGPORT   LONGPORT
        STAFFORDSHIRE

DAVENPORT
LONGPORT
STAFFORDSHIRE.

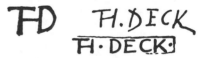

Printed

Dawson, John & Co: (*fl.* 1800–64)
English firm making pottery at Sunderland, Co. Durham.

DAWSON
Impressed

Deck, Théodore: (1823–91)
Generally regarded as the first of the
studio potters. Worked in Paris; was
appointed Director at Sèvres in 1887.

FD   H.DECK
          H·DECK

Impressed   Impressed, incised,
            or transfer-printed

H DECK
O
Impressed

Delaherche, Auguste: (1857–1940)
Made stoneware near Beauvais and
worked in Paris; in 1904 began to make
his own shapes at La Chapelle-aux-Pots
near Beauvais.

Incised or impressed

Delft: De Drie Klokken (The Three Bells)
Factory working from 1671 to 1840.
During the 18th century, mark of the three bells, rather crudely drawn, was used. About the same time Van der Goes also registered the mark WD conjoined. Van Putten & Company worked the factory from 1830 to 1840.

Delft: De Drie Porseleyne Flessies (The Three Porcelain Bottles)
In various ownership from 1679 to after 1764. Hugo Brouwer, coming into possession in 1762, registered his mark in 1764:

Delft: De Drie Vergulde Astonnen (The Three Golden Ashbarrels)
Factory founded in 1655, working under various owners, viz. the Kam family (1674–1720); Zacharias Dextra (1720–59); Hendrick van Hoorn (1759–1803). Continued for a short time by Hoorn's daughter.

G. P. Kam
(also at de Paauw)

Zacharias Dextra

Mark registered in 1764

H. van Hoorn

Delft: De Dubbele Schenkkan (The Double Jug)
Factory apparently founded in 1648, continuing until second half of the 18th century. Most important potter was Louwys Fictoor; his mark was almost identical with that of Lambertus van Eenhoorn.

Louwys Fictoor here 1689–1714 (or Lambertus van Eenhoorn)

Mark registered in 1764

Delft: De Gekroonde Theepot (The Crowned Teapot)
Managed or owned from 1671 until 1708 by Ary Jansz de Milde, followed by his son-in-law and widow.

Delft: De Grieksche A (The Greek A)
Pottery started 1658; Adriaenus Kocks owned it 1687–1701; Jan Theunis Dextra held it 1759–65; Jacobus Halder (or Jacobus Halder Adriaensz) from 1765. The factory closed down in 1820.

Adriaenus Kocks   Jan Theunis Dextra

Jacobus Halder

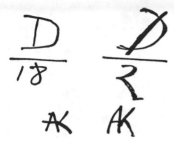

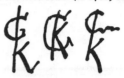

Gerrit Pietersz Kam (*c.* 1700) signed:

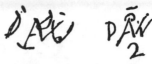

Delft: De Lampetkan (The Ewer)

Factory working from 1609 or 1637 until 1811. For most of the period, the mark was a variant of the initials L.P.K.

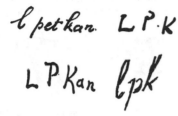

Delft: De Porseleyne Bijl (The Porcelain Hatchet)

Factory working from mid 17th century until 1802 or 1807.

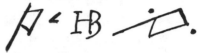

Hugo Brouwer, owner (1716–1807).

Delft: De Porseleyne Fles (The Porcelain Bottle)

Factory working from 1655 until after 1876. Owners included Dirck Harlees (1795–1800) and H. A. Piccardt in 1800.

PICCARDT
DELFT
Impressed

Delft: De Metale Pot (The Metal Pot)

Established 1638, worked under various

owners until 1764.
Lambertus Cleffius
(owner, 1660–91)

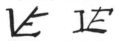

Lambertus van Eenhoorn
(owner, 1691–1721)

Eenhoorn's mark cannot be distinguished from that of Louwys Fictoor

Mark registered by Pieter Paree
(owner, 1759–64)

Delft: De Paauw (The Peacock)

Founded 1651, closed down *c.* 1779. Various owners:

Delft: De Porseleyne Klaeuw (The Porcelain Claw)

Factory working from 1662 until 1850. Claw mark used, freely rendered in many variations:

In conjunction with numerals and initials of owners.

Delft: De Porseleyne Schotel (The Porcelain Dish)

Factory flourishing from 1612 until late 18th century. Among important owners were Johannes Pennis (1702–88) from

1725 to 1764, and Johannes van Duyn from 1764 to 1777.

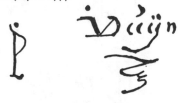

Delft: De Romein (The Rummer)
Factory under various owners from c. 1613 until 1769. Among recorded signatures:

Petrus van Marum (1756–64)

Johannes van der Kloot (1764–69)

Delft: De Roos (The Rose)
Factory working from c. 1666/7 until after 1848.

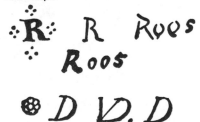

Dirk van der Does
(proprieter, 1760)

18th-century marks

Delft: De Twee Scheepjes (The Two Little Ships)
Factory working from mid 17th century until end of 18th century. Adriaen Pynacker here registered his mark as the monogram A P.

Delft: De Twee Wildemannen (The Two Wildmen)
Factory dates given variously as 1661–1780, 1704–78, and 1756–94.
Willem van Beek was connected with it from 1760 to after 1778.

$$W : V : B$$

Delft: De Vergulde Blompot (The Golden Flowerpot)
Factory working from ?1634 until c. 1741.

Blompot
De Blompot

Delft: De Vergulde Boot (The Golden Boot)
Factory recorded working from 1613 until after 1764.

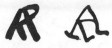

A. Reygens or Reygensberg
(owner 1663–66)

G. L. Kryck (according to Justice),
who took over in 1666; mark
similar to that of G. P. Kam

D K boot

Dirck van der Kest
(manager 1698–1707)

IDA

Johannes den Appel
(working 1759)

See also APPEL, KESSEL, KEST, KRYCK,
REYGENSBURGH.

Delft: De Witte Starre (The White Star)
Faïence factory established 1663, working
until its closure in the early 19th century.
In succession from 1720 came: Cornelis
de Berg, Justus de Berg, Albertus Kiell
(1763–72) and Johannes de Bergh.

Cornelis de   Justus de   Albertus Kiell
Berg   Berg

Johannes de   The White Star
Bergh

Delft: 'T Fortuyn (The Fortune)
Factory working from c. 1661 until after
1770.

P U B

P. van den Briel
(took over 1747)

WVDB

WVDB

Widow van den Briel
(registered mark in 1764)

't Fortuyn
J H F

J. H. Frerkingh
(here in 1769)

LVD   LV

Marks sometimes wrongly attributed to
this factory

Delft: 'T Hart (The Hart)
Founded 1661, working through the 18th
century.

t'hart
T HART HVMD

**Delft: 'T Oude Moriaenshooft (The Old
Moor's Head)**
Factory working from mid 17th century
to about end of 18th century.

Rochus Hoppestein (d. 1692)
proprietor

Del Vecchio, Cherinto:
Made cream-coloured earthenware at
Naples, late 18th century:

**F D V
N**

Standing for Fabbrica del Vecchio Napoli

*del Vecchio
N*

De Morgan, William Frend: (1839–1917)
English potter noted for making reproductions of 16th- and 17th-century Syrian
wares; rediscovered the process of re-
duced lustre decoration. Worked first in
London, then at Merton Abbey, Surrey
(1882–88); in partnership with Halsey
Ricardo at Fulham (1888/9 and again
1898/1907).

Painted

Painted

Impressed

Impressed

Initials of certain painters appear:
J.J. for **Joe Juster**
C.P. for **Charles Passenger**
F.P. for **Fred Passenger**

Denuelle, Domeniquei:
Hard-paste porcelain manufacturer at
Paris and Saint-Yrieix.

*Denuelle
à paris*

Derby, England
Porcelain made here from *c.* 1745(?) to
1848, and again from 1876.

First factory had various owners: by 1756 owned by William Duesbury (d. 1786); then his son William (d. 1796) and son's partner Michael Kean; works bought in 1811 by Robert Bloor, closing in 1848. The present Royal Crown Derby Porcelain Company was formed in 1876.

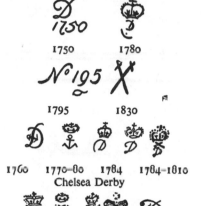

1750   1780

1795   1830

1760   1770–80   1784   1784–1810
Chelsea Derby

1795–96   Imitation

Deruta, Umbria, Italy
Decorative maïolica made here from before 1500, and continued through the 17th century.

Dextra, Zacharias:
Manager from 1712 at De Drie Porseleyne Astonnen.

Dicker, Sussex, England
Slip-decorated red earthenware made here during the 19th century.

'DICKER WARE'

Dillwyn & Co: (*fl.* early 19th century)
English potters at Swansea (q.v.) trading 1810 to 1817 (previously as Haynes, Dillwyn & Co, 1802–10); owners again from 1831 to *c.* 1850.

DILLWYN & Co

Dimmock & Co, Hanley, Staffordshire
Firm making earthenware during the 19th century.

Dirmstein, near Worms, Germany
Faïence and cream-coloured earthenware made here 1778–88; factory founded by the Bishop of Worms.

Taken from the arms of the episcopal see of Worms; very uncommon.

Dixon & Co: (*fl.* 19th century)
English firm working the North Hylton Pottery at Sunderland, Co. Durham (originally founded 1762 by C. Thompson and J. Maling); later trading as Dixon, Austin & Co; and Dixon, Phillips & Co.

DIXON & CO.
DIXON, AUSTIN & CO.
SUNDERLAND
Impressed

Doat, Taxile-Maximilien: (b. 1851)
English sculptor at Sèvres from 1879 to 1905 or later; worked in porcelain and stoneware. Mark the monogram TD:

Doccia, near Florence, Italy
Porcelain made here from 1735 onward, at first under the Ginori family; from latter part of 19th century working as Richard-Ginori.

In blue, red, 18th century Incised In red or gold

Incised

On imitation Capodimonte

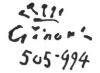

1873–1903	1847–73

1850–1903	19th century

1874–88	1884–91	1883–1900

modern marks

Dolphin mark
(For Dauphin) found stencilled in red on hard-paste porcelain made at Lille from 1784 until 1790 by Leperre-Durot, under the protection of the Dauphin.

Donaldson, John: (1737–1801)
Scotsman, enameller and miniaturist, who came to London (*c.* 1760); became a notable outside porcelain decorator, e.g. for Chelsea and Worcester.
Monogram mark recorded:

Donath: (*fl.* later 19th century)
Dresden decorator of porcelain from 1872.

Don Pottery, Swinton, Yorkshire, England
Earthenware of various types and stonewares made from *c.* 1790 until 1893; factory trading as Greens, Clark & Co (1807); as John William Green & Co (1822); remaining with the Greens until taken over by Samuel Barker in late 1830s.

Painted   Impressed

Transfer-printed

Dorotheenthal, near Arnstadt, Thuringia, Germany
Faïence made here from 1716 until the beginning of the 19th century. A number of painters are recorded:

R.L. Johann Michel Rasslender 1725–40
M F Johann Martin Frantz   1717–29
M B Johann Martin Meiselbach 1733–58

The monogram A B stands for Augustenburg, which was the seat of the Dowager Elizabeth Albertine of Schwarzburg-Sondershausen, sometime patron of the factory.

Douai, Nord, France
Two factories here made English-type earthenware: (1) Leigh's, 1781–1831; and (2) under Dammann 1799–1804, followed by an Englishman, Halfort, 1804–07.

Douai   Leigh & Cie   Halfort

Douai   Douai

Doulton: (*fl. c.* 1815–   )
John Doulton (1793–1837) became partner in Doulton & Watts (1815) at Lambeth, London, making salt-glazed stoneware; firm traded as Doulton & Co from 1854, continuing to present day. Decorative stoneware made at Lambeth from 1870 onward, and at Burslem, Staffordshire, also, from 1877. Bone china made from 1884.

DOULTON
LAMBETH

Before 1836

Artists' (Lambeth) marks recorded include:

Barlow, Arthur Bolton: 1871–78
vegetable forms of decoration

Barlow, Florence: c. 1873
animal decorations

Barlow, Hannah Bolton: c. 1870
incised animal decoration

Broad, John: 1873–1919
figure modeller

Butler, Frank A.: c. 1873

Davis, Louisa: c. 1873

Edwards, Louisa E.: c. 1873

Huggins, Vera: 1932–50

Lee, Francis E.: c. 1875

Marshall, Mark Villars:
1876–1912 figure modeller &
decorator

Mitchell, Mary: c. 1874

Pope, Frank C.: 1880–1923
modeller

Roberts, Florence C.: c. 1879

Rowe, William: c. 1883

Simmance, Elise: c. 1873

Tabor, George Hugo: c. 1878

Thompson, Margaret E.: 1900

Simeon, Henry: 1896

Tinwith, George:
1867–1903 modeller

Dresden

Number of 19th-century manufacturers
working here in Meissen style, some using
marks closely imitating original Meissen:

DONATH	KLEMM
HAMANN	LAMM
HIRSCH	MEYERS & SON
HELENA WOLFSOHN	

Madame Wolfsohn used the Augustus
Rex monogram of the Meissen factory.
Other Dresden marks included:

DRESDEN

Dresden, Saxony, Germany
Faïence made from 1708 to 1784.

Initials D.H. for "Dresden: Hörisch"
used from 1768 until 1784, when Sophie
von Hörisch was proprietor, her son
being director during 1784.

Dudson Bros: (from mid 19th century)
James Dudson made earthenware at Hanley, Staffordshire, from 1835; firm became
Dudson Bros and so continues.

Eastwood, Hanley, Staffordshire, England (*fl.* 18th and 19th centuries)
Cane and brown wares made here by William Baddeley from *c.* 1750; son continued, adding cream ware and black Egyptian; many imitations of Wedgwood made, late 18th and early 19th centuries.
EASTWOOD
Impressed

Eckernförde, Schleswig, Germany
Faïence made here 1764 to 1780.

Edge, Joseph: (1805–93)
Partnered Benjamin Cork (1847) at Burslem, Staffordshire, making Egyptian black, lustred wares, and stonewares; in 1864 firm became Cork, Edge & Malkin; in 1875 Edge, Malkin & Co; pottery was then abandoned for tile-making.

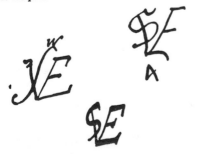

Eenhoorn family: *c.* 1658–85.
Samuel van Eenhoorn worked at De Grieksche A potworks 1674–85. His mark is frequent:

Eenhoorn, Lambertus van: d. 1721
Bought De Metale Pot, Delft, 1691. His widow continued until 1724.

Painted   Impressed on
                           red stoneware

Eichwald, Bohemia
Hard-paste porcelain made here from 1870.

Elbogen
Porcelain manufacture established in 1815, by Springer and Company.

Given by Brongniart and Riocreux

Elers, David: (1656–1742)
Elers, John Philip: (1664–1738)
Dutch brothers making pottery in England; at Fulham and Vauxhall, London, *c.* 1690 to 1700; chiefly famous for their red stonewares, e.g. red teapots made in north Staffordshire, *c.* 1693 for five years. No identifiable marks on Elers' wares.

213

Imitation Chinese marks
stamped underneath Elers' wares

Ellis, James: (*fl.* early 18th century)
Modeller (1818), and earthenware toy
manufacturer (1830), at Shelton, Staffordshire.

J. ELLIS & Co

Impressed

Emens, Jan: (*fl.* 1568–94)
German stoneware potter. Used his
initials I E, I E M, or full name Y A N
E M E N S.

Emery, James: (*fl.* 1837–61)
Made earthenware at Mexborough, Yorkshire, England.

J Emery
Mexbro
1838

Incised

Este, northern Italy
Cream-coloured earthenware made here
from 1785 by Gerolamo Franchini.

ESTE
G   Impressed   GF

Étiolles, Seine-et-Oise, France
Hard-paste porcelain made here from
1768 to *c.* 1780, by Dominique Pellevé
and Jean-Baptiste Monier, with the mark:

MP

Other marks are recorded:

E
Pelleve 1770

Incised

Etiolles
x bre 1770
Pellevé

Incised

Faber, Johann Ludwig: (*fl.* 1678–93)
Nuremberg hausmaler painting on glass
and faïence in schwarzlot, signing with
monogram or initials, J.L.F.

Fabriano, Urbino, Italy
Manufacture of maïolica *c.* 1527 inferred
from an inscribed plate:

fabriano
1527

214

Faenza, Emilia, Italy
Influential centre of maïolica production
from mid 16th century onward.

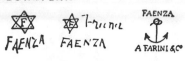

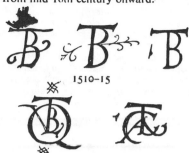

1510–15

1510
On tiles; recorded by Fortnum

Casa Pirota marks

See also FARINI, FERNIANI, CASA
PIROTA.

Farini, A.:
Potter at Faenza, from 1850.

Faubourg Saint-Denis, Paris
(or Faubourg Saint-Lazare)
Hard-paste porcelain made here from
1771 to 1810.

In blue · · · Stencilled in red · · · In colour
1771–76 · · · 1779–93 · · · 1800–10

FLEURY
early 19th century

Fell, Thomas, & Co: (*fl.* 19th century)
Made earthenware at Newcastle, England; recorded at International Exhibition
of 1861.
Marks: Fell & Co, or F. & Co; sometimes with anchor and cable, or arms of
Newcastle, in blue.

FELL

Féraud, Jean Gaspard:
Founded faïence business in Moustiers
in 1779; continued to 1874, worked by
his descendants.

Ferniani, Count Annibale:
Made maïolica at Faenza from 1693;
factory continued by descendants to
present day.

215

Ferrybridge, near Pontefract, Yorkshire, England
(*fl.* 19th century)
Earthenware made here from early 19th century, first by Edwin Tomlinson & Co. Firm traded later as Wigglesworth & Ingham, then as Reed, Taylor & Company until 1851. Other firms followed.
FERRYBRIDGE
(impressed)
TOMLINSON & CO.
(impressed)

F.F., F.F.F., and F.F.O. marks
Attributed to Flaminio Fontana:

See FONTANA FAMILY

Fishley family: (*fl.* from end 18th century through 19th century)
Made pottery at Fremington, Devon, England; five generations included: George Fishley (until 1839); Edmund Fishley (d. 1861); Edwin Beer Fishley (1832–1912).
Mark of latter recorded:
E. B. FISHLEY
FREMINGTON
Given by Jewitt

Fletcher, Thomas: (*fl.* 1786–*c.* 1810)
Black-printer, in partnership with Sampson Bagnall the younger (1786–96), making earthenware at Shelton, Stoke-on-Trent, Staffordshire; on his own account at Shelton from 1796 to *c.* 1810. His prints signed.
T. Fletcher Shelton
or
T. FLETCHER, SHELTON

Fleur-de-lis mark
At Capodimonte, Naples, painted in blue; also in gold, and impressed, 1743–59. At Buen Retiro, Madrid, 1760–1808, the same; incised fleur-de-lis rare.
At Marseilles faïence factory of Honoré Savy, *c.* 1777 onward.
At Sèvres, the fleur-de-lis above the word "Sèvres" and the figures "30", transfer-printed in blue, August-December 1830 only. The Sèvres painter, Taillandier, also used the fleur-de-lis.

Florence, Tuscany, Italy
Centre of great ceramic activity during the Renaissance. Some unidentified marks:

On early 15th-century jar made at or near Florence

Near the base of a Florentine albarello
c. 1450–70

Folche, Stephen: (*fl.* 1820–28)
Made ironstone china at Stoke-on-Trent Staffordshire.
FOLCHE'S GENUINE
STONE CHINA
Given by Chaffers

Fontainebleau, Seine-et-Marne, France
Hard-paste porcelain factory set up here in 1795. Works bought by Jacob and Mardochée Petit in 1830.

Jacob Petit

Godebaki & Co
1875

Fontana family:
Celebrated family of maïolica potters and artists, working in Italy. Originally named Pellipario, of Castel Durante, and mentioned from *c.* 1515 to 1605.
Nicola Pellipario: worked at Castel Durante, *c.* 1515–27; signature found on various pieces, some dated 1521, 1528.

1521

In the Louvre   1528
Orazio Fontana: grandson of Nicola, working from before 1565, dying in 1571.

On dish dated 1541

Other marks on face of dish,
possibly painter's signatures

Forli, Italy
Maïolica made here, 16th century or earlier.

Forsyth, Gordon Mitchell: (1879–1952)
Pottery craftsman, designer, and teacher. Connected with various firms, notably Pilkingtons, Manchester, England (1906–19); produced finely-painted lustre pottery; designed pottery shapes and decoration for Brains of Longton, Pountney of Bristol, etc. (period 1920–44); and finely-gilded and lustred pieces (from 1944) for Grimwades.
Mark: four interlacing scythes, or initials G.M.F. incised.

Incised

Fouque family: (*fl.* 1750 onward)
Made faïence at Moustiers, *c.* 1750–1852.

Fowke, Sir Frederick, Bart: (*fl.* early 19th century)
Established a terracotta works at Lowesby, Leicestershire, England, in 1835, which worked for a few years only. An impressed mark is given by Jewitt.

Frankenthal, Palatinate, Germany
Porcelain made here from *c.* 1755 to
c. 1800.

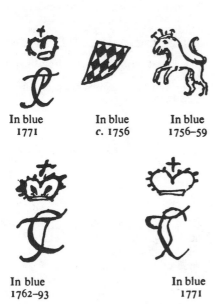

In blue   In blue   In blue
1771   *c.* 1756   1756–59

In blue   In blue
1762–93   1771

From 1770 to 1788 the last two figures of
the year were added.

Frankfort-on-Oder, Brandenburg, Germany
Faïence and earthenware made here from
1763 by Karl Heinrich, who signed H F
or F H, placed one above the other, and
separated by a stroke.

Frankfort-on-Main, Germany
Faïence made here from 1666 to 1772.
Mark: letter F with initials of painters;
dated examples are known.

F.R. or F.L.R. painter: (*fl. c.* 1522)
Initials identified as those of a notable
Faenza figure painter.

Frijtom, Frederick van: (*fl. c.* 1658–)
Delft painter.

F. V. FRYTOM

Fulda, Hesse, Germany
Faïence made here from 1741.

Given by Chaffers
Porcelain made here from 1765 to 1790.
Marks: the letters FF for "Fürstlich-
Fuldaisch", forming the letter H for
Heinrich von Bibra, who founded the
factory.

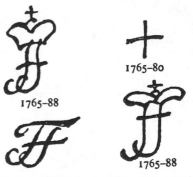

1765–88

1765–80

1765–88

Between 1788 and 1790, FF was arranged
to form a letter A, for Adalbert von
Harstall; this is rare.

Fulham, London, England
John Dwight of Fulham took out a patent
in 1671 to make "transparent earthenware" and stoneware: followed by Margaret Dwight and others of the family;
in 1862 factory owned by MacIntosh
& Clements; in 1864 by a Mr Baker;
trading today as the Fulham Pottery and
Cheavin Filter Co.
Mark recorded on a piece of brown-
glazed stoneware (British Museum,
London):

Fulham
Pottery
c. 1811
No other marks known to have been used.

Fürstenberg, Brunswick, Germany
Porcelain made here 1747–1859, and onward.

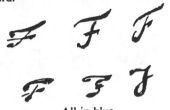

All in blue

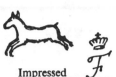

Impressed
on biscuit reliefs
   In blue on
   19th-century
   reproductions
   from old moulds

Modern mark

Gallé, Emile: (1846–1904)
Artist at Nancy; did experimental work
in the ceramic field.

**GALLE
NANCY**

E F G
Dépisé

E.Galle à Nancy

Garrison Pottery, Sunderland, Durham,
England
Various earthenwares made here from
the early 19th century; factory first owned
by Phillips & Co.
> PHILLIPS & CO.
> Sunderland (date)
> PHILLIPS & CO.
> Sunderland Pottery

Later the firm was Dixon, Austin Phillips
& Co.
> DIXON, AUSTIN & CO.
> Sunderland Pottery
> DIXON & CO.
> Sunderland Pottery

Gély, J.: (*fl.* 1851–88)
Decorative artist at Sèvres, working in
the pâte-sur-pâte technique.

J.G.

Gera, Thuringia, Germany
Faïence made here 1752–*c.* 1780.

Gien
Factory here made imitations of 16th-
century Italian maïolica.

   GIEN

Giovine, Raffaele: (*fl.* 1826–60)
His workshop decorated imported French
porcelain.

Giovine in Napoli

In red

Giustiniani family: (*fl. c.* 1760 onward)
Made porcelain and earthenware at
Naples.

Giustiniani   GIUSTINIANI
   Impressed

G   Giustiniani
   I Ọ N

Given by Chaffers
Other marks:
BG or BG over an N, for Biagio
   Giustiniani
F.M.G.N.   for Fabbrica Michele Giust-
   iniani Napoli
F.G.N.   for Fratelli Giustiniani
   Napoli

219

Glass, John: (*fl.* 1787–1834)
Made common earthenware and Egyptian black at Hanley, Staffordshire.

GLASS
HANLEY
Impressed

Glienitz, Silesia, Germany
Faïence factory established here in 1753; in 19th century turned to cream-coloured earthenware and white-glazed earthenware.
18th-century mark: letter G or GG painted, the latter standing for Gaschin-Glienitz (Countess Anna), 1767–80.
Mark from 1830: place-name GLINITZ over letter M (for Mittelstadt), or letter G impressed.

Goincourt, Oise, France
Faïence factory called "L'Italienne" started here in 1793.

L' ITALIENNE

L' Italienne

Impressed

Gordon, William: (*fl.* 1939–)
Sculptor and studio potter; experimented at Chesterfield, Derbyshire, England, in 1939, making salt-glazed stoneware at the Walton Pottery Co since 1946.

Goss, William Henry, F. G. S.: (1833–1906)
English manufacturer of ivory porcelain at Stoke-on-Trent, Staffordshire, England (1858 onward); noted for Goss's Armorial China; made decorative objects in third quarter of 19th century.

W H GOSS COPYRIGHT

Impressed

Gotha, Thuringia, Germany
Hard-paste porcelain factory established here in 1757; continues.

1757–83   1783–1805

1805–

Gouda, Holland
Tin-enamelled earthenware made here from 1621 (originator Willem Jansz). Three modern factories exist here.

ZENITH Gouda
HAND PAINTED

Goult, near Apt, France
Faïence made here from 1740 to *c.* 1805.

Given by Jännicke

Grainger, Thomas: (d. 1839)
Founded porcelain factory at Worcester, England, in 1801, decorating "white" from Caughley, etc.; later made porcelain with mark of Grainger Lee & Co; finally absorbed by Royal Worcester firm, 1889.

GRAINGER LEE & CO
WORCESTER
1801-62

GRAINGER
& Co

Grainger Lee & Co
Worcester
Printed in red

George Grainger
Royal China Works
Worcester

In red: 1801-62   Printed: after 1823

Gray, A. E., & Co: (from 1912–)
Pottery decorating business founded by
A. E. Gray in 1912 at Hanley; later at
Stoke, Staffordshire, using "white" wares
from Johnson Bros and others.

Transfer-printed
in colours

Green, Stephen: (*fl.* first half of 19th
century)
Made salt-glazed stoneware at Lambeth,
London; factory bought by John Cliff
in 1858; closed down in 1869.

Or: "Stephen Green, Imperial Potteries,
Lambeth" (impressed).

Green, T. G. & Co: (*fl.* 19th century)
Made earthenware at Church Gresley,
Staffordshire, from 1864, succeeding
previous firms.
Numerous marks used, with name of
firm, type of ware, or pattern.

Greenock, Renfrewshire, Scotland
White and cream-coloured earthenware
made here from 1810s, at several factories, including the Clyde Pottery (1816–
1903); the Greenock Pottery has worked
from 1860 onwards.

Greenwood, S: (*fl. c.* 1780–*c.* 1790)
Believed to have owned a pottery at
Fenton, Staffordshire.
Signature recorded on black basalt vase
(British Museum, London):
S. GREENWOOD
Stamped

Grenzhausen, Rhineland, Germany
Hard stoneware made in the Westerwald
district here, from 15th century onward,
and again in the 19th century.

**WESTERWÄLDER
NEVKERAMIK**

Mark of Merkelbach & Wick (from 1873)

Grocott, Samuel: (*fl.* 1822–28)
Made earthenware toys and figures at Tunstall, Staffordshire. Possibly partner in firm using mark:
EDGE & GROCOTT
Impressed

Groszbreitenbach, Thuringia, Germany
Hard-paste porcelain made here during later 18th century. From 1869 the firm was Bühl & Söhne.

Grünstadt, Rhineland, Germany
Factory run by Bordello and family flourished from 1812 to late 19th century.

Given by Jännicke

Gubbio, Urbino, Italy
Maïolica and lustred wares made here during the 16th century. Famous lustre painter Giorgio Andreoli, or Maestro Giorgio, worked here (*c.* 1518 onward), likewise his son Vincenzo.

Note also the 19th-century firm of Carocci, Fabbri & Company.

Gudumland, Denmark
Cream-coloured earthenware and faïence made here from 1804 until 1820.

In brown   Impressed

Gustafsberg, Sweden
Pottery made from 1786 and during the 19th century, up to the 1860s.
Modern revival from *c.* 1900.

Gutenbrunn
Porcelain made here 1769–75.
Mark of initials PZ found, standing for Pfalz-Zweibrücken, where the Gutenbrunn factory had originated in 1767.

Haarlem, Holland
Maïolica made here from *c.* 1572.

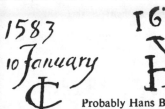

Probably Cornelis
Lubbertsz

Probably Hans Barnaert
Vierleger

In blue
overglaze or underglaze

Haile, Sam: (d. 1948)
English potter and teacher.

Hackl, Joseph: (*fl. c.* 1749–68)
Factory owner and modeller of faïence,
perhaps also an outside decorator.
German.

Mark attributed to him

Halfort: (*fl.* 1804–07)
English potter at earthenware factory at
Douai.

HALFORT

Halfort & Cie

Hackwood, William (d. 1849) **& Son:**
(*fl.* 1818–53)
Made earthenware at Shelton, Staffordshire.

Transfer-printed

Hall, John and Ralph: (first half 19th
century)
Staffordshire potters working together
(1805–22) at Tunstall and Burslem; then
separately: Ralph at Tunstall, as Hall &
Co, or Hall & Holland (*c.* 1846–49);
John, with sons, at Burslem (bankrupt
1832).
Blue-printed earthenware for the American market made by both firms.
Mark recorded on enamelled figures:

Impressed

Hague, The, Holland
Hard-paste porcelain made here *c.* 1776–
94; also decorating of Meissen and
Ansbach hard-paste porcelain and of
Tournay soft-paste porcelain.

Hamann: (working *c.* 1866)
Dresden porcelain decorator.

Hanau, Hesse, Germany
Faïence made here from 1661 to 1806.

Hancock, Robert: (1729/30–1817)
English engraver; probably at Bow 1756
briefly, then at Worcester (partner 1772–
74); joined Turner at Caughley 1775; at
Bristol 1796; at London 1808.

R. Hancock fecit

RH. Worcester

RH Worcester

R. H. f.

Hancock, Sampson: (*fl.* mid 19th century)
Owned china factory at Derby, England.

In red

Harding, W. & J.: (*fl.* mid 19th century)
Made cream-coloured and transfer-print-
ed ware, etc., at the New Hall factory,
Shelton, Staffordshire (recorded 1864–69).

Transfer-printed

Harley, Thomas: (1778–1832)
Worked as enameller, black printer, and
earthenware manufacturer (from 1801);
in 1818 the firm styled Harley and Secker-
son; at Lane End, Staffordshire.
T. Harley Lane End
HARLEY
Impressed
Given by Chaffers

Harmer, Jonathan: (*fl.* 1800–1820)
English potter making terracotta insets
for gravestones and tombs, working at
Heathfield in Sussex.
Some found signed:

HARMER FECIT

Harvey, Charles & Son: (*fl.* first half 19th
century)
Made china, earthenwares, gold lustre,
etc. at Longton, Staffordshire, from 1799
for some years; and again 1841–53.

Transfer-printed

Hauer, Bonaventura Gottlieb: (1710–82)
Painter at Meissen.
Work signed with initials B G H or,
rarely, in full.

Haviland & Co:
Founded 1892 to make Limoges porcelain mainly for the American market.

Haviland, David: (*fl.* 1842–)
American who became a naturalised
Frenchman, and founded a pottery works
at Limoges.

Haviland
France

Haviland, Theodore:
Founder of hard-paste porcelain factory at Limoges (?late 19th century).

Théodore Haviland
Limoges
FRANCE

Hawley, Thomas: (*fl.* early 19th century)
Identity doubtful. Potters of this surname working in both Yorkshire and Staffordshire in the 19th century.
Mark recorded on a bust of John Wesley:

THO HAWLEY

Impressed

Heathcote, C. & Co: (*fl.* early 19th century)
Made decorated earthenware at Longton, Staffordshire.
Mark recorded:
Prince of Wales feathers, with the name C. HEATHCOTE & CO. in an arc above.

Heel, Johann: (1637–1709)
Nuremberg decorator of faïence.

Heinrich & Co: (founded 1904)
Made hard-paste porcelain at Selb in Bavaria.

Helchis, Jacobus: (*fl. c.* 1738–*c.* 1748)
Porcelain decorator, believed to have worked some time at Vienna. Covered cup (British Museum, London) signed "Jakob Helchis fecit".

Heraldic label

Attributed to various factories:
Orléans, soft-paste porcelain (1753–70)
Boisette, hard-paste porcelain (1777–92)
Also ascribed to Chantilly and Vincennes.
Used by Vieillard (1752–90), Sèvres painter of emblems.

Herend, Hungary
Porcelain factory founded 1839, directed by Moritz Fischer; specialised in copies of European and Oriental porcelain, especially Sèvres, Capodimonte, etc.

HEREND

Herculaneum, Liverpool, England
Factory founded 1793; passing through various ownerships; made earthenware, stoneware, and, from 1801, porcelain of the Staffordshire type.

HERCULANEUM
Impressed

(so-called
liver bird)

Variants recorded:
Crown enclosed by a garter inscribed
HERCULANEUM;
HERCULANEUM POTTERY impressed;
liver bird surrounded by a floral wreath,
with the word HERCULANEUM in
an arc above, and a scroll inscribed
LIVERPOOL beneath (printed in red).

Herold, Christian Friedrich: (1700–79)
Decorator at Meissen from 1726, best
known for chinoiserie harbour scenes, etc.
Cup and saucer, with gold relief applied
to the porcelain (British Museum,
London) is signed:
C. F. HEROLD INVT. ET FECIT
A MEISSE 1750.d.12 Sept.

Herold, or Höroldt, Johann Gregor:
(1696–1776)
Director at Meissen, 1731–56, and again
1763–65. Chemist responsible for many
fine colours. Signed pieces noted: on a
vase with yellow ground "Johann Gregorius Höroldt inv Meissen den 22 Jann
Anno 1727"; on another vase "J. G. Höroldt fec. Meissen 17 Augusti 1726".

Herrebøe, near Friedrichshald, Norway
Factory founded here by Peter Hofnagel
(1721–81), making the first Norwegian
faïence in 1759; factory making domestic
ware until c. 1778.
Marks, 2-tiered arrangement of initials,
HB for Herreboe over those of the
decorator.
Artists:
Johann Georg Kreipe, foreman or manager, 1760-64
Joseph Large (1742–93), painter
Gunder Large (1744–1818), modeller
H. F. L. Hosenfelder (1722–1805) working
1762–72

Hicks & Meigh: (*fl.* 1810–35)
Manufactured decorated earthenware and
ironstone china at Shelton, Staffordshire.

Printed

High Halden, Kent, England
Country pottery existed here in the 19th
century, using slip decoration and inlaid
technique.
Mark recorded:
HALDEN POTTERY
On a moneybox, with inlaid name,
J. G. DUDEN

Hilditch: (various 19th-century firms)
English potters at Lane End and Lane
Delph, Staffordshire:
Hilditch & Co. (*c.* 1805–13)
Hilditch & Martin (1818)
Hilditch & Son (1820s)
Hilditch & Hopwood (1830–67)

Hirsch, Franziska:
Decorator of porcelain at Dresden, 20th
century.

Hispano-Moresque pottery
No potters' marks can be identified with certainty.

Höchst, near Mayence, Germany
Porcelain made here from 1750 to 1798.

Wheel mark in red or other coloured enamel, *c.* 1750–62; wheel mark in blue 1762–96; crowned wheel mark *c.* 1765–74; impressed wheel mark, of six spokes, *c.* 1760–65.
Faïence made here from 1750 to 1758. Marks used: the four- or six-spoke wheel together with painted initials or signatures. Other forms given by Chaffers include an eight-spoke wheel surmounted by a crown and a circle enclosing a six-point star:

Artists:
Georg Friedrich Hesse 1746–51
Ignatz Hesse 1746–51
Johannes Zeschinger 1748–53
Adam Ludwig 1749–58
Joseph Philipp Dannhöfer 1747–51
Pressel 1748

Holdcroft, Joseph: (*fl.* from 1870)
Made parian, maïolica, and lustre ware at Longton, Staffordshire.

Impressed

Holdship, Richard, and Josiah: (*fl.* mid 18th century)
Engravers and part-proprietors of original porcelain works at Worcester, England, 1751–59; Richard at Derby (recorded 1764). Some Worcester engravings have signature of Hancock in full, accompanied by a rebus design of R H in monogram and an anchor; these marks traditionally thought to stand for Holdship, but may stand for Hancock.

Much confusion has arisen owing to Robert Hancock and Richard Holdship having the same initials.

Holdsworth, Peter (*fl.* 1945–   )
Founded the Holdsworth Potteries at Ramsbury, near Marlborough, Wiltshire, England, in 1945.

Holitsch, Hungary
Maïolica factory founded here in 1743. Usual mark the letter H:

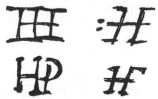

In blue, manganese purple, or light green.
Other marks included:
H.F for Holitscher Fabrik
HH for Holitscher Herrschaft
HP for Holicske Panstvi
On cream-coloured earthenware the mark
consisted of the word HOLICS, HO-
LITSCH or HOLITSH, impressed.

Hollins, T. & J.: (*fl.* second half 18th
century)
Potters making stonewares in the Wedg-
wood style at Hanley, Staffordshire;
business founded by the father, Richard
Hollins, in 1750.
T. & J. HOLLINS
Impressed

Hoorn, Hendrik van: (d. 1803)
Recorded as owner of De Drie Vergulde
Astonnen factory, Delft, in 1759.

H V̸hoorn

Hoppestein, Jacob Wemmersz:
Proprietor of T'Oude Moriaenshooft,
Delft, about 1680.

] W ⚹ ⚹ iw

Hoppestein, Rochus Jacobs: (d. 1692)
At T'Oude Moriaenshooft, Delft; his
widow carried on until 1714.

Honiton, Devon, England
Various potters recorded here, e.g. Susan
Hussey (1850); James Webber (*c.* 1880);
Foster and Hunt, taken over in 1918 by
C. Collard, who in turn sold to present
proprietors in 1947.

COLLARD
HONITON
ENGLAND

NORMAN HULL
POTTERY
N.T.S. Hull

Honoré, François-Maurice:
Founder of hard-paste porcelain factory
in Paris in 1785; also associated with
Dagoty until the 1820s.

*Dagoty
à paris*   *Ed. Hon. ...*

Hubertusburg, Saxony, Germany
Faïence factory established here in 1770,
continuing until 1814, when it passed to
the Government. Weigel and Messer-
schmidt manufactured here from 1835
until 1848.

*H
T
X S*

K S St F
HUBERTUSBURG

Wedgwood

Impressed
K.S.ST.F. stands for Königliche säch-
sische Steingut-Fabrik.

Hull, Yorkshire, England
Belle Vue Pottery
Potworks originally started here in 1802,
closing some time after 1806; William
Bell bought the pottery in 1825, working
it until 1840; decorated creamware made
here.
Marks recorded:

Impressed

Transfer-printed

Hunslet Hall, Leeds, Yorkshire, England
Cream-coloured and blue-printed earthenware made here from *c.* 1792 by Petty and Rainforth.

RAINFORTH & CO.
Impressed: 1790s

Continued until 1880 or later, under various names.

1818 Petty & Co. 1822 Petty & Hewitt
1825 Samuel Petty & Son 1847 John Mills

Hunting horn mark
Adopted by the Chantilly factory in 1725; rendered in many forms.

The mark was imitated on porcelain made at Worcester and Caughley.

Hutschenreuther, C. M.: (*fl.* 1814 onward)
Founded hard-paste porcelain factory at Hohenberg, Bavaria, which was continued by his widow and descendants. Both useful and luxury porcelain was made from 1860.

Hutschenreuther, Lorenz: (*fl. c.* 1856–)
Firm founded at Selb, Bavaria, making hard-paste porcelain.

Ilmenau, Thuringia, Germany
Hard-paste porcelain factory founded here in 1777 by C. Z. Gräbner; bought by Christian Nonne in 1808, who worked it with his son-in-law named Roesch.

i   &R   N & R

Initialist I.B.
The initials "I.B." occur with some frequency, either alone or in combination with other initials, on slipwares of Staffordshire type, some dating 1690–1700. May stand for Isaac Ball, a father and son of this name being recorded; Isaac the son (christened 1669 at Burslem) is mentioned in the Wedgwood MS list of early 18th-century potters as working at Burslem.

Initialist I.S.
Possibly for John Simpson of Chell, potter at Rotten Row, Burslem, Staffordshire (1710–15);
or for Joseph Simpson of Newcastle-under-Lyme, potting in the same locality.

Initialist R.F.
The initials R.F. which occur with some frequency on slipwares of the late 17th/early 18th centuries may stand for Ralph or Richard Fletcher, both being listed as inhabitants of Burslem, Staffordshire, in 1671.

Isleworth, Middlesex, England
Factory established here *c.* 1760 by Joseph Shore, and later owned by Richard and William Goulding; closed down *c.* 1825. Made slipwares.

S & G

Jever, Oldenburg, Germany
Faïence factory working from 1760 to 1776.

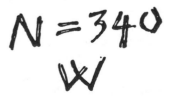

Given by Chaffers   Given by Stöhr

Johanneum mark
Named after the building in Dresden which housed the Royal Saxon collection of porcelain, including Chinese and Japanese export ware. Collection begun by Augustus the Strong, and porcelain identified by inventory marks engraved on the wheel and coloured black:

Johnson Bros: (1883–
English potters, whos
in 1883 by four brothe
wares at Hanley and
shire, continuing today

JOHNSON BR
MADE IN
ENGLAND

Johnson, Reuben and Phoebe: (*fl.* ... 8–40)
Reuben Johnson recorded as making lustred china and fancy earthenware at Hanley, Staffordshire, in 1818; factory listed in 1834 under name of his widow, Phoebe Johnson (Phoebe Johnson & Son, 1836).

JOHNSON
HANLEY
Stone China

Keeling, Anthony: (1738–1815)
Made pottery at Tunstall, Staffordshire, from 1783 to 1810; in 1802 Anthony and E. Keeling were working two factories in Burslem, with the mark:
A. & E. KEELING

Keeling, Toft & Co: (*fl.* 1806–24)
Made Egyptian black and other contemporary earthenwares; succeeded by Toft & May, working until 1830.
KEELING, TOFT & CO.
Impressed

Kellinghusen, Holstein, Germany
Faïence made here from *c.* 1765.

$$\frac{K \cdot H}{B}$$
$$E$$

Carsten Behren's factory *c.* 1765 onwards

Joachim Möller, 1785–95

Dr. Sebastian Grauer, 1795–1820

c. 1800

Kelsterbach, Hesse-Darmstadt, Germany
Faïence factory founded at Königstadt
c. 1758; transferred to Kelsterbach in
1761, closing 1835. Cream-coloured
earthenware made in the later years.

K

For Königstadt or
Kelsterbach; early mark

In blue or impressed on
cream-coloured ware
late 18th century

Hard-paste porcelain made here from
1761 to 1768, and again from 1789 to
1802.

In blue: In blue:
rare before 1789   Lay's period (*c.* 1789)

Kemp, Dorothy: (20th century)
English studio potter and teacher; makes
lead-glazed earthenware, slip-decorated
pottery, and stoneware.

(

Kiel, Holstein, Germany
Faïence factory established here in 1763,
under J. S. F. Tännich, succeeded by
J. Buchwald, and closing *c.* 1788.
Marks usually three-tiered, with initial
of factory, manager, and artist, and
occasionally, last figures of date and
other figures.

Kiel/Tännich/Christopherson
Artists
C for Christopherson
K for Kleffel
A.L. for Abraham Leihamer

Kiev, Russia
Cream-coloured earthenware made here
from end of 18th century.

KIEBZ.

Porcelain made by M. Gulina is marked:

Kilnhurst pottery, Swinton, Yorkshire, England
Kilnhurst Old Pottery established in 1746 by William Malpas; eventually taken over by Joseph Twigg & Brothers in 1839; continued in hands of Twigg family until 1881, using the marks:

 TWIGG'S

Impressed

Kishere, Joseph: (*fl.* up to 1811)
Made salt-glazed stoneware at Mortlake, Surrey, England; pieces found marked:
Kishere Pottery, Mortlake Surry
Impressed

Klemm, K. R.: (*fl.* from *c.* 1869)
Decorator at Dresden, in style of Meissen factory.

Klösterle, or Klásteric, Bohemia, Czechoslovakia
Porcelain and earthenware factory established here in 1793, continuing through 19th century.

Kloster-Veilsdorf, Thuringia, Germany
Hard-paste porcelain factory established here in 1760.

1760 onwards 1765 1760 onwards

Imitation Also used on Modern
Meissen Ilmenau, Grosz- mark
    breitenbach and
    Limbach porcelain

Kocks, Adriaenus: (*fl.* 1687–1701)
Proprietor of De Grieksche A pottery, Delft, from 1687 until his death in 1701.

Korzec, or Koretzki, Poland
Hard-paste porcelain made here from *c.* 1790 until factory transferred in 1797 to Gorodnitza, where it closed in 1870. Mark, an eye drawn in geometric convention:

Kunersberg, near Memmingen, Germany
Faïence made here from 1754 to *c.* 1768.

Other marks recorded: the initials K B, separately, or in monogram.

La Charité-sur-Loire, Nièvre, France
Earthenware factory established here in
1802.

LA-CHARITÉ
Impressed

La Courtille, or Rue Fontaine-au-Roy,
or Basse Courtille, Faubourg du Temple,
Paris
Hard-paste porcelain factory established
here in 1771, closing in 1841.

Incised   In blue   In blue

Lake, W. T.: (20th century)
English manufacturer of earthenware and
redware at Truro, Cornwall.
Mark:

LAKE'S
CORNISH
POTTERY
TRURO

Lakin & Poole: (*fl.* 1791–95)
Potters at Burslem, Staffordshire, making
blue-printed earthenware, etc.; trading as
Poole, Lakin, & Shrigley in 1795; soon
after, Lakin withdrew, Poole and Shrigley
becoming bankrupt in 1797.
LAKIN & POOLE
Impressed

Lamm, A.: (*fl.* from 1887)
Dresden porcelain decorator working in
the Meissen style.

Lammans, B., Andenne, Belgium
Made white and cream earthenware from
1794 until 1820.

BD LS & Cⁱᵉ
Impressed   On transfer-printed ware

La Moncloa, or Florida, Madrid
Factory working from 1817 until 1850.

Landais: (*fl.* 19th century)
Copyist of Henri Deux and Palissy
wares.

Landore pottery, Swansea, South Wales
Earthenware factory established here in
1848 by John Forbes Calland; closed
down in 1856.
J F CALLAND & CO
LANDORE POTTERY
CALLAND
SWANSEA

Langenthal, Switzerland
Porcelain factory established here in 1906.

La Rochelle, Charente-Inférieure, France
Faïence made here in the 18th century,
from 1722. Most important factory was
that of De Bricqueville, founded in 1743.
Marks recorded:

La Tour D'Aigues, Vaucluse, France
Faïence factory founded here in 1753,
using the mark:
Given by Jännicke, Chaffers, and others

Leach, Bernard: (1887–)
Studio potter, founding the St Ives Pottery, Cornwall, England, in 1920, making slipware and stoneware.

Bernard Leach

David Leach
(pupil of Bernard Leach)

Leach, Margaret: (*fl.* 1947–)
Studio potter, making slipware, marked:

Leeds, Yorkshire, England
The Old Pottery: (*c.* 1760–1878)
Established at Hunslet, Leeds (not to be confused with the later factories of Hunslet Hall, and Rothwell, in the same district), *c.* 1760 by the two Green brothers, later trading as Hartley, Greens & Co, and making fine cream-coloured earthenware in quantity (*c.* 1780–1820) with pierced or basket-work; sold in 1825, trading successively as S. Wainwright & Co; the Leeds Pottery Co; and Warburton, Britton & Co.

Impressed

Impressed: *c.* 1864

Lefebvre, Denis: (*fl.* 1631–49)
Painter working at Nevers.
Mark recorded:

Lei, Pietro: (*fl.* 18th century)
Maïolica painter at Sassuolo and Pesaro.
Dated mark recorded:

C:C
Pesaro
1765
P:p:L:

Leigh, Charles and James:
English potters trading at Douai from 1781; faïence factory continued to 1831.
Impressed

Le Montet, Saône et Loire, France
Mark used on white stoneware, of 9th-century date:

Le Nove, Italy
Porcelain made here *c.* 1762 to 1835. Monogram GBA stands for Giovanni Battista Antonibon, original founder. The usual mark from 1781 was a six-point star, or the word NOVE incised on

234

figures, etc. The letter N incised on later tablewares may stand for Nove or be a workman's mark.

✳	*Nove* ✳	✴
In red	In gold	In blue
✳		✳
In gold		In red

NOVE
Gio.ᵗ Marconi pinx era
In gold

G.B.
NOVE *G.B Nove* ✴
In colour In blue

Nove

Unexplained marks, possibly of owners:

MGS **X** **A.G**
B
In gold In red

Lenzburg, Switzerland
Faïence made here from 1763 for a few years by Heinrich Klug. Faïence painter Jacob Frey or Hans Jacob Frey had a workshop from 1775 to 1790.
Numerous marks; initials accepted:
  L B for Lenzburg
  H K for Heinrich Klug
  H F for Hans Frey

Leroy, Louis: (d. 1788)
Faïence manufacturer at Marseilles from 1750. Signature recorded:
Fabque De Marslle Le Roy

Lessore, Emile: (d. 1876)
Porcelain painter: at Sèvres until 1850, then in Paris; in England 1858, a few months at Mintons, then at Wedgwoods at Etruria until 1863; then returned to France.

Emile Lessore
L3 *E Lessore*
E Lessore
E. Lessore
E Lessore

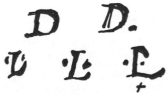

Lesum, near Bremen, Germany
Faïence factory established here in 1755 by Johann Christoph Vielstick (1722–1792 /1800). Mark: the letter V or VI over initial of the painter separated by a dash.

Liège, Belgium
Faïence made here from 1752 until 1811. The name "Boussemaert" also occurs.

L ⬒ G

Lille, France
Soft-paste porcelain made here from 1711 until 1730. Mark ascribed:

ℬ

Other marks formerly ascribed to Lille:

D **D.**
L **·L** **·L+**

Hard-paste porcelain made here by Le-perre-Durot, from 1784 to 1790; after which it passed from hand to hand, closing down in 1817.

Stencilled

The dolphin was adopted because the factory was protected by the Dauphin. Faïence made here from 1696 to 1802; a tileworks also flourished from 1740 to 1808.

by Alluaud 1788; firm traded as Alluaud during the first half of the 19th century, becoming Charles Field Haviland in 1886. A large number of factories worked from the 1820s onward, the best known being Haviland & Company, and Charles Field Haviland (1833–96).

For the Comte d'Artois protector of the factory until 1784

Selection from large number of 19th-century marks:

Limbach, Thuringia, Germany
Porcelain factory founded here in 1772 by Gotthelf Greiner, worked after his death (1797) by his sons, trading as Gotthelf Greiner-Sohne.

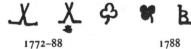

1772–88   1788

Limoges, Haute-Vienne, France
Faïence factory established here, working from 1736 to 1773.
Mark recorded:
The place-name, Limoges, with various dates.
Hard-paste porcelain factory established in 1783 by Massié, Fourniera and Grellet; taken over by the King of France, 1784; Grellet junior was succeeded as manager

Serpaut

C. Tharaud

Martial Redon
from 1853
(d. 1890)

CFH
GDM
FRANCE

Charles Field
Haviland
in green
1881–91

Porcelaine Mousseline

Theodore Haviland & Company
(Theodore died 1919)

J. Pouyat

L. Sazaret
from *c.* 1850

L. Sazaret

In green

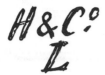

France

Impressed
Haviland and Co.

Haviland
France

A. Lanternier E. Madesclaire J. Granger
1855   jeune   et cie

Lindemann, George Christoph: (*fl.* 1758–
c. 1767)
Painter on porcelain, e.g. flowers, landscape and figure subjects, at Nymphenburg (1758–60).
Mark recorded: initials of artist, G.C.L.,
with date, 1758; another signature (Meissen) dated 1767; also occurs on Tournay
pieces.

Linthorpe, Yorkshire, England
Factory established here in 1879 by John
Harrison, making "Art" pottery of extra-
vagant form; closed 1889. Christopher
Dresser worked here.

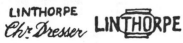

Impressed

Lisieux, France
Faïence tiles and pottery made here from
mid 17th century.
Mark recorded:

Given by Jännicke and Graesse

Lissim, Simon: (1900–   )
Stage and ceramic designer, working in
France, *c.* 1921 to 1940, in U.S.A. from
1940 onward.
Mark: the initials SL in monogram.

Liverpool, Lancashire, England
Delftware made here (*c.* 1710–*c.* 1780)
and porcelain (second half 18th century),
but marks are almost unknown; numerals
occur on various types of delftware;
numbers used are said to be higher at
Liverpool than at either Bristol or Lambeth.

Livesley, Powell & Co: (*fl. c.* 1850 until
fairly recent times)
China and earthenware made at Hanley,
Staffordshire, by William Livesley & Co
from *c.* 1850; firm traded successively as:
Wm. Livesley & Co
Livesley, Powell & Co
Powell & Bishop (from 1865)
Powell, Bishop & Stonier
Bishop & Stonier

Impressed

Lloyd, John: (1805–51)
and Lloyd, Rebecca:
Made earthenware and china toys at
Hanley, Staffordshire (*c.* 1834 to after
1851).

Impressed

Lockett firm: (*fl.* from *c.* 1786 onward)
Staffordshire potters trading successively
under the family name with variations;
Timothy and John Lockett made earthen-

ware at Burslem, Staffordshire (1786–
c. 1802); moved to Lane End (1802), then
as J. & G. Lockett; later names:
John Lockett & Co (1818–30s)
John Lockett (d. 1835) & Son
John & Thomas Lockett (recorded 1851
and 1875)
John Lockett & Co (1889 onward)
Early members apparently made salt-
glazed stoneware; mark recorded:
J. LOCKETT
Impressed

Lodi, Lombardy, Italy
Maïolica made here by Simpliciano Fer-
retti from 1725.
Mark: SF in monogram.
See also ROSSETTI

Lodovico, Maestro: (*fl. c.* 1540)
Venetian maïolica painter; inscription
recorded:
In Venetia in Cotrada di Sto Polo in
botega di Mo Lodouico

Longton Hall, Staffordshire, England
Porcelain factory established here c. 1750;
closed down 1760. William Littler in
partnership here with Aaron Wedgwood,
trading as Littler & Co, 1752–60.
Crossed L's appear in several forms, and
may stand for Littler, Longton.

In blue
under the glaze

Longwy, Lorraine, France
Faïence and earthenware made here
during 18th and 19th centuries; factory
owned by Huart de Northomb c. 1840.

Impressed

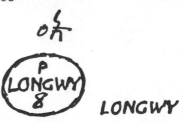

LONGWY

In black and impressed

Lovatt's Potteries, Langley Mill, Notting-
ham, England
Manufacturers of earthenware.

Another mark: words "LANGLEY
Pottery" superimposed upon a windmill.

Löwenfinck, Adam Friedrich von: (1714–
54)
First a painter of porcelain (Meissen
1727–c. 1736), then at Bayreuth and
Chantilly; made faïence at Fulda (1741–
45), where signature recorded: F.v.L.
with arms of Fulda. Made faïence at
Höchst (c. 1745–49) and later at other
places.

Lowestoft, Suffolk, England
Factory making soft-paste porcelain
established here in 1757, lasting until
1802.
No mark consistently used, but numerals
up to 28, often in underglaze blue, inside
the footring, are found on some pieces.
Factory marks of Worcester, Meissen,
and other factories sometimes imitated:

Lücke, Johann Christoph Ludwig von:
(d. 1780)
Ivory carver known to have been modeller
and repairer at Vienna in 1750; signature
recorded on Vienna porcelain figures,
etc., as "L. v. Lücke."

Ludwigsburg, Württemberg, Germany
Hard-paste porcelain made here from 1758 until 1824.

Usually in blue, occasionally in red: 1758–93

Painted in blue: 1758–93

Stags horns, from arms of Württemberg, painted in blue: late 18th or early 19th century

Duke Ludwig
1793–95

King William
1816–24

King Friedrich
1806–16
impressed, or
painted in gold
or red

A number of painters' and repairers' marks are known, including the L of Jean-Jacob Louis (d. 1772).
A painted arrow sometimes occurs on ware produced 1760–70.

Incised
Jean-Jacob Louis
oberbossierer 1762–72

The Letters WPM found under various Ludwigsburg marks indicate the modern factory at Schorndorb, and signify Württembergische-Porzellan-Manifactur. Faïence made at Ludwigsburg from 1756, using mark of Niderviller, namely that of Comte de Custine:

Lunéville, Meurthe-et-Moselle, France
Faïence made here during the 18th century from 1731; successive owners included: Cambrette, Loyal, Keller & Guerin (1788), Cyfflé, etc.

Lyons, France
Faïence made here from c. 1520s until c. 1758. Some pieces have inscriptions including name of maker, place-name, and date. Mark recorded:

Maastricht, Holland
Pottery called "De Sphinx" established here in 1836, by Petrus Regout (b. 1801).

239

Machin & Potts: (*fl.* 1818–34)
Made drab stonewares with relief decoration and blue-printed earthenware at Burslem, Staffordshire.
Mark on piece in British Museum:
PUBLISHED
AS THE ACT DIRECTS
June 20th, 1834, by
Machin & Potts
Burslem, Staffordshire
(stamped)

Mafra: (*fl. c.* 1853)
Potter working at Caldas da Rainha, Portugal; made pieces often with Whieldon-type tortoiseshell glazes; work usually marked, but otherwise might easily pass for authentic Whieldon wares.

Mafra & Son, Caldas da Rainha, Portugal
Firm making earthenware from 1853.

Magdeburg, Hanover, Germany
Faïence made here from mid 18th century for about 30 years, under direction of Johann Philipp Guichard (1726–98). From 1786 Guichard made English-type earthenware, with mark:
M
(GUISCHARD)
Impressed

Makkum, Holland
Faïence made here from *c.* 1669 onward. Modern mark used by Freerk Jans Tichelaar:

Maling family: (*fl.* 1762–mid 19th century)
English potters at North Hylton, near Sunderland, Co. Durham (1762); then at Newcastle-upon-Tyne, Northumberland, from 1818; made plain and decorated earthenware; firm known as C. T. Maling in 1853; the Ford Pottery bought in 1854.

Malkin, Samuel: (1668–1741)
Slipware potter at Burslem, Staffordshire (*fl.* 1710–30); pieces known with dates (1712 and 1726); dishes usually signed on the face S. M.

Malta

Mark recorded on stoneware jars given to Sèvres museum in 1844:

Manara, Baldassare: (*fl. c.* 1530–36) Maïolica painter of Faenza.
Mark, signature in full or initials:

Marans, Charente-Inférieure, France
Faïence made here from 1740 to 1745; factory transferred to La Rochelle in 1756.

Given by Jännicke

Marieberg, near Stockholm, Sweden
Faïence and porcelain factory working here from 1758 to *c.* 1788.
Marks on faïence:

Given by Jännicke

In blue   Given by Jännicke
MB, Marieberg-Berthevin
(Pierre Berthevin, 1766/9)

Marks on porcelain:

In pink

In blue

Marks, cancellation

Outmoded or defective wares sold "in the white" to outside decorators (hausmaler) were marked with a stroke through the original factory mark, by firms that had regard for the quality of their wares; practice originated at Meissen, where one stroke is said to indicate wares sold as defective to decorators, two or more strokes to indicate imperfectly-decorated factory products:

Similar cancellations were used at Vienna and Sèvres:

Sèvres

Vienna

Russian court inventory mark: Meissen porcelain

Made for the Château d'Anet: Sceaux

K.H.C.

Königliche Hof-Conditorei (Royal Pantry): Meissen porcelain

On Italian maïolica plate as part of decoration, and on the reverse

Marks, ownership
These include: signs of hospitals or pharmacies on Italian drugpots; names of châteaux or palaces on French porcelain and faïence; court inventory marks on German and Russian porcelain; all generally marks of ownership; not to be taken for factory marks.
Examples:

Pharmacy mark

Mark of the Carthusian order

Pharmacy mark

Mark of owner or maker: Florentine jar

Marks, workmen's
These include artists' signatures or initials, and the initials or signs of gilders, repairers, etc.; they were used to assist factory organisation, and as a means of checking faulty workmanship; artists' and gilders' signs used at Sèvres are well-authenticated.

Selection of examples:

On Sèvres porcelain

Mark of Jan Emens and merchant's mark

Pharmacy sign

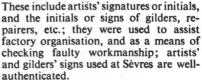

Nymphenburg: workman's mark

Höchst: repairer's mark

Pharmacy mark: Hispano-Moresque drugpot

Merchants' mark: Siegburg stoneware

Sèvres: painters' marks

Meissen: lustre mark

Meissen: lustre mark

Honoré Savy c. 1770

Marktredwitz, Bavaria
Hard-paste porcelain made here by firm of F. Thomas, from mid 19th century.

J. G. Robert c. 1750–95

Bonnefoy late 18th century

Marseilles, Bouches-du-Rhône, France
Hard-paste porcelain made here from c. 1770, by Joseph Robert:

Martin Bros: (*fl.* 1873–1915)
English potters making salt-glazed stoneware at Southall, Middlesex.

Faïence made here from 1677 until about 1827. Important factories included those of Fauchier, Leroy, Perrin, Savy, Robert, and Bonnefoy.

Incised

St Jean du Désert factory
(worked by Joseph Clérissy, 1677–85)

Mason, Miles: (1752–1822)
English manufacturer, recorded at Liverpool, Lancashire (1796–1800), and at Lane Delph, Staffordshire (1796–1813), with different partners; made bone china, a hard porcelain and earthenware.
Marks:
M. MASON or MILES MASON (impressed); a square seal with MILES above and MASON below.

Fauchier factory c. 1711–95

Factory of Veuve Perrin (*fl.* 1748–93)
These marks are said to be much forged

Pseudo-Chinese seal
Transfer-printed in blue
on bone china

Mason, William: (1785–1855)
Made blue-printed earthenware at Lane Delph, Staffordshire, from 1811 to 1824.
Mark:

W. MASON
In blue: transfer-printed

Mason family: (*fl.* 1795–1854)
Staffordshire potters; Miles Mason (1752–1822), made porcelain at Fenton (from 1800), bone china (1807–13); succeeded by G. M. Mason (withdrew *c.* 1829) and C. J. Mason (bankrupt 1848), making porcelain, bone china, and ironstone china; C. J. Mason started up again at Longton (1851), but closed in 1854.

Transfer-printed

Variations in crown

Transfer-printed

Massier, Clément and Jérôme: (*fl.* from 1870s)
Made decorative pottery, with flambé and lustre glazes, at Golfe Juan, Vallauris, France.

Painted   Impressed

Lucien Levy was artist and designer.

Mayence, Germany
Cream-coloured earthenware made here during early 19th century.
Mark: name MAINZ or initials MZ impressed.

Mayer, E. & Son: (*fl. c.* 1773–*c.* 1840)
Made earthenware at Hanley, Staffordshire.
Marks recorded:
E. Mayer
E. Mayer & Son
Impressed

Mayer, Thomas: (1762–1827) and
Newbold, Richard: (1758–1836)
Staffordshire manufacturers in partnership (*c.* 1817–33) at Lane End; made porcelain and various earthenwares.

Meakin, J. & G.: (*fl.* 1845 onward)
Earthenware factory established 1845 by James Meakin at Lane End, Staffordshire; transferred to Hanley in 1848/50; continues to present day.

Medici porcelain, Florence, Italy
Soft-paste porcelain made from 1575 until 1587, and again possibly *c.* 1613. Marks recorded included the six balls of the Medici arms, and the dome of Florence Cathedral, with or without the letter F.

Painted in blue
The initials MMFEDII stand for Franciscus Medicis Magnus Dux Etruriae Secundus.

Meigh family: (*fl.* 1790–1860)
English manufacturers of earthenware at Hanley, Staffordshire; traded as Job Meigh & Son (1812–35); Charles Meigh (1835–47); Charles Meigh, Son & Pankhurst (1850); Charles Meigh & Son (1851–60).

The firm was known as the Old Hall Earthenware Co Ltd, 1862 to 1887, and as Old Hall Porcelain Co Ltd, from 1887 to its closure in 1902.

J.M.S.   MEIGH'S
M. & S.   CHINA
  C.M.   C.M.S & P.

Job Meigh & Son: 1812–34

Charles Meigh: 1835–47

Charles Meigh Son & Parkhurst: 1850

Charles Meigh & Son

Charles Meigh & Son: 1851–60

Meillonas, near Bourg-en-Bresse, Ain, France

Faïence made here from 1761 until *c.* 1804 or thereabouts.

Meissen, near Dresden, Saxony, Germany

Red stoneware made here in early 18th century until *c.* 1730, chiefly under J. F. Böttger (*fl.* 1704–19).

Impressed, incised, or moulded

Hard-paste porcelain in production here by 1713, but not systematically marked until 1724.

Pseudo-Chinese mark occurring on blue-and-white porcelain (*c.* 1720–25) and on stoneware:

N 27 is Johanneum Inventory No. 27

So-called Caduceus mark first used *c.* 1723:

First clearly identifiable factory marks were initials, sometimes with the crossed swords:

K. P. F.

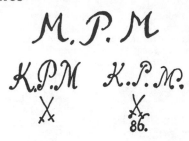

The crossed swords mark was introduced *c.* 1724, continuing in use until modern times. Various forms:

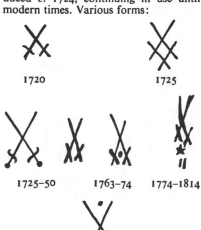

1720   1725

1725–50   1763–74   1774–1814

Modern mark

Some variations of the crossed swords mark with unexplained additions:

Variant of the gilded mark on the right

Mark in blue number in red

Crossed swords in blue. Centre mark in gold and inventory mark incised

Late 18th
century

Sub-standard ware cancelled thus:

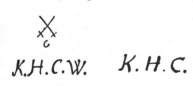

The Augustus Rex cipher was placed in blue on specially fine pieces intended as royal presents, or for the Royal Palace; much forged in the 19th century:

Rare mark is the monogram F.A. for Frederick Augustus II of Saxony (1733). Wares for special departments marked:
K.H.C.W. (Königliche Hof-Conditorei Warschau)
K.H.C. (Königliche Hof-Conditorei)

K.H.C.W.   K.H.C.

A number of pieces are marked B.P.T with word "Dresden" and date, 1739. Believed to be Palace marks:

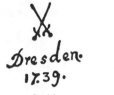

In blue   In blue

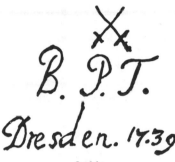

In blue

Inventory marks were engraved on the wheel and coloured over in black:

$Z\,90$ $N=494$,

J. G. Heintze frequently incorporated the factory mark and date in his paintings; artists sometimes signed their work, e.g.

C.F. Herold
invt: et.fecit a meiſsē
1750. ♃ 12 Sept:

Melchior, Johann Peter: (1747-1825)
Modellmeister at Höchst, 1767-79; at

Frankenthal, 1779–93; and at Nymphenburg from 1796 until 1822.
Signatures recorded:

fet par
I.P   *Melchior*
Melchior   *Sculptner*
'771   *1771*

Mennecy, Seine-et-Oise, France
Porcelain made here from 1734 to 1748, then at Bourg-la-Reine, 1773 until 1806.

DV   .D.V.

Incised   In blue

Mennecy

BR
B.R.   N   MŌ

Late 18th century   Initials of
Bourg-la-Reine   Christophe Mô
                        from 1767

Mesch, Quirynus: (*fl.* 1702–19)
Delft painter.

MQ
H29

Methven, David: (d. 1861)
Made decorated earthenwares at Kirkcaldy, Fifeshire, Scotland.

Metsch, Johann Friedrich: (*fl.* 1732 to after 1751)
Enameller at Dresden (1731); hausmaler at Bayreuth (1735–51); later at Fürstenberg.
Signatures recorded:

.Metzsch   F.M.
.1748.   Bäyreith
Bajr.   1744

                        On Chinese
On Meissen porcelain   porcelain

Mexborough Old Pottery, Mexborough, Yorkshire, England
Established in 1800 by Sowter & Bromley; taken over 1804 by Peter Barker, and worked by the Barker family until its closure in 1844; chiefly made printed earthenware.

SOWTER & CO
MEXBRO
Impressed

Meyers & Son: (late 19th century)
Dresden decorators in the Meissen style, using mark closely resembling the crossed swords mark:

Middlesbrough pottery, Middlesbrough, Yorkshire, England
Factory established 1834; from 1844 to 1852 traded as the Middlesbrough Earthenware Co; from 1852 as Isaac Wilson & Co; closed
Made painted and printed earthenwares.

Impressed

Milan, Italy
Maïolica made here in the 18th century.
Mark recorded of potter named Cesare
Confaloniere (1775–82), working in the
oriental style:

Firm of Julius Richard and Company
established in 1833, working until 1873,
when linked to Ginori of Doccia.
Mark:

In black

Milland Pottery, Liphook, Hampshire,
England
Earthenware potworks started 1948.
Mark, a windmill between the words:

MILLAND/POTTERY

Mintons (Mintons Ltd): (1793 onward)
English manufacturers, working at Stoke-
on-Trent, Staffordshire; founded 1793,
trading (1817) as Thomas Minton & Son;
as Minton & Hollins, or Minton Hollins
& Co (1845–68); then as Minton & Co;
from 1883 as Mintons Ltd

Transfer-printed
1800–36

Printed or
impressed
after 1851

MINTONS   B B New Stone

Impressed   Impressed
20th century

MINTON

Impressed 1861 onward

1822–36

Transfer-printed
1860–80

Transfer-printed

Transfer-printed   M : 1822–30
M & Co: 1841–44   M & H : 1845–68

Transfer-printed

Transfer-printed, uranium glaze, 1918

Year marks (impressed):

1842–50

1851–59

1860–68

1869–77

1878–86

1887–95

1896–1904

1905–13

1914–22

1923–31

1932–40

Signatures recorded:

Birks

Birks, Alboin: (1861–1941) 1876–1937
decorator, pâte-sur-pâte

A Boullemier

Boullemier, Antonin: (1840–1900)
figure painter

A CARRIER

Carrier-Belleuse, Albert: after 1854
sculptor and figure modeller

J E Dean

Dean, Edward J.: (1884–1933)
painter of fish and game

L Solon

Solon, Leon Victor: (1872–) 1909
art director

Solon, Marc Louis: (1835–1912)
1870–1904
decorator, pâte-sur-pâte

Y.

Wadsworth, John William: 1935–1955
art director

A. H. Wright   A. H. Wright

Wright, Albert:
fish and flower painter

Miragaya, near Oporto, Portugal
Faïence factory established here in late
18th century.

Mô, Christophe and Jean: (*fl.* from 1767)
Modellers and repairers working at Mennency. Jean continued as a repairer at

Bourg-la-Reine. Marks recorded include:
"J Mo" and "Mo" (incised) also e.g.
"B R, Mo" and "DV, Mo".

Monaco
Pottery established here in 1874.

Monterau, Seine-et-Marne, France
English-type pottery made here from
1748; by Clark, Shaw et Cie from 1775
and various owners afterwards.
  MONTEREAU M ᴬᵁ No 1
  Impressed

Moorcroft, William: (d. 1946)
English master potter; founded firm of
W. Moorcroft Ltd, Cobridge, Staffordshire, in 1913.

W. Moorcroft

Moore, Bernard: (1853–1935)
English china manufacturer at Stoke-on-Trent, Staffordshire, from 1905.
Factory marks:

BERNARD MOORE ≈ 1904

Painted

BM   *BERNARD MOORE*   *BM*

Artists' marks:

   Adams, John: (1882–1953)

Beardmore, Hilda

 Billington, Dora May

 Buttle, George A.: (1870–1925)

 Jackson, Gertrude

 Lindop, Hilda

 Ollier, Annie

 Tomlinson, Reginald R.

 Wilkes, Edward R.

Moore Brothers: (*fl.* 1870–1905)
English china manufacturers at Longton, Staffordshire.

Moore & Co: (*fl.* early 19th century)
English potters working the Wear Pottery at Sunderland, Co. Durham, taking it over shortly after it was founded by Brinton & Co in 1803.

MOORE & CO.
SOUTHWICK

MOORE & CO.
Impressed

Morley, Francis (*fl.* from before 1845 until 1862)
English potter, first partner in firm of Ridgway, Morley, Wear and Co; sole proprietor in 1845, trading under his own name, or as Morley & Co (1850–58), or Morley & Ashworth (1858–62); purchased the Mason moulds and engravings.

Printed

Morris, Rowland James: (*c.* 1847–1909)
English ceramic sculptor; modeller to the trade, e.g. to Bernard Moore at Longton, Staffordshire, and to J. S. Wilson, parian manufacturer at Longton.

RJ Morris

Incised

Mortlock, John: (*fl.* early 19th century)
London agent who bought undecorated porcelain from various manufacturers (e.g. Swansea, Nantgarw, and Coalport), to be painted to his order by Randall, Robins, and other artists. His name is found on various articles, including

Rockingham brown-glazed "Cadogan" teapots (made *c.* 1813–26).

Moscow, Russia
Gardner's factory established here, making porcelain from 1758.

Ç	ГАРДНЕРZ	Æ
In blue	Impressed	In blue

Transfer-printed

Popoff factory established in 1806, closing 1872.

Moseley, John: (*fl.* early 19th century)
Perhaps two English potters of this name; Moseley & Dale recorded at Cobridge, Staffordshire (1801); a John Moseley recorded as making Egyptian black at Burslem (1818); also a John Moseley recorded as an earthenware manufacturer at Cobridge.

Given by Chaffers

Moulds, marked (Staffordshire, England)
Examples dated and inscribed recorded:
A.W. Aaron Wood
R.W. with dates 1748, 1749, 1750,
1763 Ralph Wood
"Ralph Wood 1770"
J.B. 1763 John Baddeley
"William Bird made this mould," etc.
1751

Moustiers, Basses Alpes, France
Faïence made here from 1679 until 19th century, various names associated with it.

Jean-Gaspard Féraud 1779–1817	Joseph-Gaspard Guichard *c.* 1755

Jean-François Thion 1758–88	Jean-Baptiste Ferrat 1718–91

Müller, Paul:
Founded modern hard-paste porcelain factory at Selb, using marks:

Münden, Hanover, Germany
Pottery made here from 1737.
Marks, three crescents from the arms of the founder, Carl Friedrich von Hanstein.

Murray, William Staite: (*fl.* 1919–)
Studio potter, making stonewares; worked in England until 1940, then left for Southern Rhodesia.

Myatt, Richard: (d. 1804)
English potter, recorded at Lane End, Staffordshire, in 1783.
Mark recorded:

MYATT

Impressed: on
Elers-type "red china"

Myatt family: (*fl.* early 19th century)
English potters; George Myatt recorded (1830) at Bilston, Staffordshire, where he made blue-and-white earthenware; Benjamin Myatt recorded at Bilston (1834) making yellow wares.
Mark recorded:

MYATT
Impressed

Nantgarw, Glamorgan, Wales
Porcelain factory founded here in 1813 by William Billingsley; transferred to Swansea for a short time; Billingsley again at Nantgarw 1816 until 1820.

NANT GARW
G.W.

Naples, Italy
Maïolica made here from end of 17th century; notably at factory of Biagio Giustiniani (end 18th century).
Marks recorded include:

Naples, Italy: Royal Factory
Soft-paste porcelain made here from 1771 to 1807; sold to Jean Poulard Prad et Cie, working at Capo-di-monte until 1834.

In colour or gold

N	N	N
Impressed	In blue	In red
N	N	N
In blue	In blue	In blue

Neale, James: (1740–1814)
English potter making earthenware at Hanley, Staffordshire (1778); trading as Neale & Wilson after Robert Wilson made a partner in 1786; as Neale & Co when others partners admitted; factory in hands of David Wilson & Sons (1801–17).

NEALE & Co

NEALE & CO

NEALE

Impressed

NEALE & CO
G

NEALE & WILSON

Impressed

Nevers, Nièvre, France
Faïence industry founded here after arrival of Augustin Conrade from Albissola (*c.* 1585). One considerable factory working in 19th century, of H. Signoret and his successor A. Montaignon.
Marks recorded:

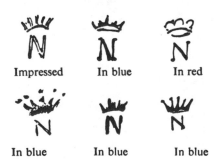

From Chaffers, Garnier, and actual pieces

New Hall, Shelton, Staffordshire, England
Factory making hard-paste porcelain, *c.* 1782–*c.* 1810; changing to bone china, from *c.* 1810 until its closure in 1835.
Marks:
On porcelain, pattern numbers prefaced by N or No in cursive style; on bone china, the words "New Hall" in a circle.

Initials and pattern number printed before 1812; circular mark transfer-printed 1812–35.

Niderviller, Lorraine, France
Faïence made here from 1754 onward; porcelain made from 1765 by Beyerlé, followed by Comte de Custine in 1770–71 (*fl.* 1770–93). Factory reopened by Lanfrey (d. 1827), followed by M.L.G. Dryander.

Beyerlé

Custine

In black
Custine

In black

Custine

Beyerlé

Lanfrey

Lanfrey
Early 19th century

Impressed

Impressed
late 18th century

Dryander

Noël, Gustave (*fl.* 1755–93)
Painter at Sèvres, using the mark:
Not to be confused with 19th-century faïence painter of same name.

Nuremberg, Bavaria, Germany
Faïence made here, 16th century onward.

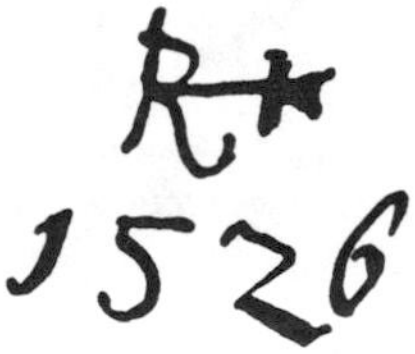

Reinhard

Nuremberg

Initials used by hausmaler working at Nuremberg include:

A.H.	Abraham Helmhack (*fl.* 1675–1700)
I.H.	Johann Heel (1637–1709)
I.M.G.	Johann Melchior Gebhard
J.L.F.	Johann Ludwig Faber (*fl.* 1678–93)
M.S.	M. Schmidt

Modern Nuremberg factory, **J.** von Schwartz used mark:

1880

Nymphenburg, Bavaria, Germany
Hard-paste porcelain made here 1755 to 1862, and onward.
Inventory marks:

$$CH.Z\ .I77\dot{s}.\qquad C.H.C\ I7\dot{7}2$$

Painted in purple

$$C_{,}H\ \mathfrak{Z}\ddot{o}\mathfrak{h}rgaden_{,}I77\dot{s}.$$

Churfürstliche Hof Zöhrgaden
(Electoral Court storeroom)

$$C.H.\ Conditorei\ \dot{j}7.\ \dot{j}7\ 7\dot{j}.$$

Churfürstliche Hof Conditoreij
(Electoral Court Confectionery)

Factory marks:

Impressed   Impressed

1763–77

Modern marks
Modellers' marks include:

F·B

Franz Bustelli
(*fl.* 1754–63)

$$J;\ Peter\ Melchior$$

Johann Peter Melchior
(*fl.* 1787–1822)

Painters' marks include:

J.W. GGL   **C Pußßer**

Hausmalers' marks include those of Amberg, J. A. Huber, etc.

**.iAH.   . Amburg 1974
K·
A:A:**

With dates 1765, 1778

Nyon, near Geneva, Switzerland
Hard-paste porcelain factory founded here in 1781 by Jacques Dortu, director until 1813.

In underglaze blue

Oettingen-Schrattenhofen, Bavaria, Germany
Pottery established at Oettingen about 1735, transferred later to Schrattenhofen. Later products marked with name "Schrattenhofen" in one or two lines, with the name of the painter or owner.

Ofen, Hungary
Factory making cream-coloured earthenware established *c.* 1795 here.
Mark: word OFEN impressed.

Offenbach, near Frankfurt-am-Main, Germany
Faïence factory established here in 1739, still in existence in 1807.

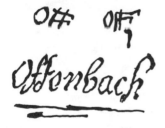

Oldfield & Co: (*fl.* early 19th century)
English manufacturers of stoneware at Brampton near Chesterfield in Derbyshire, from 1810.

OLDFIELD & CO   J. OLDFIELD
MAKERS

Impressed   Impressed
                       (sole owner by 1838)

Olerys, Joseph (d. 1749) working with Laugier, Joseph:
Made faïence at Moustiers, France, factory continuing under same name until 1790.

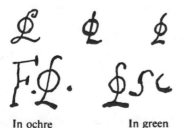

In ochre   In green

O'Neale, Jeffrey Hamet: (1734–1801)
Irish artist and ceramic decorator; worked at Chelsea (soon after 1752), and later as outside decorator for Worcester and Josiah Wedgwood; his signature is found on Worcester and Chelsea porcelain.

O.N.P

Orléans, Loiret, France
Soft-paste porcelain made here from 1753; hard-paste after 1770.

In blue   In red
          Benoist le Brun 1806–12

Faïence made here from the 17th century. Marks found on marbled ware made late 18th century:

GRAMMONT

LAINE FABQT   ORLEANS

A ORLEANS

Impressed

Ottweiller, Nassau-Saarbrücken, Germany
Hard-paste porcelain made here from 1763, but earthenware only during the

257

last years (closed down 1797).

In gold, underglaze blue or incised

Oude Loosdrecht, Holland
Hard-paste porcelain factory transferred here from Weesp in 1771, working until 1784, then transferred to Amstel.

M.O. L M:oL M.O.L

In blue

M o L M:OL.

In blue   Incised

Oxshott Pottery, Surrey, England
Founded by Denise Tuckfield in 1911, continues today.
Studio potters working individually here:

Denise K. Wren
(née Tuckfield)

Rosemary Wren

hw
OXSHOTT

Henry D. Wren (d. 1947)

The marks are scratched into the rough clay, on the base of the pot.

Padua, Italy
Maïolica and lead-glazed earthenware made here from the end of the 15th century until about the end of the 18th century.

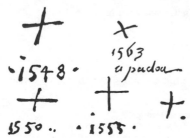

Two marks recorded on porcelain, and attributed to Padua are as follows: the date 1627 and initials I.G.P.F.; date 1638 and initials G.G.P.F. The initials P.F. might stand for "Padovano fece"; a cross potent and a hatched imitation Chinese character also appear, e.g.:

Palais Royal, Paris
Important decorating shop run here in early 19th century by Darte frères, using stencilled marks:

DARTE
Pal Royal
Nº 21

DARTE
FRERES
A PARIS

Darte also ran workshops (1790–1840) at rue de Charonne, rue de la Roquette, rue Popincourt, and rue Fontaine-au-Roi.

Palmer, Humphrey: (*fl. c.* 1760–78)
English earthenware manufacturer at Hanley, Staffordshire; rival and imitator of Wedgwood.

PALMER

Palsjö, near Helsingborg, Sweden
Faïence factory established here by Michael Anders Cöster in 1765; taken over by Heinrich Wolff in 1770, closing down in 1774.
Mark: letters P F (Palsjö Fabrik) or P F C (Palsjö Fabrik-Cöster) with date and other numerals

Pardoe, Thomas: (1770–1823)
English porcelain decorator (mostly flowers), worked for Derby, Worcester, and Swansea (c. 1785–1809); independent enameller at Bristol (1809–21); at Nantgarw in 1821.
Signatures recorded:

Pardoe
Cardiff

Passau, Bavaria, Germany
Hard-paste porcelain made here from 1840 by Dressel, Kister & Co.

Reproductions of Höchst porcelain figures made here from old moulds, using the Höchst "wheel" mark.

Patanazzi family: (at Urbino)
Had maïolica workshop; signed pieces by four members of the family are recorded; Antonio (1580); Alfonso (1606); Francesco (1617); and Vincenzio (1620).

ALF.
P.F.
VRBINI
1606

FATTO·IN VRBINO

ALFONSO PATANAZZI
FECIT.
VRBINI. 1606~

ALF.
P.F.
VRBINI
1606

Pattison, James: (fl. c. 1818–30)
English earthenware toy manufacturer at Lane End, Staffordshire.
Name and date recorded:

Painted

Pecs, Fünfkirchen, Hungary
Factory established at Fünfkirchen in 1855 by W. Zsolnay using these marks:

ZSOLNAY
PÉCS
Impressed

ZSOLNAY

In lustre   In blue

ZSOLNAY

Impressed   Impressed

Pellat & Green: (*fl. c.* 1815–20)
Dealers' name occurring as mark on
English porcelain, notably on Swansea.

Pellipario, Nicola (*fl.* 1515–*c.* 1550)
Maïolica painter, working successively at
Castel Durante, doubtfully at Fabriano,
and at Urbino.
See FONTANA FAMILY.

Pennis, Anthony: (*fl.* 1756–70)
Owner of Delft factory De Twee Scheepjes (The Two Little Ships), which continued under his widow (1770–82), and
then under his son Jan.

Pennis, Johannes: (1702–88)
Proprietor of De Porceleyn Schotel (The
Porcelain Dish) at Delft (1725–64).
Mark attributed to him:

Pesaro, near Urbino, Italy
Maïolica made here during late 15th and
16th centuries; revived in 18th century.

Painted on Pesaro maïolica
16th–18th centuries

Possibly Pesaro Gabice
16th century

Casali and Caligari

fabbrica Magrin
Pesaro

Modern mark on imitation Urbino
ware by Magrini & Co.
established in 1870

Petit, Jacob (b. 1796) **and Mardochée:**
Made hard-paste porcelain from 1830 at
Fontainebleau and later at Belleville.
This factory sold out 1862, and another
opened in Rue Paradis Poissonière. Models, moulds and marks in use until 1886
later.

Meissen models and marks copied.

Petite Rue St Gilles, Paris
Porcelain factory founded 1783 by F. M.
Honoré, working until *c.* 1822 (?).

Picasso, Pablo: (1881–)

Pijnacker, Adriaen: (*fl.* 1675–1707)
Worked De Porceleyn Schotel with his
brother-in-law Cornelisz Keyser (d. 1684)
and brother Jacobus Pijnacker; worked
De Twee Scheepjes (1690–94); foreman
of De Wildeman (1696–1707).
Mark ascribed to Cornelisz Keyser and
Adriaen Pijnacker:

Pilkington's Lancastrian Pottery:
(*fl.* from 1892 onward)
Decorative pottery was made by this firm
at Manchester, England, from 1897 until
1938.
Factory mark:

Artists' marks recorded:

 Barlow, A.

 Cundall, Charles E.

 Crane, Walter
(1846–1915)

 Day, Lewis F.

 Mycock, W. S.

 Rodgers, Gwladys

Pillivuyt & Company:
Made porcelain at three factories, at
Foescy, Mehun and Noirlac, established
in 1817.

In gold

Pinxton, Derbyshire, England
Porcelain made here *c.* 1796–*c.* 1812.

Pirkenhammer, Brezova, Bohemia
Factory established 1830 by Friedrich
Höcke; let to Granz & Brotthäuser 1800;
sold to Martin Fischer and Kristof
Reichenbach 1811; traded as Fischer &
Mieg for a time, and as Christian Fischer
1845–53.

 F&R
Impressed

C.F. F&M
Impressed

Pirotti family: (*fl.* 16th century)
Made maïolica at Faenza, from *c.* 1500. Inscriptions recorded include: FATO IN FAENZA IN CAXA PIROTA; and FATE. IN. FAEnza. IOXEF. In. CAsa PIROTE 1525.
Workshop mark: a globe scored across at right angles, with a circle or pellet in one segment sometimes with a flame issuing from it.
See FAENZA.

Plant, Benjamin: (*fl.* late 18th/early 19th centuries)
Built factory at Lane End, Staffordshire, in 1784; made table wares and lustred and enamelled figures; his son Thomas Plant (1801–53) also made pottery figures.

Painted

Plymouth, Devon, England
Hard-paste porcelain factory established here in 1768; moved to Bristol 1773; eventually sold in 1781.
A number of different marks were used, principally variants on the figure "4":

Poitiers, Haute-Vienne, France
Mark recorded:

Chaffers describes Morreine as a modeller of figures in "terre de pipe". Pasquier,

"fabricant de faïence émaillée", and Felix Faulcon, a local printer, made faïence here from 1776:

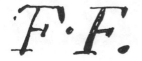

Poppelsdorf, Bonn, Germany
Earthenware made here from *c.* 1755; firm of Ludwig Kessel established in 1825.

Pountney & Co: (*fl.* from 1813 onward)
English earthenware manufacturers at Bristol, Somerset.
Marks recorded:

'mpressed   In blue   Modern mark

Pouyat, J.: (*fl.* mid 19th century)
Started porcelain factory at Limoges in 1841, which has been continued by descendants.

ENGLISH AND EUROPEAN

Pratt, F. and R.: (firm *fl.* throughout the 19th century)
English potters making china and earthenware at Fenton, Staffordshire (from 1812); specialised in multi-colour printing from contemporary narrative pictures.

PRATT
FENTON

Transfer-printed: 1830–40

Pratt, William: (1753–99)
English master potter at Lane Delph, Staffordshire, from 1783.
Mark found on some 18th-century wares:

PRATT
Impressed

Premières, Côte-d'Or, France
Faïence factory established here near Dijon in 1783, by one J. Lavalle or Laval; continued into 19th century by his descendants.

Either painted or stencilled

Proskau, Silesia, Germany
Faïence made here from 1763 until 1850.

| 1763–69 | 1770–83 | 1783–93 | 1783 |

PROSKAU
Impressed
1788–1850

Pull, Georges: (*fl.* 19th century)
Imitator of Palissy wares, working at Paris.

PULL

In relief, incised, or painted in enamels

Purmerend, Holland
Factory making peasant art types of Dutch pottery.

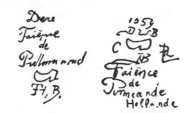

Putten, J. van, and Company, Delft (*fl.* 1830–50)
Made earthenware in Delft tradition.

"P.V." mark
Found on earthenware figures of Shakespeare (after Scheemaker's statue in Westminster Abbey) and Milton, of late 18th-century date; perhaps for "Palmer: Voyez"; unconfirmed.

Quimper, Finistère, France
Faïence made here from the end of the 17th century; stoneware was made during the 19th century.

P. P. Caussy　　　　　Hubaudière
(*fl.* 1743–82)　　　　　(1782–)

Raeren, Rhineland, Germany
Stoneware made here, *c.* 1560 until early 17th century.
Potters' initials recorded include:
I.E.　Jan Emens Mennicken (*c.* 1566–94)
I.M.　Jan Mennicken (1576)
T.W. and T.W.K. Tilman Wolf "Kannenbacker"
Also, in 19th century:
H.S.　Hubert Schiffer (fr. *c.* 1880)

263

Randall, Thomas Martin: (1786–1859)
Decorator of porcelain for London dealers; said to have started a soft-paste factory at Madeley, Shropshire, England (c. 1825), making imitation Sèvres.
Mark recorded:

TMR
Madeley
S

Painted

The firm evidently also used the Sèvres marks, e.g. when decorating Minton porcelain in the Sèvres style.

Ratcliff, William: (fl. c. 1837–40)
English potter at Hanley, Staffordshire, white and transfer-printed earthenware.

Rathbone, Thomas & Co: (fl. 1810–45)
Made earthenware with distinct Staffordshire flavour at Portobello, Scotland.

or: T. RATHBONE

Ratibor, Silesia, Germany
Cream-coloured earthenware made here by Beaumont of Leeds (1794–1803), followed by Salomon Baruch (1803); closed down in 1828.
Mark:
BEAUMONT or BARUCH
impressed

Rato, near Lisbon, Portugal
Faïence factory established here by Thomaz Brunetto in 1767; succeeded by S. de Almeida (1771–c. 1814). Rato pottery exhibited at the Paris Exhibition of 1867.

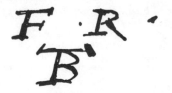

Fabrica Rato/Thomaz Brunetto

Rauenstein, Thuringia, Germany
Hard-paste porcelain factory established here by the three ·Greiners in 1783; continues today as limited company.

Ravenna, Italy
Maïolica made here during the 16th century. Mark recorded on piece not now accepted as genuine:

R·VA·1592

Reed & Taylor: (fl. mid 19th century)
Reed, James:
Reed, John: (until c. 1873)
English potters; successive owners of the earthenware factory called The Mexborough, or Rock, Pottery, at Mexborough, Yorkshire.

• REED •

Impressed   Transfer-printed

Registration marks:
These appeared on English earthenwares, and referred to the designs with which they were decorated; in two cycles, 1842–67 and 1868–83; consisted of a lozenge, with code-letters and numerals assigned by the "Registration of Designs" office;

they were arranged thus:
Cycle 1842–67

Year letters 1842–67:

X 1842	P 1851	Z 1860
Ħ 1843	D 1852	R 1861
C 1844	Y 1853	O 1862
A 1845	J 1854	G 1863
I 1846	E 1855	N 1864
F 1847	L 1856	W 1865
U 1848	K 1857	Q 1866
S 1849	B 1858	T 1867
V 1850	M 1859	

Month letters 1842–67:

C January	E May	D September
G February	M June	B October
W March	I July	K November
H April	R August	A December

Cycle 1868–83

Registration marks, contd. Cycle 1868–1883

Year letters 1868–83:

X 1868	U 1874	J 1880
H 1869	S 1875	E 1881
C 1870	V 1876	L 1882
A 1871	P 1877	K 1883
I 1872	D 1878	
F 1873	Y 1879	

Month letters 1868–83:

C January	E May	D September
G February	M June	E October
W March	I July	K November
H April	R August	A December

Note: in 1878, from 1st to 6th March, the registration letters were G for the month and W for the year.

Registration of marks
In 1764 an order regulating the use of marks was issued by the faïence potters of Delft.
In 1766, when the Sèvres porcelain monopoly broke down, potters were authorized to produce porcelain with certain restrictions, provided they registered with the police the mark or marks to be used on their wares.
It is only after these enactions that the interpretation of marks becomes trustworthy.

Reid, W. & Co: (*fl.* mid 18th century) English makers of blue-and-white wares at Liverpool, Lancashire; possibly also made bone porcelain; closed down 1759. Mark:

REID & CO.

Rendsburg, Holstein, Germany
Earthenware made here from 1765 to 1818. Marks rarely found; recorded, on faïence:
C.R. for Clar/Rendsburg, over initials of painter, and figures for year. (Christian Friedrich Clar, owner, later manager only, *fl.* 1765–98)
on cream-coloured earthenware:
REN I, or RF

Rennes, Ille-et-Vilaine, France
Lead-glazed earthenware (from 16th century) and faïence (from 1748) made here. Marks recorded:

Iᵉcitle.P.
Bourgouin

J. B. Alexis Bourgouin
modeller (b. 1734)

ℛennes
ce·12.8ᵇʳᵉ
1763

Reval, Esthonia
Faïence made here by Karl Christian Fick from *c.* 1775 until his death, 1792.

Reygens or Reygensbergh, Augustin:
Owner of De Vergulde Boot factory at Delft, 1663–66.

Ridgway, J. & W.: (*fl.* early 19th century)
English potters in partnership during the early 19th century until 1830 at Hanley, Staffordshire.

Transfer-printed
1814–30

Rie, Lucie: (*fl.* from 1938)
Studio potter working in London from 1938; Hans Coper working with her from 1947.

Hans Coper

Lucie Rie

Riley, John and Richard: (*fl.* 1802–28)
English manufacturers of china, stoneware, cream-coloured and printed wares, at Burslem, Staffordshire.

Robert, Joseph-Gaspard or Jean-Gaspard:
(*fl. c.* 1750–*c.* 1795)
At Marseilles, made faïence (from *c.* 1750) and porcelain (from *c.* 1770).
Marks:
On faïence: letter R
On porcelain: J R as monogram

Robinson & Leadbeater: (*fl.* second half of 19th century)
English manufacturers of decorative parian wares at Stoke-on-Trent, Staffordshire.

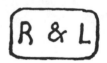

Impressed

Rogers, John and George: (*fl.* 1780–1815)
English potters making earthenware at Burslem, Staffordshire; trading as John Rogers & Son from 1815 until 1842.
Mark: name "Rogers" impressed, with sometimes also the sign for Mars or Iron added:

Rome
Porcelain made here from second half of 18th century.
Marks recorded:
ROMA I MAG 1769
with crossed CC beneath a crown (incised)
(For Carlo Coccorese, working for the Coccumos factory, 1761–69. The factory closed *c.* 1781.
G VOLPATO ROMA
(For Volpato factory, *fl.* 1785–1818)
Maïolica made at Rome from the 14th to the 17th century.

Cream-coloured earthenware made by the Volpato family 1785–1831.

Rörstrand, Sweden
Faïence factory founded in 1726; in 1926 transferred to Gothenburg; in 1932 went to Lidköping. Continues.

Very early mark

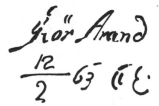

1763

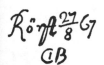

RORSTRAND   **Rorstrand**

Impressed
c. 1780

Transfer-printed

From 1884   Modern mark

GRATINA
UGNS · ELDFAST
OVENWARE

22

Modern mark

Rosenburg, The Hague, Holland: (modern)
Factory using the following marks:

Rosenthal, Selb, Bavaria, Germany
Factory established by P. Rosenthal in 1880; continues today.

Ross, James: (1745–1821)
Engraver; his signature appears on a number of pieces of Worcester porcelain.

J Ross Vigornensis sculp

Rossetti, Giorgio Giacinto: (*fl.* from 1729 to mid 18th century)
Faïence painter working at Lodi (Ferretti factory, 1729) and at Turin (his uncle Giorgio Rossetti's factory, 1737). Various signatures recorded:
Lodi G Giacijnto Rossettij fecit
Laude Hijacintus Rossetus *f.* 1729
Fabricha di G. Giacinto Rossetti in Lodi
Fabrica di Gior: Giacin: Rossetti à Tarazzi in Lodi
Hyaci Rossettas

Given by Garnier

Rotterdam, Holland
Centre of tile-making industry; tile panels and pictures made here. Artists who signed their work include:
Cornelis Boumeester (*c.* 1650–1733)
Jan Aalmis (1714–after 1788)
Signature of independent porcelain decorator recorded:

F. L. S.
A Rotterdam
W. M: 1812

Rouen, Seine-Inférieure, France
Faïence made here *c.* 1535–70; and from 1647 onward. Names connected with Rouen include: Masseot Abaquesne (*fl.* 1545–*c.* 1551/64) followed by widow and son until *c.* 1570; Edme Poterat, who had monopoly from 1647 for fifty years.

After this, many factories include:
Poterat and Letellier
Bertin, Fouquay, Heugue and Vallet
Guillibaud and Levavasseur
Pottier and Mouchard
Many marks recorded, of which large number must be those of painters or workmen.

Pinxit
1736.
◆ ₢ ◆

Claude Borne

Borne
Pinxit
Anno
1738

Claude Borne

Dieul

Dieul, painter *c.* 1755

Fossé

Fossé, *c.* 1740

va uasseur
a · Rouan

Levavasseur

E

Letellier, *c.* 1780

Mv

M. Vallet, 1756

H   *HH*

Heugue

🌿c

Heugue

JB

SJB

J. Bertin

PC

P. Caussy

MP MP

P. Mouchard, *c.* 1750

A·T.
1735

Masseot Abaquesne

B   *S·3*   *g3*

Guillibaud factory

GA

Rubati, Pasquale: (*fl.* 18th century)
Painter of maïolica at Clerici factory at Milan; set up rival establishment in 1759 or 1762.

Rubelles
Faïence factory working from 1836 until 1858.

Rue Amelot, Paris
Hard-paste porcelain made here from 1784; factory survived until 1825.

In red   In blue   In gold
stencilled   c. 1820

Rue de Bondy, Paris
Hard-paste porcelain made here from 1781 (partnered by Guerhard from c. 1786. At Rue du Temple 1795, and Boulevard Saint-Martin 1825.

Rue de Crussol, Paris
Porcelain works started here by Englishman, Christopher Potter (1789). Marks recorded:

In underglaze blue

Factory said to have been transferred to E. Blancheron in 1792.

EB

or E. BLANCHERON in relief on biscuit pieces.

Rue de la Roquette, Paris
White faïence made by Ollivier, during the second half 18th century

**OLLIVIER
A PARIS**
Impressed

ollivier aparis

Hard-paste porcelain made here from 1773.
Souroux's mark:

S

In underglaze blue

Another factory, Les Trois Levrettes, was worked by Vincent Dubois from 1774 until 1787. Mark similar to St Cloud:

In underglaze blue

Rue de Reuilly, Paris
Hard-paste porcelain made here by Jean-Joseph Lassia from *c.* 1774 until 1784.

L

In colour or gold

Given by Jacquemart

Rue de Sèvres, Paris
Factory set up here in 1859 by A. Jean to make imitation maïolica.

Marks given by Chaffers and Jännicke

Rue des Récollets, Paris
Hard-paste porcelain cameos made here by Desprès (Desprez) 1793–1825, with mark DESPREZ.

Rue du Petit Carrousel, Paris
Charles-Barthélémy Guy had decorating establishment here in 1774; continued by his son Charles until 1800.

P
C G
Mᵗⁿ du Pᵗ
Carousel
Paris

Stencilled in red
The name of the decorator, Perche, who was employed here, sometimes accompanies the mark.

Rue Popincourt, Paris
Hard-paste porcelain made here from 1772 by Johann Nepomuk Hermann Nast; continued by sons in 19th century

NAST **NAST Paris**

n nst.
p...

NAST *nast*

Stencilled in red

Rue Thiroux, Paris
Hard-paste porcelain made here *c.* 1775 by André-Marie Leboeuf; patron Queen Marie Antoinette, whose monogram with crown above was used as mark. After the Revolution, factory in hands of Guy and Housel (1797–98) and Leveillé, closing in *c.* 1820.

In red   In blue, red or gold

Also recorded:

Housel   **LEVEILLE 12 rue Thiroux**

Ruscoe, William: (*fl.* 20th century) English artist potter; Stoke-òn-Trent, Staffordshire, and Exeter, Devon.

Rye, Sussex, England
Earthenware made here during the 19th century, at the Cadborough works; and at the Belle Vue Pottery (1869 to early 20th century), the latter using the mark:

Sadler & Green: (*fl.* later 18th century) English transfer-printers, working at Liverpool, Lancashire; decorated large quantities of Staffordshire and Liverpool earthenware; Wedgwood's Queen's ware sent regularly to them; much of earlier work in black, or black and red; Sadler retired in 1770, Green continued to 1799.

SADLER
SADLER & GREEN
1756

Saint-Amand-les-Eaux, Nord, France
Faïence and earthenware made here in 18th century by Fauquez family.

Soft-paste porcelain made here by Jean-Baptiste-Joseph Fauquez, 1771 to 1778. Revived by J. de Bettignies of Tournay *c.* 1818 until 1882.

St Clément, Meurthe-et-Moselle, France
Offshoot of Lunéville, working from 1757 to end 18th century. Revived *c.* 1824.

In blue   Stencilled in blue   Impressed
                                 on figures

Saint Cloud, Seine-et-Oise, France
Faïence made here from *c.* 1670.

Soft-paste porcelain made here from *c.* 1693; factory closed 1766. Made by the Chicanneau and Trou families.
Mark of the "sun-in-its-splendour" used from *c.* 1695 until 1722.

In blue

From *c.* 1722 until 1766, the mark included the initials of the factory and proprietor:

Incised in the paste
or painted in blue

St Petersburg, or Petrograd, or Leningrad, Russia
Hard-paste porcelain made here from 18th century onward. Most important factory established under patronage of Catherine II.

Alexander III 1881–94 · 1900 Nicholas II 1894–1917 · Soviet 1917

In blue

Court inventory mark Catherine II 1762–96

Other less important factories were established by Batenin and Korniloff in the 19th century. Marks recorded:

Kuznetsoff

Корниловыхъ

Korniloff

Б

Babunin

Paul I 1796–1801

Saint-Porchaire, Deux-Sèvres, France
Earthenware made here, 1525–60.
Only one mark recorded:

Alexander I 1801–25

Salt, Ralph: (1782–1846)
English ceramic decorator, and later (from 1828) a manufacturer of figures and "porcelain tablets" at Hanley, Staffordshire.
Mark frequently found:

Nicholas I 1825–55

Impressed

Alexander II 1855–81

272

Salvini, Florence
These marks occur on reproductions of
Urbino/Gubbio lustres, and imitations of
early maïolica styles:

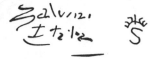

Samson, (Edme), & Co, 7 Rue Béranger,
Paris
Made reproductions from 1845 onward;
many pieces probably unmarked.

On "Chinese"   On Japanese
Lowestoft   and Chinese

On Persian and   On maïolica or
Hispano-Moresque   Palissy

On Sèvres and   On Meissen
terracotta

On Meissen   On French, English,
                      Spanish, and Italian
                      porcelain

San Quirico d'Orcia, Tuscany, Italy
Maïolica made here from 1693 until
c. 1724, and again later.

Sargadelos, northern Spain
Cream-coloured earthenware made her
from 1804 until 1875. Many marks used
mostly incorporating the name of th
town.

Sarreguemines, Lorraine, France
Factory for "faïence fine" established
here c. 1770 by M. Fabry and Paul
Utzscheider; made imitation Wedgwood
in the 19th century.

Sarguemines

SARREGUEMINES

MAJOLICA
SARREGUEMINES
702ᵖ

Sarreguemines

U & Cᶦᵉ

U & C

Savona, Liguria, Italy
Maïolica made at Savona and Albissola near Genoa, 16th century to 18th century. Marks of numerous workshops recorded·

Sceaux, Seine, France
Faïence factory working here from c. 1735 until 1793.

Painted

Conrade

Painted

Girolamo Salomini or Siccardi

Fortress mark of Guidoboni

The S.P. and anchor marks indicate the patronage (from 1775) of the Duc de Penthièvre, Grand-Amiral de France. Other initials, with conjectural meaning:
C.S. perhaps Chapelle/Sceaux
    Jacques Chapelle *fl.* here 1749–59
G.S. perhaps Glot/Sceaux
    Richard Glot, owner 1772–93
Soft-paste porcelain made at Sceaux, but surreptiously. Marks:

Pharos of Genoa mark of Levantino

Luigi Levantino

Incised

Schaper, Johann: (1621–70)
Nuremberg painter of schwarzlot on faïence.

Falcon mark of Folco

Schaphuysen, near Crefeld, Rhineland, Germany
Slipware potters worked here using sgraffiato technique; wares dating from 1713 to 1795 recorded. Potters' names inscribed include:
Christianus Lappen 1713
Johann Franssen 1749
Paulus Hammelkers 1743
Gerrit Evers 1770
Gerrit Evers, Schaphüsen 1795

Fish mark of Pescetto

Sun in its splendour Salomini

On ware signed Agostino Ratti

Schlaggenwald, Bohemia, Czechoslovakia
Hard-paste porcelain factory established
here 1792 by Paulus, Pöschl, and Reu-
mann; the letter S, painted or incised,
was used as the factory mark. Factory
owned by Lippert and Haas from 1803
until 1843; descendants continued the
business.

Johann Leihamer   Conrade Bade
(painter)   (painter)
1758   1764–91

Schlierbach
Earthenware made here from *c.* 1830.

Schney, Bavaria, Germany
Hard-paste porcelain made here from
c. 1783. Mark the word SCHNEY impressed or the letter S in blue. Modern
mark: St Andrew's cross over letter S.

Closely similar to mark used by Samson
of Paris.

Schorndorf, Württemberg, Germany
Modern hard-paste porcelain factory
established here in 1904 under name of
Bauer & Pfeiffer, using following marks:

Marks of the Württembergische Porzellan
Manufaktur given as:

Haas & Cžjžek
in
Schlaggenwald

SCHLAGGENWALD

Schlaggenwald

Schleswig, Germany
Faïence made here from 1755 to 1814.
Usual mark letter S over initials of owners
and/or painters.

Schrezheim, near Ellwangen, Württemberg, Germany
Faïence made here from 1752 until 1872.

Given by Jännicke

Schütz, Ludwig:
Made decorative faïence in the style of the Renaissance, from *c.* 1871.

Schwerin, Mecklenburg, Germany
Faïence made here from 1753 onward. Mark included the initial of the potter, J. A. Apfelstadt (d. 1771), with name or initial of the place over the painter's or decorator's mark:

Given by Jännicke and Graesse

Scott, Anthony: (*fl. c.* 1789)
English potter owning the Southwick Pottery and the Newbottle Pottery, at Sunderland, Co. Durham.
SCOTT
Impressed

Scott Bros: (*fl. c.* 1786–96)
Made stoneware, red ware, and ornamental pottery at Portobello, Midlothian, Scotland.
Mark recorded:
SCOTT BROS
Impressed

Seefried, Peter Antonius: (1742–1812)
Porcelain modeller and "repairer" working at Nymphenburg (*c.* 1756–66), then at Ludwigsburg (1766) and Kelsterbach (1767). Again at Nymphenburg, 1769 until 1810.

Mark perhaps his:
Letter S incised, repairer's mark occasionally found on Kelsterbach figures.

Segovia, Spain
Modern pottery made here by firm of Zuloaga.

Selman (Seltman), J. & W.: (*fl. c.* 1865)
English manufacturers of bronzed and earthenware toys, at Tunstall, Staffordshire.

SELMAN
Impressed

Septfontaines, Luxemburg
The brothers Boch made earthenware here from 1766; Pierre-Joseph Boch became sole proprietor in 1796.

Impressed   Impressed

          Impressed   In blue

Impressed   Impressed early 19th century

In 1841 the factory became part of the Villeroy & Boch company.

Seville, Spain
Faïence made here in 19th century in suburb of Triana; another factory was worked by M. Francesco de Aponte and Pickman & Co.

Sèvres, France

Factory at Vincennes, 1745; transferred to Sèvres 1756; moved to St Cloud in 1876. Soft-paste porcelain made 1745 to 1800; hard-paste porcelain from 1769 onward. Mark of crossed L's used in various forms at Vincennes, and from 1756 to 1793 at Sèvres.

Various forms of the crossed L's mark

Other examples, with date letters:

In blue; year 1753

In blue; year mark 1759: mark of painter Binet

In red; year 1778; mark of painter Dieu

In blue; year 1780

In blue; year 1788 mark of gilder Vincent, in gold

First Republic, 1793–1804:

Sevres

E.T.

1793–1804, in purple, mark of the gilder LF in gold

GI

1793–1804, in blue; mark of the gilder GI in gold

Jèvres

1793–1804, in blue

Jevres

In blue

RF.
de Sevres

In blue

First Empire, 1804–14:

M. Impl
de Sevres
7

Stencilled in red

Other 19th-century marks:

Printed in red
1810–14

277

In blue

In blue

1814–24
(Reign of Louis XVIII)

In red,
1848,
decoration mark

In red,
1849, year
of decoration

In chrome green,
1851, year of
manufacture

In blue: Reign of Charles X, 1824–30

In blue 1830

In gold or blue
1834

In gold or blue
1834

Year marks 1753–77:

A	1753	I	1761	Q	1769
B	1754	J	1762	R	1770
C	1755	K	1763	S	1771
D	1756	L	1764	T	1772
E	1757	M	1765	U	1773
F	1758	N	1766	V	1774
G	759	O	1767	X	1775
H	1760	P	1768	Y	1776
				Z	1777

In chrome green

In blue or gold
1845

In red
Second Empire
1852–70

Year marks 1778–93:

AA	1778	FF	1783	KK	1788
BB	1779	GG	1784	LL	1789
CC	1780	HH	1785	MM	1790
DD	1781	II	1786	NN	1791
EE	1782	JJ	1787	OO	1792
		PP		until 17th July, 1793	

Destination marks: in red

Examples with year marks:

| 1763 | 1781 | 1782 |

Date signs used from 1801–17:

Tg 1801 7 1807 tz 1813

X 1802 8 1808 qz 1814

$//$ 1803 9 1809 qn 1815

≑ 1804 10 1810 sz 1816

$-//-$ 1805 oz 1811 ds 1817

$\mathcal{W}$ 1806 dz 1812

Examples with date signs:

1803 or 1805   1804   1806

Marks or signatures of artists:

$\mathcal{N}$ **Aloncle, François:** 1758
birds and animals

$\mathcal{J}.A.$ **André, Jules:** 1843–69
landscapes

  Antheaume, Jean-Jacques: 1754
landscapes and animals

$\mathcal{26}$ **Armand, Pierre-Louis-Philippe:** 1746
birds and flowers

$A \; \mathcal{A}$ **Asselin:** 1764–1804
portraits, miniatures

   **Aubert, aîné:** 1755
flowers

$\mathcal{By}.$ **Bailly:** 1753–93

$\mathcal{B}$ **Barbin, François-Hubert:** 1815–49
ornament

=   **Bardet:** 1751–58
flowers

$\mathcal{B3. B3}$ $\mathcal{N3}$ $\mathcal{B3}$ **Barrat:** 1769–91
flowers, garlands, fruits

$\mathcal{B}$ $\mathcal{B}$ **Barré:** late 18th century
flower sprays

$\mathcal{AB}$ $\mathcal{B}$ **Barré, Louis Désiré:** 1846–81
flowers

$\mathcal{B}$ BARRIAT   **Barriat, Charles:** 1848–83
figures

$C3D$ **Baudouin:** 1750–90
gilder

♁   **Becquet:** 1748
flowers

$\mathcal{B.r}$ $\mathcal{BG}$ **Béranger, Antoine:** 1807–46
figures

$6.$ **Bertrand:** 1750–1808
detached flowers

✡ ✡   **Bienfait, Jean-Baptiste:** 1756–62
gilder and painter

$\dot{T}$ $\dot{T}$ $\dot{T}.$ **Binet:** 1750–76
flowers

$\mathcal{Sc}$ **Binet, Mme (née Chanou, Sophie):** 1779–98
flowers

$\mathcal{B.T}$ $\mathcal{B.T}$ **Boitel, Charles-Marie-Pierre:** 1797–1822
gilder

  Boucher: 1754
flowers and garlands

Bouchet, Jean: 1757–93
landscapes

Boucot, P.:
late 18th century
fruit and flowers

Bouillat: 1800–1811
flowers and landscapes

Boulanger, père: 1754–84
gilder

Boulanger, fils: 1770–81
flowers, pastorals, child
subjects

Boullemier, Antoine-Gabriel:
1802–42
gilder

Boullemier, François-
Antoine: 1802–42
gilder

Boullemier, Hilaire-François:
1813–55
gilder

Bulidon: 1763–92
flowers

Bunel, Mme (née
Buteux, Manon)
1778–1817
flowers

Buteux, Charles: 1760–
flowers and emblems

Buteux, jeune: 1759–66
flowers

Buteux, Guillaume: 1759
pastoral subjects and
children

Buteux, Théodore:
1786–1822

Cabau, Eugène-Charles
1847–84
flowers

Capelle, Mme: flowers
or
Capelle: 1746–
painter of landscapes

Capronnier, François:
early 19th century

Cardin: 1749–93
flowers

Carrier or Carrié: 1752–57
flowers

Castell: 1771–1800
landscapes, birds, hunting
scenes

Caton: 1749–98
pastorals, children, por-
traits

Catrice: 1757–74
flowers

Chabry: 1765–87
pastoral scenes

Chanou, Mme (née Durosey):
before 1800
flowers

Chapuis, aîné: 1756–93
flowers and birds

Chapuis, jeune: before 1800
flowers

Charrin, Mlle Fanny:
1814–26
figures and portraits

Chauvaux, aîné: 1752–88
gilder

Chauvaux, fils: 1773–83
bouquets

Chevalier: 1755–57
flowers
cf. mark of Boulanger, fils

Choisy: 1770–1812
flowers and ornaments

Chulot: 1755–1800
emblems, flowers,
arabesques

Commelin: before 1800
flowers and garlands

Constant: 1804–15
gilder

CT. Constantin: 1823–45
figure subject

♪ Cornaille, Antoine-Toussaint:
1755–93
flowers

L C L. Couturier: 1783
gilder

.DF DF. Davignon, Jean-
François: 1807–15
figures in landscapes

De Gault Degault, Jean-Marie:
1808–17
figures

DF Delafosse, Denis: 1805–15
figures (cf. Davignon)

DG Derischweiler, Jean-Charles
Gérard: 1838–88, gilder

Df Df Despérais or Depé-
rais, Claude: 1794–
1822, ornaments

Dl. Deutsche: c. 1815
ornament

CD Develly, Jean-Charles:
1813–48
animals in landscapes

D.I. Didier, Charles-Antoine:
1819–48
ornament

△ ⛰ Dieu: various periods, 1777–
1810
painter of Chinese subjects
and flowers; gilding

K K. Dodin: 1754–1800
figures, portraits, etc.

DR DR Drand: before 1780
chinoiseries, gilding

D7 Drouet, Gilbert: 1785–1825
flowers

🌿 🌿 Dubois, Jean-René: 1756–77
flowers

A.D. AD Ducluzeau, Mme (née
Durand, Marie-
Adelaide): 1807–48
figures, portraits

D.y Durosey, Charles-Christian-
Marie: 1802–30
gilder

D. D.. D Dusolle: before 1800
flowers

DT. Dutanda: 1765–1802
flowers

✗ Evans: 1752–1805
birds, butterflies, landscapes

F Falot or Fallot: before 1800
birds and ornament

∴∴ Fontaine: 1752–after 1800
emblems and flowers

Ft ft Fontaine, Jean-Joseph:
1827–57
flowers

♡ Fontelliau, A.: 1747–80
gilder

Y. Fouré: 1749–62
flowers

☼ Fritsch: 1763–64
figures, children, etc.

ft fx Fumez: 1777–1804
flowers

❀ Gautier or Gauthier: 1787–91
landscapes and animals

G Genest: 1752–89
figures and genre

† † Génin: 1756
flowers

G.G Georget: 1802–23
figures

Gd Gd. Gérard, Claude-
Charles: 1771–1824
pastoral subjects
and miniatures

Gérard, Mme (née Vautrin): 1781–1802
flowers

Girard: 1762–64
arabesque

Godin: 1792–1833
gilder, painter, ground-layer or
Godin, Mme

Gomery: 1756
flowers

Grémont, jeune: 1769–81
garlands and bouquets

Grison: 1749–71
gilder

Henrion, aîné: 1768–84
flowers

Héricourt: 1770–77
garlands and detached flowers (or "He")

Hilken: before 1800
figures

Houry: 1747–55
flowers

Huard: 1811–46
ornament in various styles

Joyau: 1766–75
flowers

Jubin: 1772–75
gilder

Langlacé: 1807–14
landscapes

La Roche: 1759–1802
flowers

Léandre: 1779–85
children and emblems

Le Bel, aîné: 1766–75
figures and flowers

Le Bel, jeune: 1780–93
flowers
(landscape painter of this name used this mark 1804–44)

Lecot: before 1800
gilder

Ledoux: 1758
landscapes and birds

Le Guay, Etienne-Charles: various dates between 1778 and 1840
figures

Le Guay, Etienne-Henri: 1749–96
gilder

Le Guay, Pierre-André: 1772–1812
figures

Le Grand: 1776–1817
gilder
(cf. Le Guay)

Levé: 1754–1805
flowers

Levé, Felix: late 18th century
flowers and chinoiseries

Maqueret, Mme (née Bouillat): 1796–1820
flowers

Massy: 1779–1806
flowers

Méreaud, aîné: 1754–91
flowers and borders

Méreaud, jeune: 1756–79
bouquets

Micaud, Jacques: 1759
flowers and ornaments

Micaud, Pierre-Louis: 1795–1812
painter and gilder

Michel, Ambroise: 1772–80

Moiron: 1790–91
flowers

Mongenot: 1754
flowers

Moreau, D.-J.: 1809–15
gilding

282

M   **Morin:** 1754
sea-pieces and military
subjects

V   **Mutel:** various times,
1754–73
landscapes

nq   **Nicquet or Niquet:** 1764–92
flowers

  Noël: 1755–1804
flowers, etc.

SD   **Noualhler, Mme (née Durosey):** 1775–95
flowers

P   **Parpette:** 1755
flowers

PP   **Parpette, Mlle:** late 18th century
flowers

LP   **Parpette, Mlle Louison:** late
18th/early 19th century
flowers

PT.   **Petit, aîné:** 1756
gilder

f   **Pfeiffer:** 1771–1800
flowers

P.H.   **Philippine, aîné:** 1778
pastoral subjects and
children

P.h.   **Philippine, jeune:** 1787

pe   **Pierre, aîné:** 1759–75

pq   **Pierre, Jean-Jacques:**
1763–1800
flowers

St   **Pithou, aîné:** 1757–90
figures and historical subjects

Sj   **Pithou, jeune:** 1760–95
figures and flowers

B   **Pouillot:** 1773–78
flowers

HP.   **Prévost, aîné:** 1754
gilding

Raux, aîné: 1766–79
flowers

Renard, Emile: after 1800

PR   **Robert, Pierre:** first half 19th
century
ornaments

XX   **Rocher:** 1758

Rosset: 1753
landscapes and flowers

RL   **Rousselle:** 1758–74

S.h.   **Schradre:** 1773–86
landscapes and birds

Sinsson or Sisson: 1773–95
flowers and garlands

SS   **Sinsson, Jacques:** 1795–1846
flowers

SSp   **Sinsson, Pierre:** 1818–48

SSe   **Sinsson, Louis:** 1830–47
flowers

Sioux, aîné: 1752–92
flowers and garlands

O   **Sioux, jeune:** 1752
flowers

Sw   **Swebach:** 1802–13
military subjects

  Tabary: 1751
birds

  Taillandier: 1753–90
flowers

• • •   **Tandart, Charles:** 1756
flowers

Tardi: 1755–95
flowers

• • • •   **Théodore:** late 18th century
gilder

J   **Thévenet, aîné:** 1745

jt   **Thévenet, jeune:** 1752
flowers

Troyen: 1802–17
gilder

Vandé or Vaudé: 1753

Vavasseur, aîné: 1753

Vieillard: 1752–90

Vincent: 1752–1806
gilder

Weydinger, Pierre: late 18th
century–19th century
gilder

Xrouet: 1750–75
landscapes

Marks of Modellers and Repairers:

Bono: identified by
W. Sainsbury;
given to Bachelier
and/or Brachard by
Chavagnac and
Grollier, and by
Tilmans

Bourdois: 1773

Chanou, Jean-Baptiste:
1779–1825

Collet: signed in full

Delatre: 1754–58

Duru: identified by Sainsbury

Fernex:
often attributed to Falconet
by older authorities

Le Riche, Joseph:
1757–1801

Letourneur: 1756–62

Le Tronne: 1753–57

Liance: 1769–1810

Pajou: 1751–59

Sewell & Donkin. (*fl.* from *c.* 1780)
English potters making Queen's ware
pink lustred wares, pierced baskets
(Leeds-style) etc. at Newcastle-on-Tyne,
Northumberland.
Mark, "Sewell" alone, or name of firm:

SEWELL

Sharpe, Thomas: (d. 1838)
English potter working the Swadlincote
potteries at Burton-on-Trent, Staffordshire (1821–38); firm afterwards trading
as Sharpe Bros & Co.

T. SHARPE   THOMAS SHARPE
Impressed   Impressed

Shaw, Ralph: (*fl.* mid 18th century)
English potter working at Cobridge,
Staffordshire; inscription recorded "Made
by Ralph Shaw October 31, Cobridge
gate MT 1740" (or 46); died 1754/59.

Shorthose & Co: (*fl.* second half 18th
century until 1823)
English firm, also known as Shorthose &
Heath, making various earthenwares at
Hanley, Staffordshire; specialised in
printing.
Marks recorded:

Siena, Tuscany, Italy
Pottery made here from 13th century;
maïolica made 14th and 15th centuries to
c. 1520; revived for part 18th century.

Simpson, John: (*fl. c.* 1710)
English potter making "red dishes & pans" at Burslem, Staffordshire.
Possibly his mark:

Found on certain octagonal slipware dishes.

Simpson, Ralph: (1651–1724)
English potter working in Staffordshire; name found on various pieces, notably of trailed slip decoration, may be his:

Sinceny, Aisne, France
Faïence factory established here by Jean-Baptiste de Fayard, working from 1733 onward.

In blue
The letter S sometimes occurs with the name "Pellevé" (manager 1737–   )

Painters' initials or signatures:
B.T Pierre Bertrand
Alexandré Daussy
Pierre Jeannot
Joseph Bedeaux
L M Leopold Mélériat, 1737–75
"LJLC pinxit" Joseph le Cerf, *c.* 1772
Gh François-Joseph Ghail
Philippe-Vincent Coignard
Antoine Coignard
André-Joseph le Comte
Examples:

A.Daussy P.Jeannot J.Bedeaux F.-J.Ghail

Other factories, 19th century:
Lecomte and Dantier:
              L et D
Mandois:
              Mandois

Sitzendorf, Thuringia, Germany
Hard-paste porcelain factory founded here 1850, working into 20th century.

Slee's Pottery, Leeds, Yorkshire, England
Established in 1888 for the manufacture of cream-coloured wares to the patterns of the Leeds Pottery; marks used were those of the original factory, q.v.

Smith, Sampson: (1813–78)
English potter at Longton, Staffordshire; began as decorator; specially noted for earthenware "flat back" type figures (1850–59); business continued by others after his death; figure-making ceased in 1918, but revived *c.* 1948 using some of the original moulds by Barker Bros, still trading as Sampson Smith Ltd.

In relief:
under china dogs

Smith, William,& Co: (*fl.* first half 19th century)
English potters at Stockton-on-Tees, Yorkshire, chiefly making imitations of Wedgwood's wares (from *c.* 1824); in *c.* 1848 restrained by injunction from using the latter's name (mis-spelt) on their products.
Marks recorded:
    W.S. & Co's   W.S. & Co's
WEDGEWOOD QUEEN'S WARE
                    STOCKTON

Sneyd, T.: (?early 19th century)
English potter at Hanley, Staffordshire; name found on red and other coloured jugs crudely imitating the Portland Vase.

T. SNEYD
HANLEY

Solomon s seal mark
Five-point star:

Found on maïolica made at Savona, q.v.

Solon, Marc Louis: (1835–1912)
Ceramic artist; first worked at Sèvres, developing the pâte-sur-pâte technique (c. 1859); came to England, working at Mintons (1870–1904) in the pâte-sur-pâte technique there also.
Mark recorded:

He sometimes signed his
early work "Miles"

Sölvesborg, Sweden
Faïence factory founded here by Major Gabriel Sparre in 1773; later in hands of S. Fr. von Ziepel, closing down 1793.
Mark:
The letters S B, sometimes with a numeral.

Spode, Josiah: (1733–97)
English potter who founded the Spode factory at Stoke-on-Trent, Staffordshire, in 1770; made earthenware (c. 1776) and porcelain (c. 1800); trading as Spode &

Copeland (c. 1813); as Copeland & Garrett (1833); as Copeland, late Spode (c. 1847) and thereafter by Copeland's name alone; continues today.

Printed in purple

 SPODE

Printed in blue   In red

COPELAND
& GARRETT

Stevenson, Ralph: (fl. 1815–35)
English potter at Cobridge, Staffordshire; firm noted for blue-printed wares with American and other views, portraits of eminent men, etc.

Stockelsdorf, near Lübeck, Germany
Faïence made here by Georg Nicolaus Lübbers, 1771–86; continued into the 19th century.

Stockelsdorf-Buchwald-
Abraham Leihamer

286

Other initials recorded:
A   J. A. G. Adler
S   D. N. O. Seritz
C   C. T. F. Creutzfeldt

Stralsund, Pomerania, Germany
Faïence factory started here in 1755 by
J. U. Giese (d. 1780) with J. Buchwald;
leased to J. E. L. Ehrenreich in 1766;
production ceased 1786; revived later,
finally closing 1790.

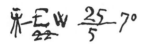

The arms of Stralsund, E for
Ehrenreich, the price, and the date

Strasburg, Alsace, France
Faïence made here in the 18th century by
the Hannong family. Marks:
PH for Paul Hannong, proprietor 1738
          (d. 1760)
JH for Joseph Hannong, proprietor
          1760 (d. c. 1790)
Painters' initials, with numerals, often
accompany these monograms.

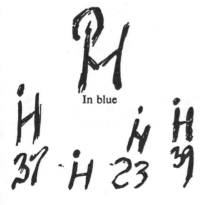

In blue

All in blue
Artists' marks recorded:
HM   **Henri Montoson** 1754
JH   **Joseph Hannsmann** 1745
NM   **Nicolas Mittmann** 1749–53
Porcelain made at Strasburg c. 1752 and
c. 1768 by Hannong family.

Studio potters (English): (20th century)
Marks recorded:

  Barron, Paul

  Bouverie, K. Pleydell-

  Davis, Harry

Dunn, Constance

Finch, Raymond

  Foy, Peggie

Hammond, H. F.

Mathews, Heber

Trey, Marianne de

Wa|ker, Agatha

Washington, R. J.

Sulzbach-Philippsburg, Germany
Faïence made here 1751–74, and porcelain 1771–74.

CT in monogram, for Carl Theodor, with or without the Electoral hat.

Swansea, Glamorganshire, Wales
Earthenware made here (c. 1764–1870) and porcelain (c. 1815–17), and a porcelain incorporating soapstone (after 1817 to 1823), at the Cambrian Pottery, under different owners: trading as Haynes, Dillwyn & Co (1802–10); Dillwyn & Co (1810–17); T. J. Bevington & Co (1817–24); and Dillwyn again (1831–c. 1850); finally in hands of David Evans, followed by his son.

SWANSEA DILLWYN & Co

ΛSEA   SWANSEA

sea Swansea

Talavera, Spain
Tin-glazed earthenware made here from c. 1560 to c. 1720, and again c. 1761. Similar industry at Puente del Arzobispo, mid 17th century until 19th century.

Blue and white faïence made during the 19th century. Marks used included the name TALAVERA.

In black   In purple-brown   In blue

In brown

Talor (Tallor), William
English name recorded on large Toft-style slipware dishes, one being dated 1700.

WILLIAM·TALOR

Tata, Hungary
Earthenware made here from c. 1756–58 until after 1811.
Mark: T incised or painted in blue.

Taunay, Pierre-Antoine-Henri: (fl. 1745–78)
Porcelain painter and colour preparer at Vincennes and Sèvres.

TANAY

Taylor, George
English name recorded on a slipware posset-pot, dated 1692, and on a dish.

Taylor, Howson: (d. 1935)
English potter who founded the Ruskin Pottery at Smethwick, Staffordshire, in 1898; closed down 1935.

Taylor, William and John: (*fl. c.* 1750)
English potters making earthenware and stoneware at Burslem, Staffordshire. Mark ascribed:

W.T. & Co
Impressed

Tebo: (*fl.* second half 18th century)
Perhaps English version of French "Thibaud"; there is evidence of a repairer at Bow (from *c.* 1750) who signed T . A Tebo was at Worcester (1760s), and the mark occurs on Plymouth porcelain (1768–70); Mr Tebo worked for Josiah Wedgwood (from *c.* 1775); later went to Dublin, into obscurity.

Teichert, C.: (founded 1864)
Modern firm, working at Meissen, using for mark word MEISSEN.

Teinitz, Bohemia, Czechoslovakia
Earthenware made here from 1801 until 1866, by Count Wrtby and F. L. Welby.

Impressed

Terchi, Bartolomeo: (*fl.* 18th century)
Italian pottery painter; at S. Quirico d'Orcia, Tuscany, 1714–*c.* 1724; at Siena 1727, and at Bassano *c.* 1744.

Tettau, Franconia, Germany
Porcelain factory founded here in 1794.

In purple or blue

Thieme, Carl: (*fl.* 19th century)
Founded hard-paste porcelain factory in 1875 at Potschappel, Dresden, making imitation Capo-di-monte wares.

Thompson, Joseph: (*fl.* early 18th century)
English potter (from 1818) at Hartshorne, Derbyshire; sons continued trading as Thompson Bros.

J. THOMPSON
Impressed

Joseph Thompson
Wooden Box
Pottery
Derbyshire
Impressed

Thooft & Labouchere, Delft, Holland
Working during 19th century, making traditional wares.

Taken from firm's advertisement 1895; usually rendered very freely:

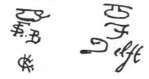

Thornhill, Sir James: (1675–1734)
English baroque painter; not ceramic artist, but there are some tin-glazed earthenware plates (British Museum) perhaps painted by him at Delft in 1711. Signed:

Thoune, Switzerland
Factory here making modern pottery.

Incised   Painted

Incised

Tiefenfurt, Silesia, Germany
Hard-paste porcelain made by P. Donath from 1808, at the Schlesische Porzellan-fabrik.

Tinworth, George: (1843–1913)
English modeller at Doulton's Lambeth (London) factory, from 1867.

Incised

Tirschenreuth, Bavaria, Germany
Porcelain factory established here in first half 19th century.

Tittensor, Charles: (*fl.* early 18th century)
English figure-maker and black-printer; in business at Hanley, Staffordshire (1802–*c.* 1813); at Shelton (recorded in 1818 and 1823).
Mark recorded:

Impressed

Tittensor, Jacob: (*fl.* late 18th century)
Marks recorded:

Incised   In relief

Toft, James: (b. 1673)
Probable maker of dishes bearing his name; dishes dated 1695 and 1705 are known.

Toft, Ralph: (b. 1638)
Name occurs on large Toft-style dishes, two being dated 1676 and 1677; a posset pot is dated 1683.

RALPH OFT

Toft, Thomas: (d. 1689)
Name occurs (to date) on 35 large dishes, 2 jugs, and a posset pot; wares decorated with trailed slip, the dishes having trellis rim borders with the name; uncertain if the name indicates maker or recipient, more likely the former.

thomas:toft

THOMAS TOFT

thomas TOFT

A A A ∂

Variations in letter A
in Toft signature

Tooth & Co Ltd: (*fl.* late 19th century)
English potters at Burton-on-Trent, Staffordshire, established 1883.

H

Toulouse, Haute-Garonne, France
Faïence made here in 17th and 18th centuries. From 1829 to 1849 made by François and Antoine Fouque, collaborating with Antoine Arnoux.

Tournay, Belgium
Soft-paste porcelain made here from 1751 to 1796 by F.-J. Péterinck; owner from 1797 to 1799, C. Péterinck-Gérard; Bettignies family worked the factory *c.* 1800 to 1850.

In gold or colour
1751–56

In blue, red, brown, or gold, 1756–81

Treviso, Italy
Soft-paste porcelain made here, 1759–77; by Andrea and Giuseppe Fontebasso, 1795–1840.

F. F.
Treviso 1799

G.A.F.F.
Treviso

G.A.F.F. for Giuseppe Andrea Fratelli Fontebasso.
Signature of painter Gaetano Negrisole occurs with dates of early 1830s.

Tunnicliffe, Michael: (*fl.* 1828–35)
English potter making earthenware toys and figures at Tunstall, Staffordshire.

Impressed

Turin, Piedmont, Italy
Hard-paste porcelain made here between 1737 and 1743; examples rare.
Maïolica made here from 16th to 19th centuries.

In blue
For the Rossetti factory, started 1725.
G.A.A. (underlined) for G. A. Ardizzone (recorded in 1765).

In black

For a 9th-century potter, D. Gionetti.

Turner, John: (1738–87)
English potter at Stoke-on-Trent, Staffordshire (from *c.* 1756); at Lane End, now Longton (1762–87); firm trading as Turner & Co in 1803; closed down 1806.
TURNER   TURNER & CO.
Impressed   Impressed

Turner's Patent

In red: 1800–1805
on stoneware

Twigg, Joseph & Bros: (*fl.* 19th century)
English potters making decorated earthenware at Swinton, Yorkshire, from 1839; Twigg family carried on until 1881.

 TWIGG'S

Impressed

Twyford (Twiford), Joshua (*c.* 1640–1729)
English potter said to have made red and black "Elers" ware and salt-glaze stoneware at Shelton, Staffordshire.
Mark ascribed:

On piece in British Museum, London

Val-Sous-Meudon, Seine-et-Oise, France
White earthenware made here from 1806 until 1818, by Mittenhoff & Mouron.

Valenciennes, Nord, France
Hard-paste porcelain factory started here by J. B. Fauquez in 1785; assisted by brother-in-law Lamoninary, 1800–1810.

In blue: for Fauquez, Lamoninary, and Valenciennes

Vallauris
Pottery made here in 19th century by Jérôme Massier and Company.
Found impressed:

*Jérôme Massier
Vallauris*

JEROME
MASSIER
VALLAURIS

Varages, Var, France
One mark cited:
"Fait par moi E. armand a varages 1698"
T. Deck says the factory dated from 1730
Mark: letter V rather freely done:

Given by Deck

Vianna do Castello, Portugal
Faïence made here from 1744.

Given by Graesse

Venice, Italy
Maïolica made here from c. 1570 until
mid 18th century.
Workshops of 18th century include;
The Bertolini brothers (first half);
The Manardi brothers (1669–1740)

Early 18th century

18th century

Venice: Cozzi factory
Factory established 1764, making porcelain; maïolica a subsidiary; closed 1812.

In red   (Figures rarely marked)

Venice: Hewelke factory (*fl.* 1758–63)
Porcelain factory established at Udine
1758–61; at Venice from 1761 to 1763;
owned by Nathaniel Friedrich Hewelke
and his wife, Maria Dorothea, from
Dresden.

Incised, and covered with
a brown-red pigment

Venice: Vezzi factory (*fl.* 1720–27)
Factory founded by Francesco Vezzi
(1651–1740) in 1720; closed in 1727
under his son Giovanni Vezzi.
Forgeries of wares and marks are known.

In blue

In red, blue or gold   In red

In colour

In underglaze blue In red   In red

In underglaze blue: other
equally fantastic forms are recorded

Lodouico Ortolani Veneto dipinse nella Fabrica di Porcelana, in Venenu

Impressed   In blue   In blue

Some modern Viennese factory marks:

Verhaast, Gijsbrecht: (*fl. c.* 1690)
Delft landscape painter.
Signature recorded on some plaques:

G Verhaast.

KNESL
WIEN

Impressed

Vienna, Austria
Hard-paste porcelain factory founded here in 1719 by Du Paquier assisted by S. Stölzel; passed through various hands, closing in 1864.
Marks:
Du Paquier period (1719–c. 1744), no marks except an occasional pseudo-Chinese one.
Shield mark used from 1744 until 1864.
1744–49   Painted in red, black, or purple overglaze colours, impressed or incised
1749–80   Painted in blue
1820s   Drawn almost as a triangle
Later,   more elongated shape, either impressed or in blue
Factory rejects marked:
On wares sold undecorated:
     a cross cut on the wheel across the blue shield mark
On decorated rejects:
     Letter A in green or red, over the blue mark
Year marks:
From 1783 to 1800, the two last figures
After 1800, the three last figures

Artist's mark recorded:

Ant: us Anreiter
VZ: 1755

Villeroy and Boch: (founded 1841)
Firm founded by families of Villeroy and Boch, to amalgate the factories working at Wallerfangen, Septfontaines, and Mettlach; new factory built at Dresden in 1853. Merzig absorbed into the business 1879, and Schramberg 1883.
     BB
     In blue
     J. F. Boch and
     Buschmann

Mettlach   Mettlach   Septfontaines

Vienne 12 July
1771

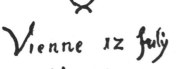

Mettlach   Dresden
    Schramberg   Schramberg

Mettlach   Wallerfangen
Dresden   Dresden

Mettlach   Mettlach   Mettlach

Villers Cotterets
These words used as mark on ware made
at Chantilly (c. 1770) for the Château
of Villers Cotterets.

Vinovo, near Turin, Italy
Porcelain (hybrid hard-paste) factory
established here in 1776, closing 1780.
Re-opened 1815, worked by Giovanni
Lomello.

Incised or   Cross of   Painted in
painted in   Savoy   blue
blue

In blue
1780–1815

Intials D G for Dottore Gioanetti (1729–
1815)
Initial L for Lomello (fl. 1815–20)

Viry family: (fl. later 17th century)
Faïence painters at Moustiers, and at
Marseilles.
Inscriptions recorded:
"Fait à Marseille chez F. Viry 1681"
"Fay a St iean du desert Viry" (on a
piece dating from c. 1690)

Viry, Gaspard:
Faïence painter at Moustiers.
Inscription recorded:

Vische, near Turin, Italy
Porcelain factory set up here by the
Conte de Vische in 1765, production
ceased after 1766.
Mark on pieces in Turin Museum:

Vista Alegre, near Oporto, Portugal
Hard-paste porcelain factory established
here by J. F. P. Basto in 1824, surviving
to present day.

Viterbo, Umbria, Italy
Inscription recorded on a maïolica dish:
"In Viterbo Diomeo 1544"

Given by Chaffers
(inscription forms part of decoration)

Vizeer or Viseer, Piet: (d. 1762)
Owner of De Kunstenaar (The Artist)
workshop at Delft, 1735–62.

Volkstedt, Thuringia, Germany
Porcelain factory established at Sitzen-
dorf c. 1760; moved to Volkstedt 1762.
Acquired 1800 by Wilhelm Heinrich
Greiner and Carl Holzapfel who contin-
ued until 1817 or later.

Marks:
Crossed hayforks from Schwarzburg arms used with a line across after 1787

Greiner & Holzapfel
1799–1817

Beyer & Bosch
decorating from 1853
manufacturing from 1890

Volpato, Giovanni: (d. 1803)
Founded earthenware and porcelain factory at Rome *c.* 1790; continued by descendants until 1832.
Mark occasionally found on figures:
G. VOLPATA. ROMA
Impressed

Voyez, John: (*c.* 1735–*c.* 1800)
Modeller and manufacturer, of French extraction, working in England; with Wedgwood (1768–69); recorded at Cobridge, Staffordshire (1772); probably modelled for the Ralph Woods of Burslem; no mention after 1791 in London.

Vron, France
Painted tiles made here, end of 18th century.
VRON
Impressed

Waldenburg, Silesia, Germany
Hard-paste porcelain made here by Carl Krister, beginning in 1831.

In green

Waldershof, Bavaria, Germany
Modern hard-paste porcelain factory established here by Johann Haviland.

Wallendorf, Thuringia, German-
Company formed here by members of th. Hammann and Greiner families, to make hard-paste porcelain. Gotthelf Greiner went to Limbach 1772. Hammann's factory closed 1833

In blue
Mark often confused with that of other factories, including Meissen.

Wallerfangen, Saar Basin, Germany
Earthenware factory established here in 1789 which passed to Villeroy and Boch.

Impressed

Walton, John: (*fl.* early 19th century)
English maker of pottery figures, from the first decade of the 19th century until 1835, at Burslem, Staffordshire.
Mark, usually on the back of the figure, occasionally underneath:

Impressed
Not to be confused with other figure-makers of the same surname:
Walton, James: (*fl.* 1848–51) Hanley
Walton, Joshua: (*fl.* 1830–35) Hanley
Walton, William: (*fl.* 1846) Shelton

Warburton, Francis: (*fl.* 1800 onward)
Made cream-coloured earthenware, first in partnership with brother Peter (1800–1802) at Cobridge, England: later at La-Charité-sur-Loire, France. Factory taken over by Le Bault in 1803.

LA CHARITE
Impressed

Warburton, Peter: (1773–1813)
English maker of cream-coloured earthenware at Cobridge, Staffordshire; at first in partnership with Francis Warburton, until 1802; afterwards on his own account; partner in New Hall company (between 1804 and 1810).

Impressed

Warburton family: (*fl.* 18th century)
English manufacturers of earthenware at Cobridge, Staffordshire; factory worked by John Warburton (from *c.* 1710) and continued by his widow, and his son Thomas (lasted more than a century).

WARBURTON
Impressed

Watcombe, Devon, England
Factory established here in 1869, making terra cotta and "art" manufactures.
Among marks used:

WATCOMBE
TORQUAY

Wattisfield, Suffolk, England
Earthenware made here during the second half 18th century; pottery taken over (1808) by Thomas Watson; worked continuously by his descendants. Thomas Harrison (1844) made brown earthenware here.

Impressed

Wayte & Ridge: (*fl. c.* 1864)
English potters making china, parian, earthenware, and lustre at Longton, Staffordshire.
Mark recorded on figures:

W & R
L
85

Impressed

Wedgwood: European imitations
Mark recorded:

WEDGWOOD
Impressed

Found on cream-coloured earthenware made at Hubertsburg, end 18th/early 19th centuries.
Also used at Bodenbach in Bohemia, 19th century, and at Schmidt's factory, Bayreuth.

Wedgwood, Josiah: (1730–95)
English potter at Burslem and Etruria, Staffordshire, making all kinds of wares (except bone china and porcelain); in partnership with Whieldon (1754–59); trading as Wedgwood & Bentley (1769–80); factory inherited by Wedgwood's second son, Josiah; continues today.

JOSIAH WEDGWOOD
Feb. 2nd 1805

Wedgwood & Bentley

wedgwood   WEDGWOOD

Wedgwood
& Bentley

Wedgwood & Bentley: Etruria

WEDGWOOD
WEDGWOOD

Wedgwood

W. & B

Wedgwood
& Bentley
356

WEDGWOOD & SONS   WEDGWOOD

E. Lifsore (signature)

Wedgwood
& Bentley

Wedgwood
Wedgwood

WEDGWOOD

WEDGWOOD

Modern marks include, where appropriate, the name of the pattern.
Examples:

WEDGWOOD
ofETRURIA
MADE IN
ENGLAND
BARLASTON

Printed:
dated 1956

WOODBURY
ofETRURIA
WEDGWOOD
MADE IN
ENGLAND
BARLASTON

Factory mark printed in grey-green; other marks painted in red; dated 1958

Other marks
A system of date marks was introduced in 1860; it consisted of three capital letters representing month, potter, and year respectively.

Month letters 1860–64:

I January	Y May	S September
F February	T June	O October
M March	V July	N November
A April	W August	D December

Month letters 1864–1907:

J January	M May	S September
F February	T June	O October
R March	L July	N November
A April	W August	D December

Year letters 1860–97:

O 1860	A 1872	N. 1885
P 1861	B 1873	O 1886
Q 186'	C 1874	P 1887
R 1863	D 1875	Q 1888
S 1864	E 1876	R 1889
T 1865	F 1877	S 1890
U 1866	G 1878	T 1891
V 1867	H 1879	U 1892
W 1868	I 1880	V 1893
X 1869	J 1881	W 1894
Y 1870	K 1882	X 1895
Z 1871	L 1883	Y 1896
	M 1884	Z 1897

Year letters 1898–1930:

A 1898	N 1911	A 1924
B 1899	O 1912	B 1925
C 1900	P 1913	C 1926
D 1901	Q 1914	D 1927
E 1902	R 1915	E 1928
F 1903	S 1916	F 1929
G 1904	T 1917	G 1930
H 1905	U 1918	
I 1906	V 1919	
J 1907	W 1920	
K 1908	X 1921	
L 1909	Y 1922	
M 1910	Z 1923	

Marks from 1930 onward:
A new and simpler method was introduced consisting of a figure to indicate the month, a letter for the potter, and two figures for the year.

WEDGWOOD
2 O 56

WEDGWOOD
2 A 58

Examples:
Impressed:
February 1956
"O" for E. R. Owen,
modeller 1947

Impressed:
February 1958

"A" for Austin Arnold
modeller 1904–47

Weesp, Holland
Hard-paste porcelain made here from
1759 until 1771; business transferred to
Oude Loosdrecht (1771) and then to
Amstel (1784).

In underglaze blue

Whieldon, Thomas: (1719–95)
English potter at Fenton Low (or Little
Fenton), Staffordshire; gave his name to
a distinctive type of earthenware, notable
for its range of colours.
No marks were used at this pottery.

Wileman family: (second half 19th
century)
English manufacturers of china and
earthenware at the Foley Potteries,
Stoke-on-Trent, Staffordshire; established
1860 by Henry Wileman; continued by
sons (1864–67); in 1867 C. T. Wileman
took over the china, J. F. Wileman the
earthenware, trade; reunited 1870 (C.
J. Wileman retired); soon after trading
as Wileman & Co.

Transfer-printed

Wilson, Robert: (d. 1801)
English potter making cream-coloured
earthenware and "dry" bodies at Hanley,
Staffordshire; partner with James Neale,
trading as Neale and Wilson, eventually
succeeding him; succeeded by David
Wilson & Sons; firm bankrupt in 1817.

NEALE & WILSON

Impressed

Impressed

Witteburg
Minor faïence factory.

Given by Jännicke

Wohlfart, Friedrich Carl: (*fl.* 1766–71)
Painted porcelain (scenes of gallantry),
etc.) at Frankenthal (1766), Pfalz-Zweibrücken (1767–68), possibly at Ottweiler
(1768–71), and at Höchst (1771).
Inscription recorded:
"Wolfart prinxit" on tureen at Hamburg.

Wolfe, Thomas, the younger: (1751–1818)
English potter making porcelain at Liverpool (1792–1818) and various earthenwares at Stoke-on-Trent, Staffordshire
(1784–1818).
Mark recorded on cream-coloured earthenware:

Wolfe

Impressed

Wolfsburg, Carl Ferdinand von: (1692–
1764)
Amateur porcelain hausmaler, *fl.* 1729–
48.
Signatures recorded:
"C. F. de Wolfsbourg pinxit 1729"
"Carolus Ferdinandus de Wolfsbourg et
Wallsdorf Eques Silesiae pinxit Viennae
Aust. 1731."

Wolfsohn, Helena: (*fl.* 19th century)
Owned factory at Dresden, where Meissen porcelain, bought in the white, was decorated.

Used indiscriminately, until prevented by injunction *c.* 1880.
Subsequent marks used:

In blue

Wood, Enoch: (1759–1840)
English potter making earthenware, cane ware, Egyptian black, etc. at Burslem, Staffordshire (from 1784); trading as Wood & Caldwell (1790–1818); later took sons into the firm, who continued as Enoch·Wood & Sons until 1846.
Marks:

E. WOOD
ENOCH WOOD
SCULPSIT
Impressed or incised
WOOD & CALDWELL
There are several variations.

Impressed

Wood, Ephraim: (1773–after 1830)
English potter making figures; enameller, gilder, and lusterer of earthenware; at Burslem, Staffordshire.
Marks recorded, which may stand for Ephraim Wood or Enoch Wood:

**EW
1788**

Impressed:
on a "Fair Hebe" jug

WOOD

π ◉

Impressed: on early 19th-century figures: bench sign and circles probably workmen's marks

Wood, Ralph: (1715–72)
English potter (established 1754) at Burslem, Staffordshire; business continued by son, Ralph Wood II (1748–95) and grandson, Ralph Wood III (1781–1801) until 1801; noted for figures and Toby jugs.

R. WOOD
Impressed

Ra Wood   Ra Wood
                      Burslem
Impressed

1770 Ralph Wood

Incised
Rebus mark (like trees) occurs on some Wood figures:

Wood, Robert: (1650–1717)
English potter making slipware at Burslem, Staffordshire; a posset-pot (Hanley Museum) is lettered THE BEST IS NOT TOO GOOD FOR YOU ROBBORT WOOD.

ROBBORT WOOD

Slip

Worcester, Worcestershire, England
Porcelain factory established here by
Dr. John Wall (d. 1776) and others;
in 1783 bought for Joseph and John
Wright (d. 1791); Robert Chamberlain
left to form a rival company; in
1792 Martin Barr joined the firm, the
successive partnerships being:
Flight & Barr 1792–1807
Barr, Flight & Barr 1807–13
Flight, Barr & Barr 1813–40
In 1840 amalgamated with Chamberlain.
Later owners were Chamberlain and Lilly
(1848), joined by W. H. Kerr in 1850;
Kerr & Binns from 1852; Royal Worcester
Porcelain Co, 1862 onwards.
Marks:

Printed   Impressed   Printed
Kerr & Binns   1852–62   James Hadley
                                          & Sons
                                          1896–1903

James Hadley   Impressed:
& Sons   since 1862

Wouters, Joseph: (*fl.* later 18th century)
Made cream-coloured earthenware at
Andenne, in Belgium, from 1783.

This mark formerly given to A. van der
Waert, Andenne, Belgium:

(According to Brongniart, Chaffers,
Jännicke)

Wright, John: (early 18th century)
Name recorded on large Toft-style slip-
ware dishes (dates 1705–07); perhaps
his initials on slipware posset-pot
(British Museum) in inscription: ANN
DRAPER THIS CUP MADE FOR
YOU AND SO NO MORE I.W.
1707

See also INITIALIST I.W."

Wright, William: (early 18th century)
Name recorded on Toft-style slipware
dishes, one being dated 1709.

About 1755–65

1760

1760–95   1755–83   1780

In blue   In red   In red
1783–89   1789–92   1792–1807

1800   1820

Incised

B.F.B.   F.B.B.

Barr   Flight,
Flight & Barr   Barr & Barr
1807–13   1813–40

301

Wrisbergholzen, Hanover, Germany
Faïence made here *c.* 1737 to *c.* 1830.
Mark: WR in monogram form, with or
without a painter's initials.

Wrotham, Kent, England
Slipware pottery made here and nearby,
in 17th and 18th centuries; no dated
pieces after 1739 are known.
Mark, the word WROTHAM, often in
conjunction with the initials of the potter
or eventual owner.

Potters recorded at Wrotham include:
Hubble, Nicholas: (d. 1689)
Ifield, John: (d. 1716)
Livermore, Nicholas: (d. 1678)
Richardson, George: (*c.* 1620–87)

Würzburg, Lower Franconia, Germany
Hard-paste porcelain made here by
Johann Caspar Geyger, from 1775 to
1780.

 C · G

Xanto Francesco, Avelli da Rovigo:
(*fl.* 1530–42)
Maïolica painter of Urbino.
Signature frequent and various, from
simple X to full signature:

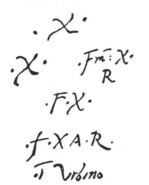

Yvernel: (*fl.* mid 18th century)
Painter of flowers and birds, at the
Vincennes-Sèvres factory from 1750.
or

Zell, Baden, Germany
General pottery established here *c.* 1820
by J. F. Lenz.
Mark: ZELL impressed
Factory continued using these marks:

(Mid and late 19th century)
(recorded by Jännicke and others)

Zerbst, Anhalt, Germany
Faïence made here from 1720 until 1861

Ziegler, Jules-Claude: (1804–56)
Made salt-glazed stoneware at Voisinlieu
near Beauvais, France, from *c.* 1839.

Zieseler, Philipp: (*fl.* mid 18th century)
Painter, working at Höchst *c.* 1749, and
at Fürstenberg from 1759. The initial
"Z" may be his mark.

Zillwood, W.: (*fl.* early 17th century)
Potter at work in the Salisbury (Wilts)
area; initials "ZW" sometimes found
incised.

Zimmermann: (*fl.* 18th century)
Signature recorded on an example of
Münden faïence (otherwise unknown):
"Zimmermann 1777".

Zittau, Saxony, Germany
Maïolica said to have been made here,
late 17th century. No marks recorded.

Zopf or Zopff, Georg Friedrich: (*fl.* mid
18th century)
Painter said to have worked at Stralsund
c. 1757, and at Eckernförde *c.* 1766.
Mark at Eckernförde thought to be his,
the initials "Z" and "J".

Zurich, Switzerland
Porcelain and faïence made here, *c.* 1763;
faïence, and lead-glazed earthenware
made *c.* 1790 to end of 19th century.
Marks recorded:

In blue, 18th century
Also the cursive letter "Z" found incised,
on soft-paste porcelain (very rare).

Japanese Date Marks

Marks on Japanese ceramics may be found stamped, painted, or incised. It should be noted that marks on Japanese wares might be found written in Chinese characters. It was not the custom for individual Japanese potters to put their names on their products before the 19th century.

あ			嘉応	1169–1171	元治	1864–1865
安永	1772–1781		嘉吉	1441–1444	[元中]	1384–1392
安元	1175–1177		(嘉慶)	1387–1389	元徳	1329–1331 [32]
安政	1854–1860		嘉元	1303–1306	元仁	1224–1225
安貞	1227–1229		嘉祥	848– 851	元文	1736–1741
安和	968– 970		嘉承	1106–1108	元禄	1688–1704
え			嘉禎	1235–1238	元和	1615–1624
永延	987– 989		嘉保	1094–1096	建永	1206–1207
永観	983– 985		嘉暦	1326–1329	建久	1190–1199
永久	1113–1118		嘉禄	1225–1227	建治	1275–1278
永享	1429–1441		(観応)	1350–1352	建長	1249–1256
永治	1141–1142		寛永	1624–1644	[建徳]	1370–1372
永正	1504–1521		寛延	1748–1751	建仁	1201–1204
永承	1046–1053		寛喜	1229–1232	建保	1213–1219
永祚	989– 990		寛元	1243–1247	建武	1334–1336 [38]
永長	1096–1097		寛弘	1004–1012	建暦	1211–1213
(永徳)	1381–1384		寛治	1087–1094	乾元	1302–1303
永仁	1293–1299		寛正	1460–1166	こ	
永保	1081–1084		寛政	1789–1809	(康安)	1361–1362
永万	1163–1166		寛徳	1044–1146	(康永)	1342–1345
永暦	1160–1161		寛仁	1017–1021	(康応)	1389–1390
永禄	1558–1570		寛文	1661–1673	康元	1256–1257
(永和)	1375–1379		寛平	889– 898	康治	1142–1144
延応	1239–1240		寛保	1741–1744	康正	1455–1457
延喜	901– 923		寛和	985– 987	康平	1058–1065
延久	1069–1074		き		康保	964– 968
延享	1744–1748		久安	1145–1151	(康暦)	1379–1381
延慶	1308–1311		久寿	1154–1156	康和	1099–1104
(延元)	1336–1340		享徳	1452–1455	弘安	1278–1288
延長	923– 931		享保	1716–1736	弘化	1844–1848
延徳	1489–1492		享禄	1528–1532	弘治	1555–1558
(延文)	1356–1361		享和	1801–1804	弘長	1261–1264
延宝	1673–1681		け		弘仁	810– 824
延暦	782– 806		慶安	1648–1652	[弘和]	1381–1384
お			慶雲	704– 708	[興国]	1340–1346
(応安)	1368–1375		慶応	1865–1868	さ	
応永	1394–1428		慶長	1596–1615	斉衡	854– 857
応長	1311–1312		元永	1118–1120	し	
応徳	1084–1087		元応	1319–1321	治安	1021–1024
応仁	1467–1469		元亀	1570–1573	治承	1177–1181 [83]
応保	1161–1163		元久	1204–1206	治暦	1065–1069
応和	961– 964		元慶	877– 885	(至徳)	1384–1387
か			元亨	1321–1324	寿永	1182 1185
嘉永	1848–1854		元弘	1331–1334	朱鳥	686

正安	1299–1302	長承	1132–1135	文安	1444–1449
正応	1288–1293	長徳	995– 999	文永	1264–1275
正嘉	1257–1259	長保	999–1004	文応	1260–1261
(正慶)	1332–1333	長暦	1037–1040	文化	1804–1818
正元	1259–1260	長禄	1457–1460	文亀	1501–1504
正治	1199–1201	長和	1012–1017	文久	1861–1864
正中	1324–1326	て		文治	1185–1190
正長	1428–1429	天安	857– 859	文正	1466–1467
正徳	1711–1716	天永	1110–1113	文政	1818–1830
[正平]	1346–1370	天延	973– 976	[文中]	1372–1375
正保	1644–1648	天応	781– 782	文保	1317–1319
正暦	990– 995	天喜	1053–1058	文明	1469–1487
正和	1312–1317	天慶	938– 947	文暦	1234–1235
昌泰	898– 901	天元	978– 983	文禄	1592–1596
承安	1171–1175	天治	1124–1126	(文和)	1352–1356
承応	1652–1655	[天授]	1375–1381	へ	
承久	1219–1222	天正	1573–1592	平治	1159–1160
承元	1207–1211	天承	1131–1132	ほ	
承徳	1097–1099	天長	824– 834	保安	1120–1124
承平	931– 938	天徳	957– 961	保延	1135–1141
承保	1074–1077	天仁	1108–1110	保元	1156–1159
承暦	1077–1081	天平	729– 749	宝永	1704–1711
承和	834– 848	天平感宝	749	宝亀	770– 780
貞永	1232–1233	天平勝宝	749– 757	宝治	1247–1249
貞応	1222–1224	天平神護	765– 767	宝徳	1449–1452
貞観	859– 877	天平宝字	757– 765	宝暦	1751–1764
貞享	1684–1688	天福	1233–1234	ま	
貞元	976– 978	天保	1830–1844	万延	1860–1861
(貞治)	1362–1368	天明	1781–1789	万治	1658–1661
(貞和)	1345–1350	天文	1532–1555	万寿	1024–1028
昭和	1926–	天養	1144–1145	め	
神亀	724– 729	天暦	947– 957	明応	1492–1501
神護景雲	767– 770	天禄	970– 973	明治	1868–1912
た		天和	1681–1684	(明徳)	1390–1394
大永	1521–1528	と		明暦	1655–1658
大化	645– 650	徳治	1306–1308	明和	1764–1772
大治	1126–1131	に		よ	
大正	1912–1926	仁安	1166–1169	養老	717– 724
大同	806– 810	仁治	1240–1243	養和	1181–1182
大宝	701– 704	仁寿	851– 854	り	
ち		仁平	1151–1154	[暦応]	1338–1342
長寛	1163–1165	仁和	885– 889	暦仁	1238–1239
長久	1040–1044	は		れ	
長享	1487–1489	白雉	650– 655	霊亀	715– 717
長元	1028–1037	ふ		わ	
長治	1104–1106			和銅	708– 715

Chinese Reign Marks

The following marks are found painted in blue on porcelain, on the bottom of the piece. Some European makers occasionally imitated Chinese marks on their own products.

Ming Reign Marks 1368–1643

Hung Wu
1368–1398

年 洪
製 武

Hung Chih
1488–1505

治 大
年 明
製 弘

Wan Li
1573–1619

曆 大
年 明
製 萬

Yung Lo
1403–1424

年 永
製 樂

Chêng Tê
1506–1521

德 大
年 明
製 正

T'ien Ch'i
1621–1627

啟 大
年 明
製 天

Hsüan Tê
1426–1435

德 大
年 明
製 宣

Chia Ching
1522–1566

靖 大
年 明
製 嘉

Ch'ung Chêng
1628–1643

年 崇
製 楨

Ch'êng Hua
1465–1487

化 大
年 明
製 成

Lung Ch'ing
1567–1572

慶 大
年 明
製 隆

Ch'ing Reign Marks 1644–1909

Shun Chih
1644–1661

正 大
年 清
製 雍

K'ang Hsi
1662–1722

熙 大
年 清
製 康

Yung Chêng
1723–1735

治 大
年 清
製 順

Ch'ien Lung
1736–1795

隆 大
年 清
製 乾

Chia Ch'ing
1796–1820

年 嘉
製 慶

Tao Kuang
1821–1850

光 大
年 清
製 道

Hsien Fêng
1851–1861

豐 大
年 清
製 咸

T'ung Chih
1862–1874

治 大
年 清
製 同

Kuang Hsü
1875–1909

緒 大
年 清
製 光

Hsüan T'ung
1909–1912

統 大
年 清
製 宣

Hung Hsien
(Yüan Shih-kai)
1916

年 洪
製 憲

Books for Further Reference

METALWORK

BRADBURY, F. *Old Sheffield Plate Makers' Marks, 1743–1860, with British and Irish Silver Assay Office Marks, 1544–1927*. 2nd ed. Northend, Sheffield. 1928.

COTTERELL, H. H. *Old Pewter, its makers and marks, in England, Scotland and Ireland*. Batsford, London. 1929.

EDWARDS, RALPH. *Shorter Dictionary of English Furniture*. Country Life, London. 1964.

GRIMWADE, A. G. (General Editor) *Faber Monographs on Silver*. Faber, London. 1965-.

HAYWARD, J. F. *Huguenot Silver in England 1688–1727*. Faber, London. 1959.

JACKSON, SIR CHARLES. *English Goldsmiths and their Marks*. Batsford, London. 1949 ed.

OMAN, CHARLES. *English Domestic Silver*. 6th ed. Black, London. 1965.

PHILLIPS, JOHN MARSHALL. *American Silver*. Parrish, London, 1949; Chanticleer Press, New York, 1949; Clarke Irwin, Toronto, 1949.

THORN, C. JORDAN. *Handbook of American Silver and Pewter Marks*. Tudor Publishing Co., New York. 1949.

YLER, SEYMOUR B. *The Book of Old Silver*. 11th ed. Crown Publishers, New York. 1949.

The Book of Sheffield Plate. Crown Publishers, New York. 1949.

FURNITURE AND TAPESTRY

EDWARDS, RALPH. *English Chairs*. 2nd ed. Victoria and Albert Museum, London 1957.

Georgian Furniture. 2nd ed. Victoria and Albert Museum, London. 1958.

HEAL, SIR AMBROSE. *The London Furniture Makers (1660–1840)*. Batsford, London. 1953.

MACQUOID, PERCY, and EDWARDS, RALPH. *The Dictionary of English Furniture*. Rev. ed. by Ralph Edwards. Country Life, London. 1954.

SYMONDS, R. W. *Furniture Making in the Seventeenth and Eighteenth Century in England*. The Connoisseur, London. 1955.

THOMSON, W. G. *A History of Tapestry*. Rev. ed. Hodder and Stoughton, London. 1930.

WARD-JACKSON, PETER. *English Furniture Designs of the Eighteenth Century*. Victoria and Albert Museum, London. 1959.

CERAMICS

BARRETT, F. A. *Worcester Porcelain*. Faber, London. 1953.

BEMROSE, GEOFFREY. *Nineteenth Century English Pottery and Porcelain*. Faber, London. 1952.

COOPER, RONALD. *Pottery of Thomas Toft*. Leeds Art Gallery. 1952.

CUSHION, J. P. *Pocket Book of English Ceramic Marks and those of Wales, Scotland and Ireland*. Faber, London. 1959.

CUSHION, J. P. and HONEY, W. B. *Handbook of Pottery and Porcelain Marks*. Faber, London. 1956.

DIXON, J. L. *English Porcelain of the Eighteenth Century*. Faber, London. 1952.

GARNER, F. H. *English Delftware*. Faber, London. 1948.

GODDEN, GEOFFREY. *Encyclopaedia of British Pottery & Porcelain Marks*. Jenkins, London. 1964.

GRAY, BASIL. *Early Chinese Pottery and Porcelain*. Faber, London. 1953.

HACKENBROCH, YVONNE. *Chelsea and other English Porcelain, Pottery and Enamel in the Irwin Untermyer Collection*. Thames and Hudson, London. 1957.

HAGGAR, REGINALD G. *English Country Pottery*. Phoenix House, London. 1950. *The Concise Encyclopedia of Continental Pottery and Porcelain*. Deutsch, London, 1960; Hawthorn Books Inc., New York, 1960.

HAYWARD, J. F. *Vienna Porcelain of the du Paquier period*. Rockliff, London. 1952.

HONEY, W. B. *The Ceramic Art of China and other countries of the Far East*. Faber, London. 1945.
Corean Pottery. Faber, London. 1947.
Dresden China. Faber, London. 1947.
German Porcelain. Faber, London. 1947.
French Porcelain of the Eighteenth Century. Faber, London. 1950.
A Dictionary of European Ceramic Art. 2 vols. Faber, London. 1962.
English Pottery and Porcelain. 5th ed. Black, London. 1962

HYDE, J. A. LLOYD. *Oriental Lowestoft (Chinese Export Porcelain)*. 2nd ed. Ceramic, Newport, Mon. 1954.

JENYNS, SOAME. *Later Chinese Porcelain*. Faber, London. 1952.
Ming Pottery and Porcelain. Faber, London. 1953.

JOHN, W. D. and BAKER, WARREN. *Old English Lustre Pottery*. Ceramic, Newport, Mon. 1951.

LANE, ARTHUR. *French Faience*. Faber, London. 1948.
Italian Porcelain. Faber, London. 1956.

MANKOWITZ, WOLF. *Wedgwood*. Batsford, London. 1953.

MANKOWITZ, WOLF and HAGGAR, REGINALD G. *The Concise Encyclopedia of English Pottery and Porcelain*. Deutsch, London, 1957; Hawthorn Books. Inc., New York. 1957.

PRICE, R. K. *Astbury, Whieldon and Ralph Wood Figures and Toby Jugs*. Lane, London. 1922.

RACKHAM, BERNARD. *Early Staffordshire Pottery*. Faber, London. 1951.
Italian Maiolica. Faber, London. 1952.

RACKHAM, BERNARD, and JEREMY, P. *Animals in Staffordshire Pottery*. Penguin, London. 1953.

SAVAGE, GEORGE, *Porcelain through the Ages*. Penguin, London. 1954.
18th Century English Porcelain. Rockliff, London. 1952.
Pottery through the Ages. Penguin, London. 1959.

TOWNER, DONALD. *English Cream-coloured Earthenware*. Faber, London. 1957.

WATNEY, BERNARD. *Longton Hall Porcelain*. Faber, London. 1957.

Index

METALWORK